JB

D0983026

January 25, 1972

To Jimm —

With sincere & appreciation
for your helping make this possible

Russ

**Political
Entrepreneurs
and Urban
Poverty**

362.5
M957p

Political Entrepreneurs and Urban Poverty

WITHDRAWN

The Strategies of Policy Innovation in New Haven's Model Anti-Poverty Project

Russell D. Murphy
Wesleyan University

Heath Lexington Books
D.C. Heath and Company
Lexington, Massachusetts
Toronto   London

Copyright © 1971 by D.C. Heath and Company.

All rights reserved. No part of this publication may be reproduced or transmitted in any form or by any means, electronic or mechanical, including photocopy, recording, or any information storage or retrieval system, without permission in writing from the publisher.

Published simultaneously in Canada.

Printed in the United States of America.

Standard Book Number: 669-75259-2

Library of Congress Catalog Card Number: 78-162641

To Sheila
Ad Multos Annos

Table of Contents

ALLEGHENY COLLEGE LIBRARY

List of Tables and Figures

Acknowledgments

"It is when I struggle to be brief," the Roman poet Horace once complained, "that I become unintelligible." Such is the danger here. My debts are considerable, the space is limited, and it is unlikely that I can express adequately my appreciation to all those who contributed to this study. Suffice to say that their assistance is no less appreciated because my gratitude is briefly stated.

I am especially indebted to my Wesleyan colleagues Fred I. Greenstein and Clement E. Vose for their continual encouragement, counsel and entrepreneurial inspiration through all the years of travail, as well as to Herbert Kaufman who nurtured and endured the study as a dissertation and saw it through to its present form. Thanks are due, in addition, to Irwin Gertzog and Peter Lupsha for their guidance and support as members of my dissertation committee, to Kenneth Dolbeare, Norton Long, James Payne, Lloyd Rudolph and Raymond Wolfinger, all of whom read and commented on the manuscript, and to Paul Heffron who, more years ago than I wish to admit, guided my first steps in academe. My appreciation also to the staff of New Haven's Community Progress, Inc., for tolerating my incessant questioning, to the National Center for Education in Politics for its support of my early field work in New Haven, and to Wesleyan University for a faculty research grant that helped defray the costs of manuscript preparation. Finally, to my wife Sheila and to our merry tribe—Russell Jr., Siobhan, Brian and Stephen, a simple thank you—for being a wife and for being merry.

Despite all the counsel and advice, imperfections doubtless remain. I apologize for these and close with Virgil's plea: "Adsum qui feci, in me convertite ferrum"—with due regard, of course, for the conventions of civil combat.

**Part I
Introduction**

1 Introduction

The Scope and the Focus

This is a study of an early encounter in the national war on poverty. The major source of information is a two-year period of observation and participation in the anti-poverty agency of New Haven, Connecticut. This city, which pioneered in urban renewal during the mid-1950s, later initiated one of the country's first anti-poverty projects. During the early 1960s this project and the agency created to administer it, New Haven's Community Progress, Inc., were being hailed by many as models and prototypes for the national war on poverty.

My concern in the following pages is twofold. The first of these is to provide an historical account of the formative years of the New Haven project. This time period spans the years during which the project was planned, 1959-1962, and the tenure of the anti-poverty agency's first executive director, Mitchell Sviridoff, 1962-1966. It was during this period that this new and at the time unorthodox confrontation with poverty took shape in the city and gained recognition nationally. To date there has been no systematic account of the project during this period[1] and one of the objectives of the study is to present such an account using the special sources made available to me during the two years I spent with the agency.

My purpose, however, is more than simply to report the historical events that occurred in New Haven between 1959 and 1966, fascinating and important though such a report might be. In writing about the agency and the project I have been guided by certain overarching questions. These questions have served as the framework for my research and for my analysis, as the organizing scheme that has led me to emphasize some facets of the encounter more than others.

Chief among these points of emphasis is the question of policy innovation. Measured in terms of dollars spent, programs initiated, and individuals reached, New Haven's anti-poverty project amounted to a major departure from the social welfare policies that then prevailed in the city. Like most innovations, however, New Haven's was beset by two major uncertainties: first, would the proposed programs make any discernible difference in dealing with the chronic and stubborn problems of poverty? Second, could these programs be instituted to begin with?

The second of these two questions is the one that will be the principal preoccupation of this study. Although the city's anti-poverty programs will be discussed in a general way, I have not attempted to evaluate them in terms of their direct social and economic value to New Haven's lower classes. Whether or

3

not the programs succeed, whether or not, for example, the efforts to improve the educational, familial, or occupation status of the community's deprived and disinherited prove efficacious, is of course a matter of no small moment, especially at this point in the city's and the nation's history when the problems of poverty are so grave. Important as these matters are, however, I leave them for others to grapple with.

My focus is rather on how these programs came to be instituted in the first place. Had they not been instituted, quite obviously there would be nothing to evaluate. And while for some analytical and political purposes it might be totally adequate to accept innovation as a given, for others it is not. Changes simply do not materialize spontaneously, automatically, and fully developed from the forehead of Zeus. Indeed, if we are to believe some political commentators, one of the principal shortcomings in American politics is the low rate of adoption of innovative proposals. As one author has noted: "Conservativism and self-preservation rather than innovation and demand for change" seem to be the modal characteristics of American politics in general and American local politics in particular.[2] In short, the system is said to be biased in favor of the status quo, with the presumption in favor of what is, and a stern burden of proof on what might be.

Underlying this appraisal of the possibilities for introducing change, given the constraints of American politics, are some familiar assumptions. For one thing, those who propose change do so, clearly, with the expectation that they will benefit more from the new order than they did from the old. It is equally clear, however, that not everyone will share in these benefits, or even prefer them if they did. For some the change will represent an unacceptable imposition on their own, or on society's, resources. Of course, few of these may be in a position to do more than complain privately, either because they lack the capacity or the inclination to do otherwise. But there are others, sufficiently numerous it would seem, whose complaints will be backed by action, by resistance, and quite possibly by a veto. This is the thrust of Wallace Sayre's and Herbert Kaufman's observation in their *Governing New York City*: "The prospects for any advocate of change are intense opposition, lengthy, costly, wearing maneuvering and negotiating, and uncertainty about results until the last battle is won."[3] Or as a political observer noted some 450 years earlier: "On every opportunity for attacking the reformer his opponents will do so with the zeal of partisans, the others only defend him half-heartedly, so that between the two he runs great danger."[4]

Despite these and other notorious constraints in American politics,[a] it is quite obvious that innovations do occur within the system. Inertia and tradition may well be the major determinants of public policy, as a number of authors have suggested they are. But they are not the only ones. How much change in public policy occurs in any given period is impossible to say in any precise quantitative

---

[a]Other constraints include the costs of gaining an understanding of the problem or problems, searching for and analyzing possible alternatives, and evaluating the performance of the alternative or alternatives actually adopted.[5]

way. Yet qualitatively such changes as do occur are probably exceedingly critical. Unless a political system continually anticipates or adapts to the social and economic conditions that are changing within and around it, there is a danger, as Sayre and Kaufman have cautioned, that it will suffer the fate of political systems of the past "whose glories are all in the archives and museums and whose significance is solely historical."[6]

It is a matter of some concern, then, to inquire under what conditions innovations can be expected. Stated somewhat differently, how is it that new issues and new alternatives come to be defined, gain recognition as legitimate and accepted items for the political agenda, and are translated into public action? That innovation is often preceded by a sense of dissatisfaction, as James March and Herbert Simon have indicated, provides us with a starting point.[7] But what we want to know is how and why this dissatisfaction comes to be articulated, by what group or groups, responding to what stimuli, with what resources and using what political strategies? More specifically, what were the characteristics of those who demanded change in New Haven? Were there any salient differences between them and other members of the community? What were their assumptions, for example, about the problem(s) or condition(s) they sought to change and about the political system within which they were operating, and how, if at all, did these assumptions influence or constrain the policies they proposed and the strategies they employed? What types of political and financial support did they possess, or develop, and how did they use this support to overcome resistance and promote the reform effort?

Viewed in this context, the account of the formative years of New Haven's anti-poverty project is a study of political behavior and specifically of the public policy-making process. As such it touches upon a number of other questions that have been of continuing interest to students of local politics in recent years, particularly those questions raised in the literature commonly referred to as community power studies. Chief among these are three studies which, fortunately for my purposes, were conducted earlier in New Haven by Robert Dahl and his associates Nelson Polsby and Raymond Wolfinger.[8] I have relied on these studies as a reference point for my own analysis for two reasons: first, because they provide important background information about the community I studied; and second, because they pose questions about the nature of policy-making that transcend the particular historical events under consideration. In addition, these studies have been widely discussed and, even where they have aroused disagreement, have provided touchstones for much of the subsequent work on community politics and policy-making.

Among the broad questions arising in the earlier New Haven studies is that of political influence in a local political system. In the early chapters of this study I will have an opportunity to examine anew the relative influence of social and economic elites and political activists. As we shall see, New Haven's anti-poverty project gave rise to a new set of political elites and a new political coalition, thus lending further support to a major point made in the earlier studies that political power is not a static, structural feature of communities.[9]

6

This new coalition, moreover, included broad categories of participants whose earlier role in the community is not at all clear in the previous accounts. For example, neither Dahl, Polsby, nor Wolfinger emphasize the role of *groups outside the city*. Although all three discuss the city's urban renewal program, a program financed principally by federal funds, they say little about the relationship between local and federal officials. This led H. Douglas Price in his review of *Who Governs?* to question Dahl's account of the local political process. Price argued that it was not so much the skill of local political leaders, as Dahl had suggested it was, that accounted for New Haven's success in redevelopment, but rather the infusion of massive federal aid.[10] Massive federal aid was also a major factor in the development of the anti-poverty project. As we shall see, in the anti-poverty case, at least, New Haven's reliance on this important and unusual resource in no way minimizes the significance of local officials in the process; on the contrary, once one takes account of the enormous variability of community capacity to exploit federal resources, it helps to clarify why their role was so critical.

The *local bureaucracy* is a second group whose influence on the outcome of local public policy is not examined at any length in the earlier studies of New Haven. This is understandable given the nature of the issues and the decisions that were studied.[11] In political nominations, for example, there simply was no relevant bureaucracy; in urban renewal there was none prior to the election of Mayor Lee in 1953.[b] In education, however, there *was* an established administrative hierarchy, but here the studies did not focus on routine or programmed decisions of the sort school officials would have been most influential in shaping. How important this routine type of policy-making can be for a local community was emphatically underlined in New Haven's efforts to launch its anti-poverty project. One of the strategic objectives of local reformers was to fashion a coalition between themselves and professional bureaucrats in the city and through this coalition to counter what local anti-poverty officials considered the deleterious effects of many existing bureaucratic policies and practices.[c]

This study will also provide a perspective on the relationship between an elected chief executive and appointed bureaucrats that differs from the perspective offered in the earlier studies. To the extent the earlier accounts consider the bureaucracy, the emphasis is on the ways New Haven's Mayor Richard C. Lee used it to further his own policy objectives. This same elected public official played a part in the development of the city's anti-poverty project. As I shall show at several points in the account, however, the relationship between the mayor and the administrators in anti-poverty was symbiotic rather than unilateral. If the mayor was adept at using these administrators, these administrators were no less adept at using him.

[b]The rise of Lee's urban renewal bureaucracy is discussed below in chapter 7.

[c]Among them such practices as the use of culturally biased testing and placement techniques by the State Employment Service, the emphasis on the athletically gifted by the Recreation Department, and the reportedly widespread policy of waiting for, rather than actively recruiting, clientele needing the assistance of public and private agencies.

Methods and Sources

The data for this study were gathered in several ways. The principal source was personal observation of top-level officials in New Haven's anti-poverty agency, Community Progress, Inc. For the better part of two years, 1963 to 1965, I was permitted to view the activities of this agency from the inside and observe the behavior of agency officials as they sought to fashion a reform effort: to develop strategies and tactics, and to negotiate and implement their programs. On several occasions I performed tasks for the agency's executive director, Mitchell Sviridoff, now vice president for national affairs for the Ford Foundation, and for Sviridoff's deputy director, Howard Hallman. Most of these tasks were inconsequential and in no way can I claim to have influenced materially the outcome of the project.

During the period I served with the agency I was given almost complete access to agency records: to files, financial reports, letters, memoranda, and working papers. These were of inestimable value, especially the papers on the planning years collected by Hallman, and the early financial records of the agency. During the first two years of the project, detailed and accurate fiscal reports were not published and it was only from lengthy and at times tedious search of the agency's files that I was able to reconstruct reliable estimates of its financial activities.[d]

Time not spent examining agency records, observing staff behavior, or performing assigned chores was devoted to extensive informal interviews with agency personnel. These took place during luncheons, coffee breaks, trips to meetings outside the city, or any other spare time staff members had away from their primary responsibility of managing a new and at the time rapidly expanding enterprise. In addition to Sviridoff and Hallman, both of whom were exceedingly patient in responding to my endless stream of questions, I am particularly indebted to Richard Brooks and Thomas Seessel, both special assistants to the executive director; George Bennett, director of manpower; Milton Brown, director of neighborhood services; Miss May White, special consultant on education programs; Isadore Wexler, special consultant on leisure time activity; Andrew Raubeson, program assistant; and the late Matthew Schecter, training assistant. It can be safely said that out of all this immersion in the "innards" of New Haven's anti-poverty agency emerged an account which could not possibly have been reconstructed from the public record.

As an insider, my perspective was analogous to the researcher who, in Norton Long's quasi-irreverent phrase, "hides under the mayor's bed."[12] No one is more aware than I of the discomforts of such a posture. Among other things, being on the scene exposes one to a constant, almost overwhelming flow of fascinating information about political personalities and political happenings. These often crowd upon the observer and tempt him to pursue questions that are fascinating and intriguing but at best peripheral to his central concern.

Yet such discomforts and diversions must be endured. If there is any merit to

---

[d]A detailed list of the sources on Community Progress, Inc. is presented in the Bibliography.

the counsel of the late V.O. Key, who urged students of politics to devote more time to learning about "that thin stratum of persons referred to variously as the political elite, the political activists, the leadership echelons, or the influentials,"[13] then it is exceedingly important that this "thin stratum" occasionally be observed close-up in its natural habitat. For one thing, political leaders are extraordinarily busy people—those who ran New Haven's anti-poverty project frequently worked well into the evenings and devoted many of their weekends and holidays to the project—and as such often do not have the time or the endurance for extended interviews by outsiders. Moreover, the rapid pace of their activity and the many rough-hewn procedures they use for simplifying their perceptions and expediting decision-making sometimes make them poor judges in retrospect of the factors that have influenced their decision. Finally, political leaders are of course extremely circumspect about what they will discuss openly with researchers. Trust and reliability rank high in their codes of behavior, and until rapport has been established, through frequent daily contact, for example, the flow of information is likely to be severely curtailed.

To supplement information I gathered through agency sources—as well as to provide a check on incomplete or partial accounts of events that respondents close to them might be inclined to report—I relied on interviews with individuals outside the agency who were either familiar with or who had themselves actually participated in the project, on an extensive file of newspaper clippings from *The New Haven Journal-Courier* and *The New Haven Register*, the city's two newspapers, and *The New York Times* and *The Wall Street Journal*, all of which carried items on the project, as well as information contained in the reports of several federal agencies and congressional committees. In addition, as already noted I have drawn on recent accounts of New Haven politics. The three academic studies by Robert Dahl, Nelson Polsby, and Raymond Wolfinger have been especially useful for the background information they contain on New Haven politics. None of these, however, deals with the anti-poverty project, since the research for them was completed before this project came into being. Two other recent studies, William L. Miller's *The Fifteenth Ward and the Great Society*[14] and Allan Talbot's *The Mayor's Game*,[15] do discuss the anti-poverty project, but in a rather brief and cursory fashion. Both these books appeared *after* I had completed my own research on the project, and where appropriate I have cited them as either confirming or disputing my inferences about events whose interpretation I had arrived at independently.

Part II
Mounting the Reform Effort

2

The Origins of New Haven's Anti-Poverty Project

Beginnings

On April 12, 1962, some two years before the passage of the Johnson Administration's Economic Opportunity Act, New Haven's Mayor Richard C. Lee announced to the press that the city was "embarking on a demonstration program to attack and overcome basic human problems . . . and to create a new urban environment and climate for better human development."[1] For the vast majority of the city's residents, the mayor's announcement was the first indication that New Haven was to be the setting for a new and ambitious type of urban reform. Prior to this there had been no public discussion or debate either about the project itself or about the conditions the project was intended to deal with.

The significance of this silence lies primarily in what it reveals about non-events, namely that *there had been no organized and explicit demand, either by the poor themselves, by their spokesmen, or by an outraged and troubled public*, for social reform of the sort that the new demonstration program constituted. The initiative in this case came from the Lee administration itself, and more precisely from a small group of officials within Lee's urban renewal bureaucracy. Acting informally and unofficially, this group established the foundations for an anti-poverty project that later would be cited nationally as a model for the country.

Poverty and the New Haven Community

Post-War Trends

New Haven is an old New England city (1638) situated along the eastern seaboard some 75 miles north of New York City, some 150 miles south of Boston, part of what the French geographer Jean Gottman has termed the eastern megalopolis. A city which in 1960 contained some 152,000 people in 17.9 square miles, New Haven ranked eighty-first among the nation's urban places in population, and twenty-ninth in population density.

Like many other urban centers within the eastern megalopolis, New Haven was afflicted by a general malaise that pervaded its social, political, and economic life. By 1950 the "sheltered harbor and broad valley with streams, framed by wooded hills and abrupt cliffs" that had "invited the early

11

colonists,"[2] had been all but obliterated and obscured by intensive residential and industrial development. In its place stood a crowded, antiquated, stagnant, and unattractive community, burdened by its past and challenged by the surrounding suburban communities for industry, residents, and retail trade.

In the early 1950s the community began to stir and by the mid-sixties the city had embarked on one of the most ambitious and famous urban renewal programs in the state (Table 2-1) and indeed in the country. By 1965, new construction in redevelopment and renewal areas valued at $228.0 million was underway, completed, or committed, a striking figure in a city whose real property tax base or Grand List the same year was only $582.8 million.[3] During the same year, visitors to New Haven could view the nearly completed Church Street Project, one of the first projects in the country in which a major portion of a city's central business district had been razed and then rebuilt; or they could tour nearby Wooster Square, one of the city's most charming residential areas consisting of handsome brownstone townhouses facing a gardened mall, where Lee and his developers earlier had embarked on a novel restoration of a deteriorated neighborhood with minimum use of the bulldozer.

Urban renewal, of course, dealt with but one facet of the general malaise besetting the community. In addition to dilapidated buildings and antiquated and inadequate public and private facilities, there were the stubborn and chronic problems of poverty and near poverty. Compared to other cities in the country, to New York's Harlem or Bedford Stuvyesant, Chicago's West Side, Washington's Southwest Area, Boston's Roxbury section, or Philadelphia's North Side, New Haven was relatively well-off. Compared to its own immediate area, however—to the New Haven metropolitan region or to the state—the city had, as can be seen in Table 2-2, more than its share of poverty. Within the city, for example, the median family income was more than $1,000 less than the median income of the State. Close to 17 percent of the city's population earned less than $3,000 a year, a proportion that was roughly two and a half times greater than that of other towns in the metropolitan region. One of every four, or 25 percent, of all dwelling units in New Haven was classified by the U.S. Bureau of Census as substandard compared to 8 percent in the surrounding suburban communities. And of all the children who in 1960 were receiving public assistance from the Connecticut State Welfare Department, some 16 percent were from New Haven, thus making New Haven the second largest contributor to the rolls of the Aid to Dependent Children program.[4]

The Inner City

Quite obviously, these aggregate statistics on New Haven conceal much of the reality of poverty within the city, since some areas and some groups within the community were worse off than others. Broadly stated, poverty assumed two dimensions in the city, one of them geographic, the other racial. Geographically, the city was divided into two roughly distinct areas, one of which, the so called

Table 2-1

Comparison of Connecticut's Urban Renewal Efforts in Cities of over 50,000 Population: 1964

City	Population (1960)	Rank in State	Acreage Under Renewal			Expenditures[a]		
			Total City Acreage	City Total as Percent of State Total	Rank in State	Total City Expenditures	City Expenditures As Percent of Total State	Rank in State
Hartford	162,178	1	185.0	3.8	4	$ 26,800,000	7.4	4
Bridgeport	156,748	2	106.0	2.1	6	17,600,000	4.9	5
New Haven	152,048	3	2,019.0	42.0	1	102,000,000	28.0	1
Waterbury	107,130	4	33.0	.6	8	3,400,000	.9	8
Stamford	92,713	5	147.1	2.9	5	33,700,000	9.2	3
New Britain	82,201	6	416.6	10.8	2	35,032,075	9.6	2
Norwalk	67,775	7	68.7	1.4	7	14,054,859	3.9	6
Meriden	51,850	8	236.0	4.8	3	11,705,207	3.3	7

Source: Connecticut Development Commission, *Urban Renewal in Connecticut, Statistical Report* (Hartford, June, 1964), pp. 3-4.

[a]Expenditures do not include private investment in urban renewal areas.

Table 2-2

Selected Socio-Economic Indicators of Poverty for Connecticut, the New Haven Standard Metropolitan Statistical Area, and the City of New Haven: 1960

Socio-Economic Indicator	Connecticut	Metropolitan Area (Excluding New Haven)	New Haven
Population (Total)	2,535,000	159,000	152,000
Population as percentage of total state population	100%	6.3%	6.0%
Non-white population as percentage of total population in specified area	4.4%	1.1%	14.9%
Population with incomes of less than $3,000, as percentage of total population in specified area	9.8%	6.9%	16.6%
Unemployment (1960) as percentage of total population in civilian working force in specified area	4.6%	3.1%	5.6%
Sub-standard housing as percentage of total housing in specified area	15.2%	8.2%	25.5%
Population living in structures built since 1950, as percentage of total population in specified area	26.9%	35.3%	7.1%
Median Income	$6,887	$6,620[a]	$5,864
Median Education of population over 25 in specified area	11.0	11.0[a]	10.1

Source: U.S. Bureau of the Census, *County and City Data Book, 1962* (Washington: Government Printing Office, 1962).

[a]Includes New Haven.

"inner-city neighborhoods," was to be the focal point of reform. There were six inner-city neighborhoods where more than half the city's total population lived in less than a third of its total land area. Here lived the unemployed, the elderly, the marginal and broken family, the welfare recipient, the unmarried mother, the juvenile delinquent, and the school drop-out in overcrowded and sub-standard housing (Figure 2-1).

That these were not the most favored of neighborhoods in the city is illustrated by the data in Table 2-3. In one neighborhood, Dixwell, over half the families had annual incomes under $4,000; in another neighborhood, Wooster Square, the proportion was 43 percent. For the inner city as a whole the figure

Figure 2–1. Inner-City Neighborhoods of New Haven, Connecticut.

ALLEGHENY COLLEGE LIBRARY

Table 2-3

Poverty in New Haven: Selected Socio-Economic Characteristics of the City of New Haven and New Haven's Inner-City Neighborhoods: 1960

Characteristic	New Haven	Inner City	Dix-well	Dwight	Hill	Fair Haven	Wooster Square	Newhall-ville
Population (000)	152.4	76.9	10.2	6.9	19.8	19.4	10.7	9.5
Black population as percentage of total population in specified area	14.9	24.5	73.0	22.0	13.0	4.0	22.0	42.0
Families with incomes of less than $4,000 as percentage of total families in specified area	25	32	52	37	28	26	43	25
Population over 25 with less than 12th grade education as percentage of total population over 25 in specified area	62	77	74	55	75	75	81	67
Percentage of 6th grade population scoring less than 6th grade level of achievement on Stanford-Binet Paragraph Interpretation test (1963)[a]	57	NA	81	56	68	58	77	65
Children under 18 living with one parent as percentage of all children under 18 in specified area	17	22	35	31	18	16	24	20
Unemployment as percentage labor force in specified area[b]	5.6	NA	10.3	6.4	7	3.6	9.1	6.1
Population age 15-24 registered with State Employment Service as "actively seeking work" as percentage of total population age 15-24 in specified area[c]	16.6	36	NA	NA	NA	NA	NA	NA
Juvenile offenders, age 8-21, as percentage of total population age 8-21 in specified area[d]	5.0	6.4	9.9	9.4	5.8	5.2	5.1	6.5

Table 2-3 *(Cont.)*

Source: U.S. Bureau of the Census, *County and City Data Book, 1962* (Washington: Government Printing Office, 1962). U.S. Bureau of the Census, *U.S. Census of Population and Housing: 1960 Census Tracts, Final Report, PHC (1)-102* (Washington: Government Printing Office, 1961). Community Progress, Inc., *New Haven Youth Development Program*, Part 1 *(The Setting)*, Chapter II, III, and V. (New Haven: Community Progress, Inc., 1963).

[a]Community Progress, Inc., *New Haven Youth Development Program*, Part 2 ("Programs"), Chapter V, "Education" (New Haven: Community Progress, Inc., 1963), p. 20.

[b]Community Progress, Inc., *New Haven Youth Development Program*, Part 1 ("The Setting"), Chapter II, "The Inner-City" (New Haven: Community Progress, Inc., 1963), pp. 1-21, passim.

[c]Community Progress, Inc., *New Haven Youth Development Program, Part 1 ("The Setting"), Chapter III, "Special Youth Studies" (New Haven: Community Progress, Inc., 1963), pp. 9-13.*

[d]Ibid., pp. 1-9.

was 32 percent, whereas for non-inner-city neighborhoods the rate was 17 percent. Almost eight of every ten adults in these areas had never finished high school; close to six out of ten had never completed the eighth grade. Within these neighborhoods the rates of unemployment, both among adults and teenagers, of school drop-outs, of juvenile delinquency were nearly twice what they were in other areas of the city, all of which was not unrelated to the lower level of school achievement among inner-city students and the relatively widespread instability among inner-city families.

The Blacks

The second dimension of poverty in New Haven was racial. From its early years New Haven had always had a relatively small black subcommunity, one consisting of slaves or ex-slaves, or members of the black "colony" established in the 1820s by one of the city's "advanced abolitionists," the Reverend Jocelyn Smith. Until the 1950s, however, the blacks constituted only a small proportion, roughly 4 to 6 percent, of the city's population.

In the decade of the fifties, the city underwent a major shift in its racial distribution. During this period, the number of blacks in New Haven more than doubled, partly as a result of natural increase and partly as the result of the immigration of some 8,000 blacks, many of them from the rural south. This growth in the number of blacks in the city, coupled with the out-migration of one of every four whites, resulted in a twofold rise in the proportion of blacks in the city. By 1960 some 15 percent of the city's population was black and it was predicted that by 1980 the proportion would rise still further to approximately 40 percent.[5]

Most of this growth took place in the inner-city neighborhoods. During the post-World War II years, neighborhood blocks that had been predominantly white were transformed into small black ghettos. The most dramatic change occurred in Newhallville, where only 3 percent of the population had been black in 1950, but by 1960 the proportion had jumped to 42 percent. Other neighborhoods were not far behind, however: by 1960 Wooster Square, once known as "little Italy," was no longer a homogeneous community of southern Italians as it long had been; nearly a quarter of the population in this neighborhood was black. Similar changes took place in Dwight, an area bordering on Yale University; in the Hill; in Fair Haven; and in Dixwell. Even in Dixwell, a neighborhood that historically had housed the largest percentage of the city's black population, the proportion of blacks rose from 62 percent in 1950 to 73 percent in 1960.

What conditions were like within the black neighborhoods is suggested by the data in Table 2-4. Using 1960 data from the city's twenty-eight census tracts, rank order correlations were computed for the percentage of blacks in each tract exhibiting seven measures of poverty. In each case the results indicate a close relationship between the racial composition of the neighborhood and the socio-economic characteristics selected as indicators of poverty. Thus, for example, the higher the proportion of blacks, the higher the rate of family separations and divorces, of families with incomes of less than $4,000 a year, of unemployment, and of adults with less than an eighth grade education.

Table 2-4

New Haven Census Tracts: Rank-Order Correlations (r and r^2) : Percentage of Blacks with Specified Characteristics : 1960

Characteristic[a]	r	r^2
Marital breakdowns	.74	.55
Families with annual incomes of less than $4,000	.73	.53
Adults (over 25) with less than 8th grade education	.72	.52
Overcrowded housing	.68	.47
Semi- and unskilled workers	.64	.40
Unemployment	.57	.33
Sub-standard housing	.47	.22

Source: U.S. Bureau of the Census, *U.S. Census, Population and Housing Census Tracts, 1960, Final Report, PHC (1)-102* (Washington, Government Printing Office, 1961).

[a]The following definitions were used for this table: *Marital breakdowns*: those separated or divorced; *Overcrowded housing*: units with more than 1.01 individuals per room; *Sub-standard housing*: units lacking complete plumbing.

This is not to say that poverty was or is only a racial problem. It was not, in New Haven, any more than it was or is in the rest of the country. As a group blacks were simply by far the *most* disadvantaged, to use the term currently in vogue. Moreover, from all indications blacks were the least well equipped of the diverse urban groups to deal with contemporary urban life, and, in New Haven at least, this was critical.[a] There was no room for complacency, since, as I have already noted, population projections indicated that within twenty years the blacks would constitute almost a majority of the population.

The Public's Response

It is impossible to say how the average New Haven citizen viewed poverty during the postwar years, for the evidence is scant and indirect. But it is reasonable to assume, I believe, that before 1962 and the formation of the city's anti-poverty agency, Community Progress, Inc., the general public's awareness and concern were both limited. For one thing, the problems of the poor and especially of the black poor were low in visibility, not ones the ordinary citizen encountered in his normal daily life. He frequently saw the physical decay of the city and often became snarled in a downtown traffic jam or searched long, and perhaps unavailingly, for a parking space. Seldom, though, was he exposed personally to poverty: to unsanitary and overcrowded housing, to hunger and malnutrition, to the high infant mortality rate, a rate that in one heavily black neighborhood, Dixwell, was 47.9 per 1,000 live births, nearly twice the national statistic. Second, little had happened prior to 1962 to focus the population's attention on the poor. Urban renewal apparently had not done so. In 1959, for example, a sample of residents was asked to identify the city's most important problems: 38 percent cited redevelopment, 27 percent traffic and parking, 12 percent the shortage of housing. Only 8 percent mentioned unemployment and fewer still, 1 percent, the need for more welfare.[6] Nor had any crisis situations or social unrest developed in the lower class neighborhoods, no organized protest by the poor that would have dramatized their plight and brought it into sharper focus for the community. Even the events that led to the city's anti-poverty project did little to educate the general public about poverty, since there was little public discussion of the project or the project's plans.

Among the city's organized interest groups, the reaction was apparently much the same as it was among the general population. Groups that since have become outspoken champions of the poor had not yet been heard from in New Haven. The communications media, for example, had not launched a public crusade for better conditions in the lower class neighborhoods; the churches had not been preaching social reform; college students had not yet turned to political and social activism, and begun to toil and organize in the slums; business and unions had not initiated recruitment and training programs or undertaken special advertising campaigns for qualified workers "regardless of race, color, or creed"; and private welfare agencies were still preoccupied largely with their traditional

[a]The point is discussed in more detail in chapter 4 along with other assumptions underlying the programmatic aspects of New Haven's anti-poverty project.

clientele, specifically with the older, more well-established white middle- and working-class groups in the city.[7]

Governmental Initiative

The Lee Administration

The Lee administration's response to poverty contrasts sharply with that of the population in general and the city's organized interest groups. Lee was a reform mayor, not in the tradition of New York City's Seth Low, Philadelphia's Joseph S. Clark, or other local chief executives whose administrations were marked by crusades against municipal corruption and inefficiency, but rather in the tradition of the New Deal, emphasizing a coalition of liberal and working class forces bent on a politics of income redistribution. Since his election in 1953, the mayor had manifested a continuing deep, personal interest in the expressions of human misery he confronted in the city's lower-class neighborhoods, and he coupled this interest with a political commitment to transform New Haven from a city that once had seen better days into a city whose history was in the future.[8]

Despite the mayor's longstanding interest in the poor, it was not until the late 1950s and early 1960s that poverty itself became an important public issue. Before this, the Lee administration, preoccupied as it was with the launching of its extensive urban renewal program, had dealt with poverty in a highly conventional manner. Caring for the poor meant caring for them through such traditional programs as general public assistance, aid to families with dependent children, or public housing.[9]

Beginning in 1959, however, a significant change in the city's definition of poverty occurred as poverty began to assume an identity of its own as a problem, or more precisely, as a cluster of problems, that warranted special consideration and action. As a result, from 1959 on city officials began devoting more of their time, energies, and attention to a search for new ways of dealing with the problems.

Two factors played an especially important part in bringing about this change in New Haven's orientation toward poverty. One of these was the Oak Street renewal project, the other the Ford Foundation.

Oak Street

Oak Street was the focal point of Lee's first redevelopment efforts. By all accounts, this 44.4 acre section that bordered on and included part of the city's central business district was New Haven's worst slum and had been for some time.[10] Beginning in 1956, Lee and his redevelopers completely transformed the area. Within ten years they had cleared Oak Street of its decaying and dilapidated buildings, its overcrowded housing, its saloons, its houses of prostitution, and its narrow and tortuous streets, and replaced all these with new office buildings, new apartment houses, new commercial establishments, and part of a new major highway. So extensive were the changes wrought in the area that a newcomer to the city is hard pressed to envision Oak Street's inglorious past.

There was another facet to Oak Street, however, one partly obscured and overshadowed by the area's advanced state of physical decay. This was the human misery and human degradation that abounded in the area. Oak Street was, according to one observer, little more than a "social cesspool," a dumping ground for a variety of human misfits and predators.[11]

Plans to redevelop Oak Street called for the displacement of the neighborhood's more than 4,000 residents, and this prospect occasioned Lee and his developers no few anxious moments. The relocation of any sizeable population is, as the experience of urban renewal across the country amply testifies, itself a sufficiently dangerous political proposition. For one thing, it disrupts the lives of the relocatees themselves, and the various social, economic, and political institutions that serve them. Second, it exerts pressure on other neighborhoods, on their inhabitants and their institutions, and threatens their established way of life. From this second perspective, Oak Street was, potentially at least, an especially perilous undertaking, for it entailed the relocation of a population consisting in large part of social outcasts and social undesirables.

This potential for conflict over the relocation of the Oak Street population never fully materialized. As far as can be determined, there was little opposition to the move, either from the relocatees themselves or from the residents of other neighborhoods. The reasons for this are not entirely clear, though it is highly probable that the dispersion of relocatees throughout the city served to lessen the pressures on, and hence the threats to, any given neighborhood. Of the 886 families that were relocated, 6.6 percent moved outside the city and 14.6 percent to public housing. The remaining 756 (Table 2-5) were moved to private housing throughout the city, no more than 23 percent of them to any single neighborhood.

Whatever the explanation for the absence of conflict over the relocation of the Oak Street population, the point of interest here is the reaction of the Lee administration. Though unscathed, Lee and his developers were unrelieved. If anything, their concern about relocation was heightened. Oak Street brought into sharper focus than before the nature and complexities of social problems in the inner city and reenforced the conviction held by Lee and others that physical renewal alone would not cure the city's ills. "If New Haven's redevelopment program is to obtain for the community the optimum benefits to be expected," one public official observed, the city had to "launch an all-out attack on social problems."[12]

Behind the administration's concern over the Oak Street relocation was the realization that this particular project was but the first of several renewal projects then being planned by the city. At the time, 1959, four additional

Table 2-5

Distribution of Families Relocated from New Haven's Oak Street Renewal Project to Private Housing within the City, by Neighborhoods

Neighborhood	Percentage of Relocated Families
The Hill	23
Dwight	16
Wooster Square	16
Dixwell	13
Newhallville	9
Fair Haven	7
State Street	7
Westville	4
Edgewood	3
Beaver Hills	1
East Shore	1
Whitney	1
	N=756

Source: Computed from data in: City of New Haven, Redevelopment Agency, Office of Family Relocation, "Where Families Have Moved from Redevelopment and Highway Construction Areas" (mimeographed), April 30, 1964.

Note: This table does not include families that either moved outside the city or to public housing within the city. Most of those who moved to public housing moved to the Elm Haven Housing Project in Dixwell neighborhood. Roughly 75 percent of the 130 families relocated in public housing were relocated in this project.

projects, each requiring the relocation of residents, were on the drawing boards. It was anticipated that 3,000 families, in addition to the 886 from Oak Street, would be relocated from the four project areas. Such a move, as the Lee administration was well aware, had profound implications. As one internal staff memorandum summed it up, "if no more service is provided these 3,000 families than was provided when 800 families were moved from Oak Street, some families will find their problems intensified and some neighborhoods will suffer further or new blight."[13] In other words, the problems encountered in Oak Street would be encountered again, the only difference being that in the future they would be multiplied and magnified, and quite possibly less manageable.

Initial Failures

Confronted by the experience of Oak Street and by the expectations about the future, the Lee administration began searching for ways to handle relocation in a more effective and humane manner. The initial response was perhaps predictable, for like many problem solvers Lee and his planners first sought more systematic information about the dimensions of poverty within the city. Early in 1959, for example, a "limited follow-up study of families relocated from Oak Street" was proposed, but quickly rejected as "totally inadequate [for] preparing to meet the very real needs facing New Haven in the next few years."[14] During the summer and autumn of the same year discussions were held with the New York City-based consulting firm, Community Research Associates, Inc., about the possibilities of a more comprehensive and ambitious study of "the human needs of the entire city."[15] Here too one of the administration's objectives was to increase its understanding of poverty in the city by determining "the nature and severity of the problems" and by identifying the availability of public and private resources for dealing with these problems.[16] As these discussions made clear, however, information was not an end in itself but rather a means to a more general political objective, for the study proposed to

provide a framework for a reallocation of resources to provide improved practices for dealing with multi-problem families by City, State, and private agencies concerned. In so doing, the study will endeavour to clarify public and private responsibilities in this field.[17]

That these twin objectives—reallocating resources and clarifying public and private responsibility for the poor—would not be easily realized was underlined emphatically by the abortive effort on the part of the Lee administration to enlist the support of private agencies in the relocation process. While other alternatives such as the Community Research Associates proposal were being explored, an official in the Redevelopment Agency, Howard Hallman, complained to the city's development administrator Edward Logue, "relocation is proceeding at the rate of several hundred families a year and therefore something needs to be done immediately."[18] What Hallman proposed was to

get five or six key welfare agencies to take action on those multi-problem families who are coming into the relocation work load. We would give each agency a complete list of the families to be relocated and have them sort out the ones which would be in the multi-problem category. Then, by mutual agreement, each family would be assigned to a single agency which would have primary responsibility for working with that family as a whole.[19]

With the backing of Frank Harris, then a staff member of the Council of Social Agencies and subsequently its executive secretary, Hallman's proposal went before the Council's Board of Directors. At the time, Hallman reported to Logue that "things are on the right track for this project."[20] If by this he meant the private agencies could be expected to cooperate, his expectations proved far too sanguine. Contrary to his predictions, the agencies simply refused to join in. As Paul Nagel of the United Fund later put it "we got a C for effort and a D for performance."[21] Whatever the reason for this behavior, its implications were perfectly clear: care for the well-being of relocatees, then at least, was not considered the responsibility of the private agencies. If Lee and his developers were serious about remedying the social and economic problems facing them in the slums, they would have to look elsewhere for the resources to do the job.

Continuing the Search: The Ford Foundation

Early Contacts

Lee and his developers were serious indeed and already had begun to expand the search for ways to complement their well proven techniques in physical renewal with programs for social and economic reform. In December 1959, Logue, responding to a memorandum from the city's welfare director Francis Looney suggesting a meeting with Community Research Associates, noted cryptically, "I'd like to hold off the meeting you propose for a little bit while we try to work something else out."[22] What Logue was trying to work out was outlined the following month in a document entitled "A Program for Community Improvement in New Haven."[23] Unlike earlier documents on the problem of relocation—documents whose main emphasis was information-gathering, albeit information with considerable political value—the Community Improvement proposal contained a rough blueprint for a broad-scaled program of social action. To be sure, the discussion was brief (seven pages) and in places quite vague. But brief and vague though it was, it contained many of the ideas that later found expression in the city's anti-poverty project, among them a suggestion that a private, non-profit corporation be established to administer the program.

"A Program for Community Improvement in New Haven" was an outgrowth of discussions between city officials and staff members of the Ford Foundation. In December 1959, a three-man delegation from the New Haven Redevelopment Agency met in New York City with Foundation officials to discuss the possibility of Foundation support for a program to combat the social problems of the central city. Heading the New Haven Delegation was Edward Logue, and among those present at the meeting was Dr. Paul Ylvisaker, then associate director of the Foundation's Public Affairs Division.

The presence of both Logue and Ylvisaker was neither coincidental nor without significance. The two had known each other for some time and indeed were quite friendly. Moreover, they shared a common interest in American cities and the problems confronting them. Since coming to the Foundation in 1955 from Swarthmore College where he had been a professor of political science, Ylvisaker had been urging the Foundation to assume greater responsibility for the country's urban areas. So too had Logue. In fact the December 1959 meeting was part of a continuing effort by Logue and Lee to persuade the Foundation to redirect its attention, and of course its substantial resources, toward urban problems in general, and in particular toward those in New Haven. As early as 1954, for example, Logue had approached the Foundation with a request for money to help in the planning of the city's urban renewal project.

Again in 1957, Lee tried to interest the Foundation in a physical fitness program for the city's teenagers. Neither effort was successful. While the Foundation had, since the mid-fifties, shown a more active interest in the problems of the city—between 1955 and 1961, for example, it sponsored some seventy-three research projects dealing with urban questions at a cost of more than $10.9 million[24]—still it had not yet fully abandoned that policy of caution engendered during the McCarthy era by right-wing critics and by threats of congressional investigations.[25] In the late 1950s, however, the Foundation began to assume a more aggressive and reform oriented posture. In March 1959 it allocated $1.25 million for the "great cities school project," a project designed to assist forty-one slum schools in ten large urban centers. The same year Ylvisaker and other Foundation officials began hinting publicly they were interested in the human side of urban renewal. Logue, sensing this shift, renewed his efforts to convince the Foundation that it should not overlook New Haven. This time the Foundation's response was more encouraging and the December 1959 meeting set in motion the process that eventually led to New Haven's receiving a $2.5 million social renewal grant.

The first and indeed only immediate concrete result of the December meeting was the Community Improvement proposal cited above. Logue, who had been the chief liaison with the Foundation and one of the moving forces behind the efforts to bring about changes in relocation practices, was at the time negotiating about a new job with the Boston Redevelopment Authority. In February 1960, he announced his resignation effective at the end of the year and during the remainder of 1960 he divided his time between Boston and New Haven. In New Haven he devoted most of his time and energies to the lagging Church Street renewal project and as a result work on the Ford proposal was temporarily at least suspended. The January draft was never submitted to the Foundation, nor for that matter ever seriously discussed locally.

Despite this, the December meeting between city officials and the Foundation staff proved to be highly significant. The prospect of Foundation support, uncertain though it was at the time, acted as a powerful and enduring incentive. Even without Logue, hopes for Foundation backing persisted, and a year later work began anew on the plans for a social renewal program in New Haven.

A Bureaucrat's Initiative: Howard Hallman

Had outside observers been asked in 1960 to predict who, among Lee's urban renewal bureaucrats, would be most likely to provide this renewed impetus for social reform, few in all probability would have nominated Howard Hallman, the director of the Redevelopment Agency's Division of Neighborhood Improvement. For one thing Hallman was relatively young (thirty years old) and a newcomer to the city and to Lee's urban renewal team. Born and raised in the rural midwest, the son of a banker, educated at the University of Kansas where he earned a Master's degree in political science, Hallman had moved to New

Haven in 1959 from Philadelphia, where he had served as metropolitan consultant to the Philadelphia Housing Association, a United Fund agency. Since his arrival in New Haven he had earned a reputation within the agency as an effective and competent, if somewhat aloof and quiet administrator. Yet his record had not been spectacular and his behavior lacked the dramatic flair that had helped make his superiors Logue and Lee well known to the population. It would have been understandable, then, if outsiders had failed to nominate him, for in all probability few had ever heard of him.

Nor would they hear of him in the future, for the part he played in the development of the city's anti-poverty project has gone largely unnoticed in the few accounts that have been published.[26] Yet Hallman was one of the project's principal initiators and organizers. To be sure there were others who contributed to the project's ultimate shape. But apart from Lee, whose role will be examined presently, no single local participant was more central to the process than this obscure bureaucrat who combined what can only be termed an intense sense of social justice with a skill for translating his humanitarian concern for the poor into concrete reality. "Without him," Mitchell Sviridoff, New Haven's first anti-poverty director once observed, "there never would have been a project."[27]

For Hallman, as for Logue before him, the immediate stimulus had been Oak Street. As director of the Division of Neighborhood Improvement, Hallman was responsible for housing code enforcement and housing surveys in renewal areas and in this capacity had come face to face with conditions in the slums. As director he also had participated in the early deliberations over relocation, in the discussions with Community Research Associates, and in the early efforts to enlist the support of the Council of Social Agencies. Finally, and perhaps most significantly, he had accompanied Logue to New York in December 1959 for the meeting with Foundation officials, and along with Logue's administrative assistant Robert Hazen, had drafted the proposal for "Community Improvement" that had grown out of this meeting.

One year later Hallman revived the idea. In December 1960 he resurrected the earlier draft, revised it, and circulated it quietly among a small group. To Isadore Wexler, Principal of New Haven's Winchester School, he wrote on December 6:

Dear Wex:

We are resurrecting our ambition to get some money from the Ford Foundation to do some additional things on the human and social side of city revitalization. As a point of departure I have written the enclosed draft, and I would like your comment on it.

At this stage, it should be considered confidential and not for any wider distribution.[28]

Confidential it remained, or at least unpublicized, until the announcement a year and a half later that the Foundation had awarded New Haven a grant. During the intervening months, Hallman gradually refined and reformulated the proposal, piecing together a diverse set of programs and activities drawn from a number of sources. Some of these sources were outside the city as he wrote or visited individuals whose record or reputation suggested they might be of some help. At first these included individuals active in the area of social welfare: Mr. Alec Rosen, dean of the School of Social Work at New York University, Miss Fern Colburn of the National Federation of Settlements and Neighborhood Centers, and Rev. C. Kilmer Myers, an Episcopalian priest active in Harlem. Later he drew on the assistance and advice of the Ford Foundation staff; of Paul Ylvisaker, who since had risen in the Foundation hierarchy to the position of director of the Foundation's Public Affairs Division; and of Ylvisaker's associates Henry Saltzman, David Hunter, and Richard Boone. For the most part, however, he relied on his personal resources and on those of a small, unofficial group he had organized to work with him on the proposal.

The New Haveners to whom he turned initially in the winter of 1960-1961 had several common characteristics.

1. They were all professional administrators—more specifically, to use Hallman's term, "social worker and educator types." Among them were three representatives from the Department of Education, six from private welfare agencies, including Frank Harris of the Community Council, who became one of Hallman's principal allies, and five members of the Redevelopment Agency.
2. Most of these individuals were already known to one another and to Hallman.
3. More importantly, all of them shared, at least in a generalized way, Hallman's belief that social change was needed. "We have a fairly good idea of the problems we are looking at and the needs we are interested in," one member of the group observed at an early meeting; "We now need to try some sort of program."[29] This was no mere coincidence. Convinced as he was of the pressing need for action, Hallman was more interested in examining the question "What should be done?" than in debating the issue "Should anything be done?" For this reason he deliberately sought out those known to be sympathetic to reform. More than this, he consciously excluded those considered hostile or merely indifferent to the types of changes he envisioned for the city.

There was some danger in this choice of action, for among those excluded were individuals whose backing, or at least neutrality, eventually would be needed. Neither the superintendent of schools nor the director of public health, for example, were included in the group despite the fact the agencies they headed were expected to play key roles in the reform. The sympathies of both officials were much in doubt, and in a move to protect the fledgling enterprise it was decided to postpone their participation to a later time. By then, it was hoped, the reform group would be in a position to advance concrete proposals from a firmer political base.[b]

[b]Hallman's decision was predicated on another factor, namely an expectation that the heads of both these agencies would be replaced by more sympathetic officials. This in fact occurred (see below, chapter 7), but just how certain this contingency was in early 1961 is unclear.

The group Hallman assembled was thus in fundamental agreement about the need for reform. Individually, its members were favorably predisposed to change, and whatever differences there were (and an examination of the minutes Hallman maintained suggests the differences were few), they were not sufficiently intense to disrupt the group and divert it from the task Hallman had defined for it. Meeting informally, either at Hallman's home or at the Redevelopment Agency offices, the group gradually sharpened its own understanding of the social problems confronting the city and of the measures that might be taken to alleviate them. By late spring a new document entitled "A Program for Educational Improvement and Human Development in New Haven" had been prepared, and in June 1961, contact with the Foundation was re-established.

As Hallman himself readily admitted, the Foundation's response to this revised draft was hardly enthusiastic. While the document contained some specific proposals—among them a proposal for a "comprehensive program for community organization workers" in the inner-city neighborhoods—its main thrust was toward planning. Having identified general problem areas, among them education, housing, the elderly, and unemployment, the group had proceeded to urge further study of existing policies and practices with a view to developing programs that would, according to the document, "make an essential contribution to creating a better life in the city."[30] "Creating a better life in the city" was, of course, what the Foundation wanted. But in addition to noble sentiments it also wanted a more complete set of concrete proposals that would help lead to this broader social goal.

If the Foundation's response was not overly enthusiastic, still the response did not constitute an outright rejection, or at least it was not so perceived. Having renewed his contact with the Foundation and having acquired some indication of what the Foundation did *not* want, Hallman intensified his own efforts to fashion a viable proposal. Once again he relied primarily on local individuals, albeit, as we shall see presently, on some who until this point had not participated directly in the planning. By October 1961, a new draft of the proposal had been readied[31] and forwarded to the Foundation, and in November a second meeting was held between city and Foundation officials. This time, Hallman recorded, the "Foundation expressed serious interest in New Haven's proposal."[32] One month later his language was less measured. After a discussion with Henry Saltzman of the Foundation's Public Affairs Division he reported back to his colleagues in New Haven: "I talked with Saltzman today, and things look very good for New Haven. . . . He gave me the feeling that our chances are very good."[33]

Nor was his optimism premature. Indeed, the substantive programs contained in the revised October draft were, in all but minor details, the very ones the Foundation eventually agreed to fund.

The "Community Power Structure"

In the year that elapsed between his letter in December 1960 to Isadore Wexler and his discussion in December 1961 with the Foundation's Henry Saltzman,

Hallman had seen his hopes for a "human renewal" effort move from vague theorizing about the nature of a good community into a set of concrete proposals. As he was well aware, however, the mere development of a set of proposals was not sufficient in and of itself to ensure acceptance. However well intentioned or sophisticated the enterprise might otherwise appear, it would founder if those who proposed it failed, as Hallman put it, "to gain the support of elements in the community power structure."[34]

What he meant by this term—despite its overtones from Floyd Hunter of a small, all-powerful social and economic elite[35]—is best suggested by his own behavior and by the identity of those whose support he actively sought. Rather than seeking out businessmen, bankers, industrialists, or others commonly listed as community and civic leaders, he relied principally (Table 2-6) on individuals who occupied positions of authority in the city's public and private agencies. In other words, he turned to those in the community with specialized political and bureaucratic roles, not to those with economic status.

The prevalence of political and bureaucratic types was in evidence from the very start of the planning process. As I indicated earlier, the working group Hallman organized in the winter of 1960-61 was drawn exclusively from the membership of local public and private agencies. So too were those outside of this group whose advice and counsel he sought. Here again he looked to agencies and institutions he thought could benefit the undertaking and within these to individuals he expected would be sympathetic. These included the director of the Grace-New Haven Hospital's Psychiatric Clinic, two Protestant ministers

Table 2-6

Institutional Affiliation of Individuals Contacted by Hallman: December 1960-December 1961

Institution	Working Group 12/60-6/61	Advisory Group	Total
Public Agencies:			
Development Admin.	5	9	14
Education	3	3	6
Mayor's Office	1	3	4
Other	0	1	1
Private Institutions:			
Health and Welfare	6	8	14
Yale University	0	6	6
Others	0	3	3
Identity Unknown	0	3	3
N=	15	36	51

Note: The table does not distinguish among the types of participation, nor among the types of influence. Its sole purpose is to indicate the character of the groups that were involved.

active in inner city parish work, the director of the Neighborhood Music School, the director of a neighborhood settlement house, and several Yale faculty members. Included also were several additional staff members of the Redevelopment Agency and the Community Council, as well as representatives of the New Haven Board of Education, among them the board's president, Mitchell Sviridoff.

Of all those in the "power structure," none was considered more important than the city's elected chief executive, Richard C. Lee. For Hallman as well as for others, the backing of the mayor was considered essential. His opposition, indeed even his mere neutrality, would have been fatal, for the planners assumed the Foundation's interest in New Haven was predicated on the mayor's actively supporting the project.

That Lee supported the project there can be no doubt, but that he did so in the way many published accounts claim he did is open to some question. According to these accounts, among them those published by the anti-poverty agency itself, it was Lee's initiative and leadership that brought the city's anti-poverty project into being in much the same way as it had been his leadership and initiative that had brought about New Haven's redevelopment program.[36]

Actually, Lee's contribution to the anti-poverty project was quite different from his contribution to urban renewal. Above all else, urban renewal was *his* program, one with which he had become identified even before his election as mayor and one which since his election as mayor had been closely associated with his political fortunes and ambitions. As such he took a direct personal interest in its functioning, maintaining a careful watch over its operation, at times attending to the smallest detail.[37]

This was not the case in anti-poverty. The mayor's support for this project was far more generalized and his participation in its operation far more limited and indirect. This was especially true during the planning stages, that period between December 1960 and December 1961 when the substantive features of the project were taking shape. Throughout this year of planning Lee remained quite apart from the deliberations of Hallman and his group. To be sure, he was kept informed about the progress of the proposal, usually by Thomas Appleby who had succeeded Logue as the city's development administrator, and he did take part in the preliminary discussions held in June 1961 with the Foundation. In all this, however, he did not lend the effort the personal attention and drive that he had urban renewal. Even in the case of the early negotiations with the Foundation, according to Hallman, Lee's participation was marginal. As one of Lee's biographers observed:

Lee was not always helpful in the negotiations. He would show up at the Foundation's Madison Avenue offices with his staff, make a general appeal for quick action and a brief request for support of his homemaking program and then take off for Roger Stevens' office several blocks away on Broadway to check on Church Street progress.[38]

Checking on Church Street was one of Lee's chief preoccupations during this period and it may help explain his seeming lack of interest in the budding anti-poverty project. Throughout 1961 Lee and his urban renewal staff had been plagued by one set-back after another in their drive to renew the city's central business district. As the November, 1961 election drew near, the project area was, in Talbot's words, "a wasteland of cleared buildings with little construction activity" and Lee faced the prospect of "carrying an apparent fiasco into the elections."[39] Lee won the election—though by what for him was a narrow margin of 4,000 votes. But to win the election, it seems, he had to focus his attention and energies on immediate problems and forego those of the more distant future.

Whatever the explanation for his behavior, the important point is that during this formative period the mayor's participation in the project was quite limited. The initiative for reform, the definition of the problems, and the articulation of specific programs to deal with these problems rested largely in the hands of a small group of public and private bureaucrats in the city.

If Lee's participation during the planning stages was limited, his contribution was nonetheless considerable. For one thing, Lee, more than anyone else in the city, had been responsible for urban renewal and it was urban renewal that led to the "discovery" of poverty in New Haven. Second, it had been the mayor who had created the city's urban renewal bureaucracy, who had recruited the administrators and technicians—"planners with a social conscience," Frank Harris of the Community Council once called them[40]—who had played such a major part in the actual formulation and articulation of the city's response to conditions in the slums. Finally, and no less importantly, Lee had allowed the planning process to proceed, though he made it perfectly clear he would not tolerate any interference with the work of the Redevelopment Agency staff on the Church Street Project.

Once agreement on the substance of the project had been reached, but before the grant was actually awarded, Lee's role changed from that of an interested on-looker to that of an active participant. It was at this point, the period roughly between December 1961, when Hallman reported that "things look very good for New Haven," and the following April, that the mayor was to contribute most directly to the project. In January 1962, for example, he and his staff staged an elaborate visit for members of the Foundation. For two days, Foundation officials were exposed to an intensive campaign arranged to demonstrate that the proposal developed by a small group of bureaucratic planners had broad backing in the community. In all some thirty-five local "leaders" participated, among them the late A. Whitney Griswold, then president of Yale University; Richard M. Grave, the president of the Community Council; John Braslin, the president of the Board of Education; and the superintendent of schools-elect, Lawrence Paquin.[41] Of those who participated, however, the mayor was the most prominent. According to Hallman and others who were present, Lee dominated the proceedings as he cast himself in a role at which he was a proven master, namely salesman par excellence for New Haven and the Lee administration.

Lee's support for the proposed enterprise went beyond his mere wooing of the Foundation, and in the weeks that followed the January conference he demonstrated in what perhaps were more meaningful terms the value of his backing. Lee was instrumental, for example, in obtaining local money to satisfy the Ford Foundation's requirement that its own grant be matched by funds from other sources. In February he went before the Distribution Committee of the New Haven Foundation, a local philanthropic organization, and, using the prospect of the Ford Foundation grant as leverage, persuaded the Foundation to commit some $100,000 to the proposed undertaking. To this he was able to add financial commitments from several local public agencies, among them the Board of Education and the Redevelopment Agency, as further evidence of his own support for the project.

Lee's final touch, and in view of subsequent developments perhaps his most important one, was the selection of the anti-poverty agency's first executive director, Mitchell Sviridoff. Sviridoff, who had resigned in 1961 as president of the New Haven Board of Education to accept a position with the Agency for International Development, was like Lee a New Haven product. The two were close in age—a year separated them—had grown up together in the same neighborhood, Newhallville, and had attended the same public school. While Lee was serving his apprenticeship in the city, first as a reporter for *The New Haven Journal-Courier*, then with the Yale News Bureau, and finally, just before his election as mayor, as a city alderman, Sviridoff was pursuing a career outside the city in the state labor movement. In 1946, at the age of twenty-six, he was elected president of the state CIO and continued as president of the AFL-CIO after the two labor organizations merged in 1956. In 1954 the mayor appointed him to the Board of Education—the first union representative on the Board in the city's history—where as a Board member and later as Board president he had pressed for reforms within the school system, among them plans for rebuilding 40 percent of the city's school buildings. By selecting Sviridoff, Lee entrusted the project to a close friend and ally, as well as a proven administrator and politician. His trust was not misplaced. As we shall see in later chapters, once appointed, Sviridoff took firm control of the project and under his leadership New Haven's anti-poverty effort became a prototype for the Johnson administration's national war on poverty.

Lee's behavior during the planning process was in marked contrast to his behavior during the selling and appointing stages. Once the reform proposal had taken form and the Ford Foundation had expressed serious interest, the mayor's seeming indifference shifted to constructive and galvanic intervention. As a result the Foundation's backing was secured and the mayor ensured an agency leadership he would be able to work with as well as one with much greater political standing than the initiating bureaucrats themselves could have fashioned.

The Beginnings in Perspective

In a sense the beginnings of New Haven's anti-poverty project were somewhat prosaic. Missing was that dramatic "stirring among the people," that shared sense of dissatisfaction with the status quo, and the common resolve and collective action to alter certain social institutions that are associated characteristically with broadly based social movements. This is not to say that New Haven's population, and in particular that segment of the population directly affected by the progress of urban renewal, was perfectly content with its lot. If there was dissatisfaction, however—and given the objective conditions prevailing in the inner city one assumes there was—it had not yet been clearly articulated, much less explicitly organized. Indeed, it would be several years before the interests of the poor and racial minorities in New Haven and in other urban communities would come to be articulated by indigenous spokesmen or by self-styled representatives of the oppressed and the disadvantaged. Missing also were the political conflicts, the struggles, debates, recriminations, and objections that frequently accompany innovative proposals. Indeed, that a proposal of the dimensions and significance of New Haven's anti-poverty project could have emerged in an atmosphere of relative quiet and calm may strike some as unreal. But such in fact was the case.

If the beginnings of the project were less than spectacular, still they are of considerable interest for what they reveal about the patterns of decision-making in a local community. For one thing, they suggest that leadership roles, rather than being a fixed part of the governmental or social structure, are or can be quite variable. During this period a new group, or to be more precise a new coalition of already existing interests, emerged within the community and asserted itself as the chief proponent of reform. Of these interests two stand out: first, New Haven's elected chief executive Mayor Lee; and second, members of the bureaucratic establishment he had created to carry-out his urban renewal program. Thus with respect to anti-poverty, at least, the chief participants turned out to be, as Robert Dahl had suggested they might, "bureaucrats and experts—and politicians who know how to use them."[42]

That Lee knew how to use his bureaucrats and experts is clear from his intervention during the final stages of the planning process. From this it should not be concluded, however, that these bureaucrats and experts were simply neutral instruments in the hands of the mayor. Quite the contrary. While they were used, they were used quite willingly and they demonstrated that they themselves were capable of using the mayor, among other things to gain final Foundation approval for the programs they had fashioned. In short, the relationship between the two, between Lee on the one hand and the bureaucrats on the other, was highly reciprocal or, to use a biological analogy, symbiotic.

That the initiative for reform came largely from Lee's urban renewal bureaucrats suggests a final, albeit tentative, proposition about decision-making, and specifically the decision to innovate or to propose change. The events surrounding the origins of the project indicate that the more recent one's exposure to problems, the more inclined he is to advance new methods of dealing with them. For the initiators of the project, for Logue, and, following him, Hallman, direct exposure to the slums and to the conditions of poverty was a quite recent experience. In a sense, they were "quasi amateurs" who had ventured into the area of social welfare. As amateurs, however, they were under fewer restraints than their professional counterparts in the public and private health and welfare agencies. For one thing, the renewal bureaucrats had less of a commitment to established welfare practices and policies; for another, they had not as yet become preoccupied with the daily routine of caring for the poor; and finally, being inexperienced, they were less likely to perceive obstacles that stood in the way of change. In short, the renewal bureaucrats were unaffected by tradition, routine, or fear of defeat, all three of which operate as strong deterrents to innovation.

While undeterred by these factors, the renewal bureaucrats were sufficiently realistic to appreciate that the path to reform would be arduous. Even with the Foundation grant and the backing of the mayor in hand there were obstacles and dangers yet to be faced. Among other things, an ambitious social welfare program initiated by newcomers was likely to occasion disagreement, hostility, and opposition. As Logue and especially Hallman and Sviridoff realized, if their energies were to be devoted to fighting poverty rather than opposing political groups, measures would be necessary to protect the fledgling enterprise and their own interests in it. What these measures were and how they developed will be examined in the following chapter.

3

The Genesis and Control of A Reform Agency

On the day he made public the award of the Ford Foundation grant, New Haven's Mayor Richard C. Lee revealed that a new agency had been created to administer the city's anti-poverty project. "I am pleased to announce the completion of the legal steps," the mayor's statement read in part, "creating a new, non-profit corporation.... Papers of incorporation for Community Progress, Inc. were filed this morning in the Secretary of State's office in Hartford by a member of my staff."[1]

In and of itself, the form chosen for New Haven's anti-poverty agency was not unique. Private, non-profit corporations are commonplace indeed throughout the country; this is the legal form under which private charitable, scientific, and educational institutions operate. Still, Community Progress, Inc. (CPI) *was* different and what made the difference was *the extent to which this new agency actually participated in the governmental process.* To anticipate what will be discussed later in detail, New Haven's anti-poverty agency participated continuously in the shaping of public policy, among other things by financing the activities of local public agencies. Indeed, so extensive was this participation that the legally untrained mind strains to understand how this new agency qualified as a private non-stock corporation, given the legal prescription that "no substantial part of the activities of [such corporations] is carrying on propaganda, or otherwise attempting to influence legislation."[2]

This is not the place, however, either to puzzle over the meaning of the law or to wonder at its elasticity. New Haven's anti-poverty agency was in form, if not in fact, a private, non-profit corporation, and what is of interest here are the calculations that led to the choice of this particular form and the ways in which agency officials used this form to enhance their own control over the project.

Institutional Form and Political Strategy

Political Calculations

Community Progress, Inc. was designed as an instrument of executive leadership, or to state it more precisely, as a device to promote and preserve a particular style of executive leadership. At first glance this may sound surprising. As the authors of a widely used textbook in public administration once observed: "Proposals for independent agencies . . . are often advanced by groups that are opposed to a particular administration in power."[3] Indeed, there were some in

New Haven who claimed this is precisely what happened in the case of Community Progress, Inc. Prior to the 1965 municipal campaign, for example, an aspirant for the Republican mayoralty nomination charged that national groups funding the city's anti-poverty project "felt that Mayor Lee and his long entrenched administration were not qualified ... to spend funds wisely and therefore turned control of the money over to a private agency."[4] His charge was as wide of the mark as was his subsequent bid to oust Lee—he lost the election by more than 16,000 votes. CPI was located outside the traditional framework of municipal government not out of fear of Lee, but out of a fear that he might leave the city.

The overwhelming concern of those who planned New Haven's anti-poverty project was the type of executive leadership that might emerge if and when Lee himself left office. At the time, Lee's future role in the city was particularly uncertain, as was the future of New Haven politics generally. In the municipal election held in 1961 just before the award of the Foundation grant, Lee had been returned to office by a slim margin of 4,000 votes, the lowest (Table 3-1) since his first victory in 1953. To some it appeared as though the mayor had finally begun to lose some of his political glamor, and although predictions of a further decline in his electoral fortunes proved premature—in 1963 the Mayor returned to form and again won handily—for those planning the project such a decline had to be considered a distinct possibility.

So too was the possibility that Lee would relinquish his office voluntarily. For one thing, it was no secret that Lee was an ambitious politician, and few believed he had any intention of devoting his entire political career to New Haven. The mayor's future was perennially discussed in terms of higher office and occasionally in terms of a high position outside of government. It was known at the time, for example, that he was interested in the United States Senate and was considering a bid for the seat occupied by Republican Senator

Table 3-1

New Haven's Mayoralty Elections: 1953-1967

Year	% Democratic		% Republican		% Other	
1953	53.3	(Lee)	46.7	(Celentano)		
1955	65.5	(Lee)	34.5	(Mancini)		
1957	65.0	(Lee)	28.7	(Cook)	6.2	(Malkan)
1959	61.8	(Lee)	38.2	(Valenti)		
1961	53.4	(Lee)	46.6	(Townsend)		
1963	59.3	(Lee)	39.5	(Townsend)	1.2	(Paige)
1965	66.0	(Lee)	34.0	(Einhorn)		
1967	61.8	(Lee)	38.2	(Whitney)		

Prescott Bush, a bid he never made in part because of his poor showing in the 1961 municipal election. Apart from the United States Senate or other high elective office, there was a possibility he would accept a position with the Kennedy administration. Lee had been an early Kennedy ally, one who had supported the late president before the West Virginia primary, and shortly after Kennedy's election Lee reportedly was offered a position in the new administration.

Finally, if the mayor did not relinquish his post for political reasons it was conceivable he would do so for reasons of health. Throughout his political career he had been plagued by stomach disorders and these were a continuing source of personal concern both to Lee himself and to the men closely associated with his administration.

If Lee's future was uncertain, so too was the nature and character of future New Haven administrations. Like many strong political figures, Lee had no heir apparent and it was a matter of no little concern that if the mayor either resigned or was defeated City Hall could easily fall into unsympathetic or hostile hands. In the Lee administration, progressive bureaucrats like Logue and Hallman had been encouraged to innovate, and, more importantly, had found backing for their innovations from a strong and resourceful chief executive. But there was no assurance a future mayor would be as receptive. In another administration there might be no place for programs such as the anti-poverty project, and it was to guard against this contingency that a new, private corporation was created to manage the project. In Hallman's words, the administrative form adopted "was structured so as to survive a change in city administration."[5]

Alternative Forms and Alternative Structures

Of course, this particular objective could have been reached in other ways, for example by using such urban forms as the board, commission, or special authority, all three of which have been employed in the past to frustrate executive control and blunt the effects of the electoral process.[6] That these particular urban forms were not selected—indeed, as far as can be determined they were never seriously considered—is understandable given the planners' objective of minimizing external interference in the administration of the project.

The choice of any one of these alternative forms would have made the agency, and hence the project, more a part of the governmental process, thereby increasing the number of voices in agency decision-making. One such voice would have been the governor, another the state legislature, still another the New Haven Board of Aldermen, since the creation of a board, commission, or special authority would have required authorization from one or all these general institutions of government. Moreover, as a public agency, a board, commission, or special authority would have been subject to continuing governmental supervision and intervention. The institutions that participate in the formation of such agencies continue to have an influence over their activities either directly, through legislative review and the budgetary process, or indirectly through stipulations in the agency's organic law regarding such matters as the appointment of personnel. So too do other governmental institutions, among them the courts and such specialized overhead agencies as civil service commissions, departments of purchasing and accounting, comptrollers' offices, and corporation counsels. In short, while any one of these traditional urban forms would have been preferable to direct executive control, each had its costs. Each would have made the agency subject to a variety of administrative regulations and political checks and in so doing would have lessened the freedom of action New Haven's planners sought.

All this was avoided, or at least minimized considerably, by the decision to create a private, non-profit corporation. For one thing, the creation of such a corporation is a fairly routine matter, merely requiring the filing of incorporation papers with the secretary of state, the payment of an incorporation fee, and a ruling of tax exemption from the United States Internal Revenue Service. For another, the corporate form offered distinct operational advantages over the traditional urban forms mentioned above. As a private, non-profit corporation the agency enjoyed the same legal status as the churches and many private universities. As such it also shared, at least indirectly, in their political power, since any attack on this particular non-profit corporation could have been a threat to the autonomy and independence of the others. This is not to say that had there been such an attack other private, non-profit corporations would have automatically rallied to support New Haven's anti-poverty agency. Quite possibly this could have happened. But at the very least, by sharing a legal form with well established institutions, the agency had a *potential* set of influential allies and a powerful argument for mobilizing them, namely that maintaining the corporate integrity of Community Progress, Inc. was in their own best interest.[a]

Community Progress, Inc. vs. the
Citizens' Action Commission

While the decision to locate the anti-poverty agency outside the formal structure of local government had been made quite early in the planning[7] it was not until late January or early February 1962, just two months prior to the award of the Foundation grant, that the exact nature of the private corporation was settled. Before this there had been two conflicting schools of thought within the planning group: one, represented by Howard Hallman, advocated the creation of a new private corporation; the other, whose chief spokesman was Frank Harris of the Greater New Haven Community Council, urged that an existing one be used.

---

[a]It should be stressed that this sharing was a potential resource only. Whether the agency ever uses it and with what results is another matter.

More specifically, Harris proposed that New Haven's Citizens' Action Commission (CAC) be used as the institutional base for the city's anti-poverty project. The commission, whose membership included some of the city's leading bankers, lawyers, and businessmen, had been created by Lee in 1954 to help win community support and acceptance for his urban renewal program.[8] Since it already existed and since it already enjoyed a corporate tax exempt status, the commission could provide the protection desired from the governmental and political process. In addition, it was well-suited to the uncertainties surrounding Lee's future in the city. "I assume we will not always have Dick Lee to push things through for us," Harris cautioned, and given this assumption the project would need, in Harris' words, "people who could render effective support." It was precisely this type of person, Harris felt, that served on the Citizens' Action Commission and he urged his fellow planners to take advantage of this group "whose personal, business, and professional contacts bring them frequent opportunities to develop understanding and support of the program."[9]

The commission also had its disadvantages, at least in Hallman's mind, and these disadvantages "far outweighed its advantages."[10] For one thing, its political currency had been debased. In urban renewal, the commission had been, as one author noted and as Hallman himself agreed, "a brilliant invention . . . a manufactured pressure group . . . which had increased support for Lee's programs without in any way extending control over them."[11] For this very reason, however, the commission's reputation had been damaged. "CAC has a rather poor public image," Hallman claimed, "because it has been so inactive and because of its role as a rubber stamp."[12] In a sense the commission had been too successful; it had served Lee's purposes in urban renewal but in serving them it had lessened its credibility and effectiveness.

Nor was there much else to recommend the commission. It was a large organization, "too big for fast and effective action"; it was "dominated by conservative elements . . . who would be difficult in certain areas of the program"; and it had "an incumbent executive director who could not run such a program [anti-poverty]."[13] Whatever the past political value of the commission, Hallman considered it an inappropriate and undesirable base for the anti-poverty project. And his argument carried the day. Harris's proposal was rejected in favor of the new, private non-profit corporation.

Hallman's objection to the Citizens' Action Commission went beyond the specific points he raised in his debate with Harris. Indeed, these points were secondary to his argument. His basic objection to the commission was the very fact that it existed, and Hallman opposed making the anti-poverty project the responsibility of any existing agency. What was needed for the proper administration of the project, he maintained, "was an agency without a tradition that would inhibit it,"[14] an agency "free from the commitments of existing programs."[15] Otherwise, he predicted, the anti-poverty project "would get lost in the shuffle by not being given adequate attention."[16] If assigned to an existing agency the project might, for example, be neglected by the agency's top executives. Moreover, as part of such an agency the new project would have to compete for resources with the agency's established programs, among other things for money, personnel, political support, and even office facilities and office supplies. Such competition could be costly, quite possibly fatal, since there was no assurance the new project could survive if forced to struggle for its existence with an established agency. Indeed, the odds were against survival, for if faced with a choice between old programs and new ones, an established agency could be expected to opt for the former. In short, if the project were assigned to an existing agency there was a danger its objectives would be nullified, a danger that could be minimized by creating an entirely new and separate organization.

Control of Personnel

Creating an institutional base was the first step in ensuring that the project would be controlled by sympathetic administrators. A second was the appointment of personnel. Availing themselves of the agency's newness and of its private status, Lee and, most especially, his appointee as the agency's first executive director, Mitchell Sviridoff, used the appointment process to protect further the integrity of the project.

The Board of Directors

In a purely formal sense the key decision-making group in New Haven's anti-poverty agency was the Board of Directors of Community Progress, Inc. Legally, the board acted as authoritative spokesman for the project. The board officially applied for and received outside grants and contracts, allocated funds, and directed the agency's professional staff members who themselves served at the pleasure of the board. As is so often the case, however, the formal organization of authority within the agency did not correspond with the effective distribution of power. In actual practice, board members had little to do with the determination of agency policies, nor, it appears, were they expected to do so.

According to its Certificate of Incorporation the agency was to be governed by a nine member board, three of whom were to be selected by the mayor, and one each by the New Haven Board of Education, the New Haven Redevelopment Agency, the United Fund, the Citizens' Action Commission, the Community Council, and Yale University. Board members were appointed to three-year terms to serve, among other things, as links between established institutions and the new agency, and as a visible manifestation of community support for the enterprise.

The board's institutional ties made it a legitimating device, as did the character of those who were chosen to serve.[b] Its members, who more than anyone else closely associated with the project represented those in New Haven

---

[b]This and other efforts to "legitimate" the project are discussed in more detail in chapter 8.

Robert Dahl has termed the "social and economic notables," were chosen to lend an element of respectability to what the planners feared might be an unpopular, and politically suspect and vulnerable, undertaking. As described in the press release announcing the project, these were "some of New Haven's most outstanding citizens."[17]

The very qualifications of this board, however, reduced the likelihood that it would provide the agency and the project strong leadership and direction. To be sure, both individually and collectively board members possessed important and salient resources. But based on past behavior and existing commitments it was unlikely they would use these resources to intervene extensively in agency affairs. For one thing, none of the members had a record of political activism; their political participation was an avocation rather than a vocation. Moreover, what limited time board members *did* have for community projects was already distributed rather widely among other activities. All nine original board members belonged to other organizations (some sixty in all!) not counting their professional associations or their membership on the board of the anti-poverty agency. If nothing else, any major participation in the business of the new agency would have been costly for board members. Spending time on the agency, on learning about and planning for this new enterprise for which there was no precedent, no established policy, and few routinized decisions, would have detracted substantially from their other commitments.

If there were doubts as to the role board members were expected to play in the project, they must have been quickly resolved with the appointment of the new agency's first executive director. For one thing, even before the selection of board members themselves, the mayor and his planners, along with staff members of the Public Affairs Division of the Ford Foundation, began searching on their own for someone to fill the post. At the board's first meeting on April 16, 1962, its members were presented with a *fait accompli* and their first official act was to ratify Sviridoff's appointment.[18] Second, Sviridoff was close to the mayor and a political force in his own right, an individual whose past record and experience as president of the state AFL-CIO, and member, then president, of the New Haven Board of Education were clear indications that he, and not the board, was to be *the* major influence within the agency.

The Professional Staff

And the major influence he was. Between 1962, when he accepted Lee's invitation to head the new agency, and 1966 when he left New Haven to head New York City's Human Resources Commission, Sviridoff *dominated* New Haven's anti-poverty project. No other single individual or group, neither the board to whom he was formally responsible, nor Lee who had chosen him, nor Hallman, who along with Lee had played a central role in launching the project, equalled Sviridoff's influence over the reform effort. Once appointed he devoted himself entirely to the project, making social reform both an occupation and a preoccupation. To be sure, there was a large element of risk in such a commitment. The enterprise was new and untested, and the problems to which it was addressed seemingly intractable ones. Yet his commitment paid off handsomely. Under his leadership New Haven's anti-poverty project was hailed as a model for the country and Sviridoff gained recognition as one of the nation's foremost experts on social renewal, a recognition that eventually led to his appointment as a key vice president of the Ford Foundation. In short, Sviridoff put CPI on the map and his CPI performance moved him from an influential role in the state of Connecticut to a position that enabled him to act on a national scale.

As executive director of the New Haven agency Sviridoff had considerable freedom with respect to personnel matters and he used this freedom to strengthen his own hand within the agency. The agency's non-profit corporate form gave Sviridoff a critical resource: *unlike his counterparts in the regular municipal agencies, he was not constrained in personnel decisions by formal laws and regulations*. Community Progress, Inc. was not bound by the requirements of the classified service, requirements such as public notification of job openings, competitive examinations, job classifications, or job security. Nor were there any statutory or municipal charter provisions restricting agency appointments to certain categories of individuals—for example, to residents and voters of New Haven, or to those who satisfied stipulated professional criteria, all of which serve to limit the appointing power of officials in the regular municipal departments.

In addition the agency was new—"without a tradition," as Hallman maintained it should be—and one of the traditions it lacked was a set of expectations about who should be appointed to the staff.[c] Within the agency itself there was no established social structure, at least no inherited one, no established loyalties to organizational sub-groups, and *no established claim associated with any individual or group to a voice in personnel decisions*. Outside the agency conditions were much the same. True, there were occasional referrals from the mayor and other local political leaders. But these referrals were few in number and as far as I could determine no outside individual or group challenged Sviridoff's control over personnel. If it is true, as Herbert Kaufman claims, that "rarely . . . does an appointing officer have an opportunity to make a selection that is his own free choice,"[19] then Sviridoff's experience was strikingly unique and atypical.

Free of formal governmental and informal political constraints, Sviridoff recruited a staff that was largely of his own making and shaped to his own

---

[c]Of those who planned the project, only Howard Hallman had any aspirations concerning the role he would play in the new agency. Reportedly, Hallman expected to head the new agency, but Lee denied him the appointment in preference for Sviridoff. Instead of being executive director, Hallman was appointed Sviridoff's deputy director and worked closely with him during the formative years. In 1965 Hallman left the agency to work as a private consultant for community action programs across the country. He was subsequently named president of the Center for Governmental Studies in Washington, D.C.

specifications. Like Lee and Logue before him in urban renewal, he relied heavily on imported talent, particularly at the agency's upper echelon, a practice that would have been virtually impossible for a government organization working through partisan channels. All but three of the agency's highest ranking officials (*N*=13), officials who served as program directors, assistant directors, or special assistants (Table 3-2), came from outside the city, as did the vast majority of those who served in the agency's middle range positions, thirty-two out of forty-four. Most of these top and middle range officials (fifty-two out of the fifty-seven in grades 6-12) were college educated and of these fifty-two, over half held advanced professional and/or graduate degrees in such diverse fields as education, law, English, philosophy, sociology, social work, public adminis- tration, and political science. And while college education alone is not an unambiguous measure of skill and competence—after all, Sviridoff himself had but a high school education—still, all indications are that the men Sviridoff selected to help him mount New Haven's anti-poverty effort were an exceptionally able group.

Table 3-2

Distribution of Community Progress Inc. Personnel, by Grade Level and Place of Origin

Place of Origin	Percentage in Grade Levels[a]			
	1-2	3-5	6-9	10-12
Local Residents	31.0	53.0	22.5	23.0
Importees	14.0	13.0	71.0	77.0
Not Ascertained[b]	54.0	34.0	6.5	0.0
	N=57	N=76	N=44	N=13

Note: Data are based on personnel listings as of January, 1965 and includes only full-time personnel employed between 1962 and 1965.

[a]Grade levels were salary classifications and corresponded roughly to the levels of responsibility within the agency. The salary ranges, including within-grade steps, were as follows:

Grades 1-2	$ 3,500 to $ 5,100
Grades 3-5	$ 4,500 to $ 8,000
Grades 6-9	$ 7,000 to $12,500
Grades 10-12	$11,000 to $20,000

[b]During the first two years the agency did not maintain systematic personnel data. As a result, I was forced to rely on information supplied informally by members of the staff about some earlier employees. Frequently, staff members could not recall much personal information about former secretaries, clerks, and the like. Hence the large number of "not ascertained" for the lower grade levels.

Sviridoff's policy of recruiting top level talent from outside the city was in fact a potential threat to his own control of the agency. Even if all men of talent do not tend toward independence and insubordination, the probability of deviation and challenge is probably greater among such a group than it is among the less talented. Moreover, as with any agency serving the public, there was a constant danger the staff would over-identify with its clientele, in this case the poor—or that short of this, staff loyalties would be torn between the agency and its director on the one hand and on the other those the agency was serving.

Sviridoff was well aware of these dangers and he guarded against them in a number of ways. First, he insisted that the recruitment and appointment of top level agency personnel[d] be a highly centralized process. Most prospective candidates were interviewed personally by Sviridoff, typically at a luncheon in his office attended by Sviridoff himself, the candidate and a small group of staff members. If these gatherings were relaxed and informal, as indeed they were, they were nonetheless political in the sense that Sviridoff used them to judge the candidate's qualifications, to test his overall capabilities, and to compare these qualifications and capabilities with those of other staff members present.

Seldom, however, did Sviridoff rely solely on interviews to select new staff members. Although the ultimate decision was his, and his personal evaluation weighed heavily in this decision, still it was not his practice in this or any other matter before the agency to deny himself the opinion of others. Staff members were asked to evaluate the candidate as were individuals outside the agency. Over the years Sviridoff had developed an extensive and impressive network of personal contacts with men and women in government, industry, labor, and academia and whenever possible he used these contacts to add to his knowledge of a job applicant.

As screening devices, interviews were not totally adequate, at least not from Sviridoff's point of view. To be sure they were probably more effective in terms of executive control than even the most elaborate and systematic procedures used in many other bureaucracies. Few agency chiefs, one suspects, have the opportunity to confront prospective employees the way Sviridoff did. Whatever the case, Sviridoff did not trust interviews completely and he used them principally as a means of selecting out those he judged definitely unsuited to his purposes.

In fact, the final aspect of the evaluation of staff members occurred *after* they had been appointed to the agency. Having passed the initial screening and having been accepted tentatively by Sviridoff, new staff members served what amounted to a probationary period. Upon arrival a new staff member was normally assigned to work on a project, the preparation of an agency report or grant proposal, for example, and his performance on this task was scrutinized carefully both by Sviridoff and by other staff members.

There was another facet to the probationary period, a facet that in political terms overshadowed the evaluation of new staff members. The probationary

[d]Specifically, personnel in pay grades 6-12. See above, Table 3-2, note *a*.

period was the time Sviridoff cultivated and developed personal loyalties among new staff members. Whatever his divisional assignment within the agency, a new staff member initially could expect frequent personal contact with Sviridoff himself; he could expect, for example, to participate with him in agency strategy sessions, to accompany him to meetings outside the agency, or to lunch with him informally. Through these early contacts the agency's executive director controlled the socialization and indoctrination of new staff members. Through these contacts a new staff member learned something of Sviridoff's resources and how he used them: learned among other things and Sviridoff controlled both salaries and assignments, and that loyalty and productivity would be rewarded by increased pay and/or increased staff responsibility. He also learned of Sviridoff's reputation and standing outside the agency, of his political and governmental contacts that might be useful in future career plans, and he learned finally that Sviridoff had, in the words of one staff member "a highly seductive personality," that he was a man capable of immense charm that he used to cultivate loyalties within the staff.

All this is not to say the early months were the only time Sviridoff concerned himself with the staff, with evaluating performance and developing loyalties. On the contrary, the process was continual. But the early months were critical. By controlling the socialization and indoctrination of new members he not only fashioned strong personal ties within his staff, but what is equally important, effectively undermined the development of sub-groups and sub-group identifications within the agency that might have competed with him for staff loyalties.[e]

As a result of such efforts, Community Progress, Inc. was, during Sviridoff's tenure, an agency manned by individuals whose principal allegiance was to Sviridoff. This does not mean, as some critics complained, the staff consisted of underlings who did Sviridoff's bidding without thought or criticism. Unlike Shakespeare's Caesar he did not fear men who thought too much. He personally relished challenges from his staff; as director of an organization that was expected to be innovative he depended on this staff as a kind of brainstorming team that would continually generate new ideas and programs. What it *did* mean, however, was that Sviridoff insisted that his be the ultimate voice in agency policy, most especially in cases involving the agency's dealings with external groups. In this sense there was but a single dominant influence within the agency, Sviridoff himself, and his domination was in no small part based on the ways he developed and maintained the loyalties of the staff members he selected and socialized into his work team.

---

[e]Two additional characteristics of the staff—one, the predominance of outsiders in high-level agency positions, and, second, the diversity of professional backgrounds among these outsiders—may also have served as a safeguard for Sviridoff's leadership. The former practice minimized the possibilities that staff members would divide their loyalties between the agency and other local organizations or groups; the latter reduced the likelihood that professional sub-groups would develop within the agency to challenge his authority.[20]

The Strategic Use of Information
Dissemination

Open Covenants . . .

"Open covenants openly arrived at" has a powerful democratic normative appeal. Empirically, however, it falls far short of describing the actual behavior of public figures. Officials typically display a marked predilection for acting under conditions wherein, as one member of the Kennedy administration put it, policies and programs can be fashioned "free from political pressure, from critics, and from the corrosive compulsion toward simplicity that marks public debate."[21]

Freedom from such a "corrosive compulsion" was characteristic of New Haven's Community Progress, Inc., and constitutes a third way local agency officials tried to protect the project and enhance their own control over it. Until 1966, when the federal Office of Economic Opportunity ordered all local anti-poverty agencies to "open their books" to the public,[f] New Haven officials severely restricted the flow of publicly available information about the agency and the project. We have already seen that the project was planned without publicity and that it was not until the actual award of the Ford Foundation grant in April 1962, a year and a half after planning had begun, that the community was apprised officially of the proceedings. Once the project had begun, the practice of minimizing publicity on intraagency deliberations continued. To be sure, absolute silence was no longer feasible at this point, nor, indeed, was it desirable, as agency officials acknowledged by mounting a "public information" campaign to alert the community to the nature and merits of the new enterprise. This "public information" campaign, however, was a promotional effort and its purpose was more to persuade and convince than it was to debate and analyze. And like all promotional efforts the information this one communicated was highly selective and quite limited.[g]

Strategic Omissions

Just how selective and limited this campaign was is suggested by an examination of the agency's *1964 Program Report*.[22] This was the first extended discussion

[f]*The New York Times*, March 24, 1966. By 1966, New Haven had supplemented Foundation funds with federal. See below, chapter 5. The federal directive did not result in full disclosure by New Haven. Agency officials claimed it applied only to federal funds and hence continued to withhold information on funds received from the Ford Foundation.

[g]The promotional efforts employed by New Haven will be examined more fully later in the study along with other strategies agency officials used to win community acceptance. See chapter 8. For the present, the discussion will be restricted to the promotion's other side, specifically the types of information not revealed, and the calculations that entered into the adoption of this particular political strategy.

of the anti-poverty project issued by the agency.[h] But as even the most cursory reading reveals, the document was conspicuously lacking in certain highly pertinent information.

Most conspicuous of all was the absence of information on the financial structure of the anti-poverty project. While the *Report* alluded to the support of the Ford Foundation—and the federal government, which by this time had added its financial support to the effort—there was no indication of how much money had been allocated to each of the programs or activities described in its pages. Nor, for that matter, was there any indication of just how much money overall was involved—no indication, that is to say, that by the spring of 1964, when the *Report* was issued, more than $7.0 million had been invested in the city's anti-poverty project.

Admittedly, despite the *Report's* uninformativeness, the silence surrounding CPI's financial structure was not total. Had an individual been especially attentive to the local press during the preceding two years, he would have had at least a general idea of the magnitude of the project's budget. The total amount of the Ford Foundation grant was, for example, public knowledge, as were the total amounts awarded by some of the federal agencies. Even here, however, budgetary details were not reported. Like the *Report* itself, the press releases announcing the grants contained no information on the distribution of grant money within or among various facets of the agency's operation. Neither the *Report*, nor the press releases, nor any other publicly available source revealed how much money had been allocated to such general program areas as education, employment, or recreation, let alone how much had been allocated within each of these general areas to specific activities such as pre-kindergarten classes, tutorials, or remedial reading, or within these specific activities for such expenses as personnel, office supplies, or rent.

Nor was the CPI any more open about other aspects of its affairs. The public was not informed in any detail about the agency's transactions with the Ford Foundation or the federal government, the two principal sources of project funds, about the amount of money requested, or the alternatives proposed, examined, modified or rejected. Indeed, the very fact that negotiations had been in progress was not revealed until these negotiations were successfully concluded and the grant awarded. Even less was disclosed about personnel matters or the agency's purchase of goods and services. Staff openings, whatever the level, were not advertised, and it was a rare occasion when the appointment, promotion, or

---

[h]Prior to this, most information about the project had been disseminated through press releases prepared by the agency staff. This information was piecemeal and non-cumulative, with bits of information scattered throughout articles published over a two year period. Even if this information had been complete—which it was not—obtaining a comprehensive picture of the project from the press would have been extremely costly. The only other published source of data on the project was *Opening Opportunities*, a document prepared by Hallman and issued in May 1962, a month after the announcement of the Ford Foundation grant. This described the project in broad terms, and, like the *1964 Program Report*, omitted information on its financial matters.

transfer of an individual was reported to the press. And there were no open competitive bidding procedures for such items as office space, equipment, and supplies. These were bought and sold at prices agreed upon in private negotiations where the only participants were the agency and the suppliers.

Of course, at the time the agency was under no legal obligation to reveal or discuss these or any other matters publicly. Prior to the 1966 ruling by the federal Office of Economic Opportunity, Community Progress, Inc. enjoyed the same freedom from public scrutiny as did other private, non-profit corporations. The agency was not a governmental bureau, and the public as yet had no more legal right to know about this agency's activities or inner workings than it did, for example, about the financial affairs or hiring practices of a private university or a church. Still, given the nature of CPI's mission, the absence of detailed public scrutiny of its activities during this period is worth stressing, the more so since it operated in a diverse and open community with a major university, a contentious two-party system, two newspapers, radio stations, and a television channel. Whether for lack of attention or for lack of interest, those institutions in the city most concerned with disseminating information did not themselves produce or generate detailed coverage or accounts of the project, and instead relied primarily on what the agency staff decided to make public.[i]

The Implications of Strategic Omissions

There were a number of advantages to the freedom and flexibility agency officials enjoyed in communicating with the external world. Free of the constraints public agencies encounter in continually working in the proverbial "goldfish bowl," anti-poverty officials were able to pursue a strategy based on the political maxim that the best time to manage conflict is before it starts.[23] To this end, agency policies and practices that were susceptible to political exploitation simply were not widely advertised. A case in point was the appointment of outsiders to all but a few high level agency positions, a practice which if publicized might easily have stirred xenophobic sentiments against the agency in the community. Another was the high salaries and liberal fringe benefits that agency personnel received. In 1965, for example, the highest paid *public* official in the city, the superintendent of schools, received $20,000. Next in line was the mayor at $18,000, followed by the chiefs of the Fire and Police Departments at $14,500 each, and the corporation counsel at $10,500. By contrast Sviridoff's own salary was in excess of $25,000; Hallman's $20,000, and the salaries of at least six other agency officials in the $14,000 to $17,500 range. And while these high salaries and liberal fringe benefits were probably necessary to attract qualified personnel, had they been made public it would have been difficult to counteract the cynic's charge that anti-poverty officials were really enriching themselves rather than helping the poor.

By not raising these and other issues publicly, agency officials shifted the

[i]See footnote h above.

burden of discovery on potential critics and in so doing reduced the likelihood that specific agency policies would be subject to open and possibly damaging debate. At the same time, agency officials spared themselves the cost of preparing and presenting their case publicly, a case that, however well-reasoned or well-articulated, still might have been insufficient to convince every listener of the merits of the agency policy under attack.

There was a further, more general advantage in being able to manage the flow of information, namely, that restricting information about the project restricted the scope of participation in agency decision-making. More complete information, for example, on pending grant negotiations or on job openings, would have been an encouragement to individuals and groups outside the agency to press their cases. As a result, the number of competing demands and claims on the agency's resources would have increased. To be sure, such an eventuality might not have altered the outcome of decisions, though quite obviously a different set or mix of programs and policies was more likely, the larger the number of participants. But even if the outcomes were the same, the costs of decision-making would have risen substantially. Among other things, more time would have been required to reach decisions, and under the circumstances this would have been injurious to the agency. For, as we shall see in a later chapter, one of the ways agency officials were able to obtain the funds necessary to support the anti-poverty project was by demonstrating to the Ford Foundation and the federal government that New Haven was capable of acting quickly.

Challenge to Control

The Early Years

For almost five years, control over the planning and administration of New Haven's anti-poverty project was restricted to a relatively small group of men, among them Hallman, whose initiative had led to the formation of the agency, and Sviridoff, whose personality and politics dominated the functioning of the agency itself once it was in being. Although CPI spent government funds and tried to influence government policy, there were few opportunities either for the public at large or for special elites to learn about the project, to raise questions, to offer suggestions, to scrutinize activities, or to express disapproval, let alone to veto what the agency proposed to do.

Beginning in 1965, however, this control over the agency came under fire. In January a local conservative group, the Better Education Committee, challenged the role of Community Progress, Inc. in city government, charging the agency with usurping many of the functions of municipal government. The challenge, as we shall see in chapter 8, was unsuccessful. Later, during the summer of the same year, the agency came under attack from a different quarter, in this case the inner city.[j] This attack was more successful and resulted in some modifications in the formal structure of control over the agency. The success of this attack is, however, of less interest here than the philosophy it expressed. This philosophy contrasted sharply with that held by anti-poverty officials themselves, and as such helps delineate further the considerations that led agency officials to restrict access to decision-making.

Participatory Democracy

At the heart of the inner-city challenge was the issue of participatory democracy. Under the Economic Opportunity Act of 1964, local anti-poverty projects were to be "developed, conducted, and administered with maximum feasible participation of the residents of areas and members of groups to be served."[24] As *The New York Times* put it, this was "the most controversial and confusing aspect of the national war on poverty,"[25] a proposition fully borne out in the New Haven experience.

Publicly, agency officials denied that resident participation was at issue in New Haven. In fact, they claimed, the city had pioneered in this respect, setting an example for the nation. According to one agency publication: "New Haven's 'resident participation' . . . began years before the establishment of the Office of Economic Opportunity and the announcement of its nationwide policy of 'maximum feasible participation' of representatives of the poor."[26]

What agency officials meant by "resident participation" was, however, something less than a full, formal voice for neighborhood residents in the management of the project. While residents were asked informally to voice their opinions about the project, these opinions were not binding on agency officials, and as far as is known there were no occasions on which the poor actually

---

[j]Prior to this there had been only one controversy involving "inner-city residents" and the anti-poverty agency. This dispute did not, however, center on the control of the agency or on its reform policies, but rather on a complicated personnel question. More specifically, the controversy entailed the appointment of John Barber, a former president of the New Haven chapter of the National Association for the Advancement of Colored People, as an administrative assistant to Connecticut's U.S. Senator Thomas Dodd. Barber's appointment was opposed by the president of the New Haven Central Labor Council, Vincent Sirabella, on the grounds that Barber had engaged in scab labor practices during a strike in New Haven. Sirabella was a labor consultant to the anti-poverty agency and NAACP officials demanded that the agency terminate its association with him. Sviridoff refused, and this led to a bitter public dispute between Barber and his successor as president of the NAACP, and the agency. The agency eventually won. In late 1964, a small group challenged the incumbent NAACP leadership and in a special election managed to replace this leadership with one more favorably disposed to the anti-poverty agency. *The New Haven Register*, August 31, 1964; November 20, 1964. Sviridoff's position throughout the leadership struggle was one of utmost caution. While he stood to gain from a change in leadership, he maintained a publicly neutral posture and refused either to support or oppose those on his own staff who had helped mount the challenge.

initiated proposals that were later adopted by the agency.[k] If more than 100 agency staff members lived in the inner-city neighborhoods, as agency officials claimed they did, still none of these held positions in the higher ranks of the agency hierarchy.[27] However meaningful this type of participation might have been, and agency officials insisted it was quite meaningful, it was participation on terms set by the agency, not by the residents of the inner city.

It was this lack of direct, formal, grass-roots-initiated participation that led to demands from the inner city for a complete redistribution of authority and control over the anti-poverty agency and its activities. In July 1965, a neighborhood group, the Hill Neighborhood Union, challenged agency policy in a formal complaint to the federal Office of Economic Opportunity.[28] Noting that control over the agency was restricted to a few non-residents, the Hill group asked that the agency's then pending application for grant renewal be held in abeyance until "as a minimum a majority of the Board of Directors of CPI . . . be elected by the residents of the neighborhoods that CPI serves."[29]

Agency Reaction

If agency officials responded angrily, as they did, it was only partly due to their concern that their national reputation might be damaged. As we shall see in a later chapter, this reputation had been carefully cultivated and was one of the most important resources the agency had in its quest for outside funds. Equally important, the demand for formal resident participation was at odds with their own philosophy of reform and they feared that such a change in the control of the agency would seriously hamper efforts to aid the poor.

Part of this philosophy was that the poor themselves were ill-equipped to participate in decision-making. Meaningful participation in the management of programs, according to some agency officials at least, presupposed a certain level of social and educational achievement, and however noble their intentions, the poor lacked this prerequisite. Because of their condition, the poor lacked the political motivation and the political skill needed for sustained action: for defining, selecting, and articulating program alternatives and program priorities, and for seeing these through to completion. "For the vast majority of the poor," Hallman once wrote, "poverty is a disability that precludes meaningful participation in planning."[30] As a result, responsibility fell to what Hallman

---

[k]Agency officials credited inner city residents with the initiative in supporting, though not proposing, state legislation aiding inner city public schools. On March 3, 1965, a group of about 150 inner-city residents, most of them women, travelled to Hartford, there to voice support for the bill. Agency officials claimed the demonstration of support had been spontaneous. In fact, it had been initiated and organized by agency officials themselves. For the agency's account of the event see: Community Progress, Inc., *The Human Story* (New Haven: Community Progress, Inc., 1966), p. 55. The part New Haven played in the formulation of this legislation is discussed below in chapter 6.

termed a "democratic elite," "a group of individuals with superior talent who have achieved their positions on the basis of ability and achievements."[31] These were the ones who would have to act on behalf of the poor.

While there is no reason to doubt the sincerity of those who held this particular view, it is clear that other considerations entered into the agency's opposition to a formal role for the poor in decision-making. One of these was the *identity* of those demanding an increased role for the poor. This was of no small moment, for many on the CPI staff seem to have objected as much, if not more, to the *source* of the demand as they did to the demand itself.

The source in this case was what political commentators and journalists had just begun to call the "new left."[32] In New Haven, as elsewhere, the term was little more than a handy label denoting a rather heterogeneous collection of individuals and groups whose political attitudes and behavior belie any simple categorization. On one point, however, they apparently agreed, namely, that the political "establishment" was not to be trusted. Public officials, government agencies, political parties, and, for some, even the electoral process, were operating against the poor. Almost by definition, whatever those in power did was suspect, including the war on poverty. At best the latter was an effort by the local "power structure," specifically the mayor and officials at Community Progress, Inc. to coopt the poor and thereby forestall more extensive and radical changes in the system.

This view of politics in general and New Haven politics in particular clashed sharply with Sviridoff's own. For more than sixteen years he had actively participated in mainstream politics and during the preceding three years had seen this participation bear fruit in the anti-poverty project he administered. Little wonder, perhaps, that he viewed the new left's philosophy as alien and its members as suspect Johnny-come-lately's. He considered them more raucous than representative, and construed their demands for "resident participation" as simply a ploy by members of this vocal group to be recognized as putative grass-roots leaders and to gain control of the agency and its resources.[l] Once in their hands, he feared, the agency and its resources would be used by the new left as a base from which to actually attack the system of which he was so much a part, and in so doing undermine efforts to alleviate the conditions of the poor.[m]

The agency's first line of defense against a formal role for neighborhood residents was to argue that it had already more than satisfied the statutory requirements. Since at the time neither the Economic Opportunity Act nor the federal Office of Economic Opportunity had specified the precise meaning of "maximum feasible participation," local agency officials saw no reason for not

---

[l]Sviridoff had done battle with the left before. As president of the state CIO, he had led the fight in 1948 against "Communist" take-over of labor unions in Connecticut. *The New Haven Register*, July 12, 1964. Whether these earlier struggles influenced his response to the "left" of the mid-1960's is unclear.

[m]For a discussion of these efforts see chapter 4. The agency's rejection of confrontation politics is analyzed below in chapter 8.

advancing their own. This they did, claiming that such practices as informal consultation with neighborhood residents, and most especially the hiring of indigenous personnel, albeit in low echelon positions, in effect afforded residents a voice in the administration of the project.[33]

This interpretation was rejected by the new left and, more importantly, by the Office of Economic Opportunity.[34] The latter stipulated that neighborhood residents should have formal representation on the board and, faced with this stipulation, agency officials eventually yielded. On November 12, 1965, the agency officially agreed to expand the board of directors from nine to sixteen members, and to provide for the election of one additional member from the seven neighborhoods then being served by the project. This of course fell short of what the agency's local critics had demanded, a clear majority on the board. But the change satisfied the federal Office of Economic Opportunity, and with its approval the question of whether and how many residents would have a formal voice in the administration of the project was settled.[n]

Strategies for Control: Implications

Although for almost five years, agency officials successfully restricted access to the planning and administration of the project, they did so at no small risk to themselves and their programs. To be sure, this strategic choice had its advantages. Among other things it reduced the cost of decision-making[35] and increased the influence of agency officials themselves over the city's anti-poverty programs. But the strategy could have been self-defeating, especially for an agency such as Community Progress, Inc., whose mission it was to encourage innovation in an established governmental system. Located outside the framework of local government, lacking formal authority, and without any claim to a regularized source of income, the agency might well have become isolated and impotent.

And it would have, if agency officials had not developed, among other things, powerful alliances with groups outside the city. While consolidating power over the CPI locally, anti-poverty officials were cultivating important groups outside New Haven, specifically the Ford Foundation and the federal government. Both these had what local officials needed most, namely, funds, and one of the continuing tasks local anti-poverty officials defined for themselves was to

---

[n]Not, however, the matter of who would represent the neighborhoods. According to one official, the elections provided a second line of defense against encroachments from the new left. Reportedly the agency's neighborhood staff, which by 1965 numbered over 100 full-time workers, were instructed, in the words of one neighborhood coordinator, "to keep the lid on things." This apparently meant the staff was to campaign, albeit quietly, against individuals known to be hostile to the incumbent agency leadership. How successful they were in this is not known. In the period just after the elections, however, it appears that elected Board members, like their appointed colleagues, served as instruments rather than masters of the professional staff.

demonstrate to these funders that New Haven's undertaking was worth supporting.

Before considering the ways anti-poverty officials developed these crucial sources of support, it is necessary to pause momentarily to examine the policy implications of the local reform effort.

4 New Haven's Anti-Poverty Project: Policy Implications

"Looking at CPI is like looking through a kaleidoscope," Mitchell Sviridoff, the executive director of New Haven's anti-poverty project, once remarked. "At first glance it's a jumble of shapes, sizes and colors. But turn any kaleidoscope around slowly and an interesting and rational ... and sometimes even beautiful ... pattern will eventually emerge."[1]

Beauty, of course, is in the eye of the beholder; but in his momentary flight of poetic fancy, Sviridoff's characterization of the New Haven project was not very wide of the mark. At first glance the project did indeed appear jumbled and confused, as a random collection of programs and personalities, and not a few observers puzzled over the meaning and purpose of this new program as well as the objectives of the men associated with it. Like the view through the aperture of a kaleidoscope, however, there were recognizable patterns in the agency's activities; and the patterns, like the kaleidoscope's, depended in large part on the observer's perspective.

Strategic Focus: Poverty among the Young

From one perspective, the anti-poverty project was a social and economic reform program, a welfare effort to improve conditions among the lower classes in the city. These are generic terms, however, and though commonly used to describe the enterprise, they tell us little about its actual parameters.

First of all, the project was addressed to the *problems of intergenerational poverty*, and in this respect at least, differed radically from the New Deal and its concern for the displaced middle and working classes.[a] Of principal interest to anti-poverty officials was that segment of the population for whom poverty had become an inherited way of life, individuals who were unable to move out of the slums where they and their parents before them had been raised, individuals who seemed unaffected by general economic prosperity nationally or by existing public and private assistance. These were the inhabitants of Michael Harrington's *Other America*, the hidden poor, generations of whom had never made it in the past and who, given their record, seemed unlikely to make it in the future.

---

[a]Like the New Deal, however, the anti-poverty project was both redistributive and reallocative. It was not purely redistributive as are such recently proposed policies as the negative income tax and the guaranteed annual income. Funds were redirected to the poor, but only indirectly in the form of programs and services. Individuals within the poverty class were not given money and left to decide for themselves how this money would be allocated, as would be the case with the guaranteed annual income.[2]

Of those who had "never made it," one group in particular was of primary concern to the local staff—namely, the young. Operating on the premise that, for the young, poverty had not yet become a habitual and total way of life, anti-poverty officials focused their energies and resources on this group in an effort to break the "cycle of poverty." According to 1965 staff estimates, for example, some 60 percent of annual expenditures, including administrative costs, was being earmarked exclusively for programs to assist those under eighteen, and an additional 15 percent for activities that served all age groups.[3] In short, the major theme in New Haven's social and economic reform program was prevention, its principal goal to improve the life chances of a new generation of poor and to make this generation self-sufficient in a highly competitive society (See Table 4-1).

Table 4-1

Allocation of New Haven Anti-Poverty Funds by General Program Areas: 1962-1966

Program Area	% Total Budget
Manpower/Employment	32.6
Education	36.6
Neighborhood/Social Services	9.9
Health	1.8
Legal/Correctional	8.5
Research	1.7
Community Action Institute	2.7
General Administration	6.2

Source: Community Progress, Inc., *The Human Story* (New Haven: Community Progress, Inc., 1966), p. 99.

To achieve this long-term social objective, local anti-poverty officials fashioned what they called a "comprehensive attack on poverty through a simultaneous and coordinated series of interrelated activities."[4] Bureaucratic rhetoric aside, in actual practice this amounted to a reform effort of considerable magnitude and scope. By 1965, for example, there were more than sixty separate anti-poverty programs, some of which, such as a pre-kindergarten with eighteen neighborhood centers, operated at various locations throughout the city. Between 1962 and 1965, over $10 million had been spent for programs in education, employment, job training, recreation, and law enforcement, all focused on the New Haven's inner-city neighborhoods.

Although the project was broad-gauged, some program areas were emphasized more than others, in particular education and employment. In agency parlance, education and employment constituted "opportunity programs" and as such were designed to equip the poor, and especially the young, with the basic skills that would allow them eventually to make it on their own. Other programs, in health, welfare, recreation, or law enforcement, were considered supportive: recreation and leisure time activities to facilitate access to school drop-outs and potential juvenile delinquents who might then be persuaded to participate in an employment program or to return to school; day-care centers to enable mothers to work or to enroll in job training or education programs; a neighborhood services program to establish and maintain a "bridge between . . . New Haveners who [lived] in the inner city and the opportunity programs available to them."[5]

Viewed in terms of social and economic reform, New Haven's anti-poverty project represented an effort to repair, or more precisely, to build the functional equivalent of what Samuel Lubell once termed the "old tenement trail."[6] To be sure, there was no effort to encourage geographic mobility, at least not directly. But indirectly, by facilitating efforts at upward social and economic mobility, anti-poverty officials were trying to lay the foundations for a modern-day trail out of the slums.

A Community Action Program

Efforts to facilitate upward social and economic mobility through programs in education, employment, or recreation suggest another feature of the local anti-poverty effort, a feature that can be easily missed if one dwells too long on the characteristics of the population served or the programs designed to serve them. After the passage of the Economic Opportunity Act, New Haven's anti-poverty project was known officially as a "Community Action Program", and, while this term in itself reveals little, what it meant in actual practice was *an expanded role for society generally and especially for governmental institutions in shaping the lives of the poor*—paradoxically, as we have seen, through a "democratic elite" during the early stages.[b] Thus by turning Sviridoff's kaleidoscope a few degrees a broader and politically more richly colored pattern emerges.

The best, though by no means the only, illustration of this dimension of the local project is provided by the New Haven Board of Education. As a result of the anti-poverty project, the scope of public school activity was broadened both quantitatively and qualitatively: quantitatively by the infusion of additional funds for already existing programs, such as reading and adult education; qualitatively by the initiation of new programs and the assumption of new

---

[b]At least in New Haven. In some other communities, Community Action meant participation of the poor in the administration of anti-poverty projects. As I noted in the previous chapter, the poor had no direct voice in the administration or planning of New Haven's project until late 1965 and early 1966, some three years after the project became operational, and some six years after the planning had actually begun.

responsibilities that hitherto had not been borne by any local public institution. In this latter respect, the reform project can be viewed as part of a broader, long-term trend toward making the schools increasingly central in the life of the child. Because of the ready access they provide to the young, schools have traditionally been a major target of specialized interest groups. As a result their responsibilities have grown enormously and now embrace a range of activities far beyond the teaching of the three R's.

Pre-kindergarten is the most obvious example of a qualitative change wrought in the public school system. The program was designed to offset the educational and cultural handicaps of pre-school children between the ages of three-and-a-half and four-and-a-half. Through this program the schools were to become a force for the socialization and assimilation of an age group that previously had been socialized and assimilated by private institutions, principally the family.[7]

Even more radical and ambitious was the proposed use of the school as a means of restoring and refurbishing a sense of community in the city's lower-class neighborhoods.[8] Under the Community School program, one school in each of seven designated inner-city neighborhoods was transformed from a regular educational facility into a general, multi-purpose, year-round facility, available for public use twelve to sixteen hours a day. As such it continued its regular educational program during the school day; but during the school day and particularly after school hours, the Community School was to function as a neighborhood center that would serve as a "unifying force" or "common denominator" for the neighborhood's heterogenous population, and as a "stabilizing influence" for the community.[9]

Underlying the general thrust of the local anti-poverty project toward new and expanded roles for governmental agencies was an assumption that traditional institutions and processes were functioning imperfectly among the poor. This was particularly true of the black poor, a group whose well being, or lack thereof, was of major concern to anti-poverty officials. Among the blacks, the basic social unit, the family, was believed no longer capable of meeting demands placed on it by society. Here, for example, parental and especially paternal authority had been weakened to a point where the community at large could no longer count on it alone to acculturate the young. Beset by unemployment, poor housing, illiteracy, and a high desertion rate, blacks faced insuperable odds in their quest for a better life for themselves and for their children.[10]

If the family was functioning imperfectly, so, too, agency officials believed, were other black institutions, such as the church, the small business establishment, the fraternal organization, the mutual aid association, or the neighborhood club.[11] These institutions, whose counterparts in the white community had helped provide jobs, housing, medical care, food, and counselling for earlier migrants to the cities,[12] in the black community were either all but nonexistent (small businesses), lacking in resources (churches), or concerned primarily with the welfare of the relatively small black middle class (fraternal organizations).[13] For all practical purposes, social and economic life among the blacks was disorganized and the blacks themselves incapable of "bootstrap operations."

Until conditions changed, outside assistance would be necessary; more to the point, conditions would not change unless the poor and the blacks received massive aid from the outside.

Like many other social and economic reform efforts, the programs and ideas that found expression in New Haven's war on poverty had their parallels elsewhere. The assumption about the black family, for example, although at the time (1959-1964) not as well publicized as it would be after the publication of the Moynihan Report in 1965, was nonetheless not an unfamiliar one.[14] Neither were the assumptions about black social life in general and in particular the social disorganization of neighborhood life. This latter theme, in fact, has long been popular among both critics and champions of city life.[15] In the diagnoses and remedies advanced by New Haven's reform advocates, one can find traces of an older tradition, with roots in the work of such earlier urban reformers as the social worker Jane Addams, the philosopher-educator John Dewey, and the sociologist Robert Park. Indeed, in both design and purpose, New Haven's Community School was similar to the Settlement House developed by Miss Addams. Both idealized the city as a collection of relatively small, self-contained neighborhoods where residents were known to each other personally and shared a sense of common identity and purpose.[16] Nor was the New Haven project unique in other respects: job training, vocational guidance, day-care centers, neighborhood libraries, and municipal public work projects—all had been used in past reform efforts. Even pre-kindergarten had its historical dimensions, or so some could argue, as a modern day application of an educational philosophy first expressed in Plato's *Repbulic*.

Whether and to what extent the substantive aspects of New Haven's anti-poverty project were borrowed from other sources is not known precisely. Given the fact that none of the city's programs seems to have been unique, and that most if not all of them enjoyed currency at least among some reformers and students of the city, it is possible that what local anti-poverty officials did was to draw, albeit selectively, on ideas advanced by others. But the evidence is not conclusive; similarity does not mean imitation and it may well be, as a few local anti-poverty officials claimed, that some of the programs were discovered independently and *de novo* in New Haven.

Whatever the case, the question need not detain us here, for the main interest is the implementation of these ideas, not their invention or intellectual history. Ideas are not self-executing, and there is a vast difference between thinking of or even proposing a particular alternative and translating this alternative into action. If New Haven's anti-poverty officials did not discover or invent the individual programs that were eventually incorporated into the city's reform enterprise, still, they were among the first to *propose* a project that embraced such a broad and comprehensive array of individual programs. Moreover, they were among the first to *implement* their proposals, and in so doing developed an operational model for the national war on poverty. This model, as we shall see in the next chapter, was one of the key elements in New Haven's strategy for dealing with the Ford Foundation and various federal agencies.

Part III
Establishing
an External Base
of Support

5

A Local-National Alliance Against Poverty

Of all the facets of New Haven's reform effort, none was more fascinating nor indeed more central to the development of the project than the local agency's access to sources of money outside the city. This access was critical. Without these funds it is unlikely there ever would have been a reform undertaking at all, certainly not one of such magnitude. With these funds the anti-poverty staff was able to embark on a massive social and economic reform effort while minimizing demands on the local budget and therefore on those local political groups with already established, potentially competitive claims on existing sources of municipal revenue.

How important this support was for New Haven can be judged from the extent to which outside money was used by local anti-poverty officials. Between 1962 and 1966 the city's social renewal effort was *almost totally* supported by non-local funds. In all some $16.3 million was spent during this period, of which roughly $15.5 million or 94 percent came from outside the city. In 1965 alone, outside money amounted to approximately $7.7 million, or nearly $7,700 for every family in New Haven with an income under $4,000![1]

However impressive or extensive the amount of outside support, or however significant this support for the workings of the project locally, what needs to be examined here is the way in which groups outside the city were made part of the local effort. How was it that these groups came to invest their funds in New Haven's anti-poverty effort, and what, more generally, was the nature of the relationship between New Haven and the groups that helped fund the city's reform effort?

What made the difference for New Haven was the initiative and skill of the anti-poverty staff itself. To be sure, local officials benefited considerably from developments both in New Haven and in the broader arenas of state and national politics. But these developments would have had little meaning in terms of financial support for New Haven had it not been for the staff's recognition of the opportunities these developments afforded and its ability to turn these opportunities to the best advantage of the city and its programs. To state it somewhat differently, the financial backing New Haven received for its anti-poverty project was neither chance nor good fortune. Rather *it was the outgrowth of a deliberate and persistent policy of seeking out and exploiting financial support from outside groups and, more importantly, of fashioning alliances with them.*[a]

[a]Compare this general proposition with Hugh Douglas Price's criticism of Robert Dahl's *Who Governs?* Price criticized Dahl's analysis of New Haven politics on the grounds that it

These alliances were central to the New Haven strategy, and, given what the city stood to gain, it is hardly surprising that CPI officials placed as much emphasis as they did on developing and maintaining them. But an alliance is a relationship in which both parties stand to benefit, and at first glance, at least, it would seem that New Haven had little to offer in return for the support it was seeking. For one thing, it was a relatively small city, with only 6 percent of the state's population and, what is more salient in political terms, only 6 percent of the state's registered voters (1960). Moreover, there were no major concentrations of poverty in New Haven. Located in a state with the highest per capita income in the country (1965), New Haven was, as I noted earlier, mildly well off compared to other cities nationally. Considering its size, its electoral importance, and its need, New Haven's attractiveness as an ally was marginal. Had the city's planners based their alliance strategy on these considerations alone, they would have fared far less handsomely than they did.

Obviously, these were not the sole considerations, for despite its size and relative well being, New Haven's strategy of seeking outside funds was eminently successful. What the city lacked in terms of size or electoral power was more than offset by its aggressive political leadership and the ingenuity of this leadership in selling New Haven to national funders. New Haven cast itself in the roles of *prototype* and *promoter* for the national war on poverty and it was in these capacities that local anti-poverty officials made their principal contribution to the alliances through which funds crucial to the project were channelled to the city.

The National War on Poverty: 1958-1966

The New Frontier and the Great Society

New Haven's quest for a social and economic reform program coincided with what many local staff members considered a radical shift nationally in the definition of domestic problems. From the close of World War II, and most dramatically during the early years of the Eisenhower administration, the country had been preoccupied with the question of internal Communist

---

was not so much the mayor's leadership and political skills that accounted for the city's success in urban renewal (as Dahl had argued it was) as it was the financial backing of the federal government. "Is the New Haven Story," Price asked, "a sort of miracle to be attributed to a great-man theory of political leadership, or more simply a case of massive outside funds serving as a sort of *deus ex machina*?" According to Price, it was the latter, for "the more emphasis one puts on the important and unusual resource base of federal funds the less weight one need attach to the Mayor's particular talents." Hugh Douglas Price, Review of *Who Governs?* by Robert Dahl, *Yale Law Journal* 71 (1962), p. 1593. What Price fails to account for is the city's good fortune in having an "important and unusual resource base." As we will see in this chapter, the backing of outside groups, at least in anti-poverty, was not chance good fortune, not a *"deus ex machina*," but rather the fruits of local initiative and local strategy.

subversion, and one of the consequences of this preoccupation was a suspicion of social reform efforts. By 1955, the political climate had begun to change. Fears that domestic communism threatened the very existence of the nation were on the wane, as was the influence of the Senate Government Operations Committee's Permanent Investigations Subcommittee and its chairman, Senator Joseph McCarthy. In the place of communism and subversion, new issues began to emerge, among them the conditions of the city, civil rights, and poverty.

One reflection of this changed climate, and the one most relevant to New Haven's planners, was the appearance in the late 1950s and early 1960s of four social reform programs, one sponsored by the Ford Foundation, the other three by the federal government. During the 1950s, the Foundation abandoned its previously cautious posture toward controversial enterprises and began earmarking funds for demonstration programs in urban ghettos.[b] Shortly afterwards, a similar shift occurred in the federal government. With the Democrats' return to power in 1961, the national government began striking out in new directions in social welfare, at first modestly with the Juvenile Delinquency and Youth Offenses Control Act[2] of 1961 and the Manpower Development and Training Act[3] of 1962, and then more ambitiously with the Economic Opportunity Act[4] of 1964 with its declaration that

it is . . . the policy of the United States to eliminate the paradox of poverty in the midst of plenty in this nation by opening to everyone the opportunity for education and training, the opportunity to work, and the opportunity to live in decency and dignity.

These four programs, which constituted what I shall term in the following pages the "national war on poverty," were the main financial base for New Haven's reform effort between 1962 and 1966. To understand how this financial base was developed, however, one must first understand how local anti-poverty officials defined the administrative and political contexts of the national programs.

An Uncertain Start

Despite the heightened sense of social responsibility for the poor that marked the country's mood in the early sixties, a mood most evident in the high moral fervor that accompanied the civil rights movement during these years, the national war on poverty began in an atmosphere of much uncertainty.[c] True, the

[b]See above, chapter 2.

[c]The following sections record the perceptions of local staff members—record, for example, how Sviridoff, Hallman, and other agency officials defined the political trends and the political conditions of the 1950s and early 1960s. How well the perceptions accord with reality is not discussed at any length. The important point is what anti-poverty officials believed and how they acted on these beliefs.

bold national policy of the Economic Opportunity Act, committing the nation to the elimination of "the paradox of poverty in the midst of plenty," enhanced considerably the prospects for successful social reform. So, too, had the earlier commitments of the federal government and the Ford Foundation. But these commitments were only the beginning—clarion calls, so to speak—announcing the onset of the struggle. And a lengthy struggle it promised to be. Like other ambitious national commitments, most notably perhaps the as yet unfulfilled promise of the Housing Act of 1949 that every American family should have "a decent home and suitable living environment,"[5] the realization of the national goal of ending poverty was confronted by innumerable obstacles.

One obstacle was the complex nature of poverty itself. To be sure, the broad statistical outlines of the problem were sufficiently clear. As the Council of Economic Advisors noted in its 1964 *Annual Report*, one-fifth of the nation's families and nearly one-fifth of its population, or more than 30 million people, subsisted on an annual income of under $3,000. Poverty, the council noted, was a social problem, national in scope, a condition endured by people "in many places . . . and in many situations." At the same time, it was a problem that was especially acute among particular sub-groups in the population. One-third of the nation's poor families, for example, were headed by individuals over sixty-five; roughly the same proportion were headed by individuals with only a grade school education; and close to half of all non-white families were poor.[6]

Clear as these statistics were, there yet remained much that was unknown about poverty. The poor lived "in a world apart . . . isolated from the mainstream of American life and alienated from its values,"[7] in a world that fostered such difficult-to-measure phenomena as defeatism and despair. There were no data on these subtle but key dimensions of the problem, and as the national war on poverty began, it was unclear how the poor, having lived "in a world apart," would respond to the incentives and opportunities the rest of society was preparing to offer. Though the nation was committed to ending poverty, as Michael Harrington had hoped it would be in his *The Other America*, there was no guarantee this commitment would be sufficient to strike a responsive chord in a population that over the years had been, as Harrington put it, "maimed in body and in spirit."[8]

Compounding this uncertainty was the absence of a reliable, continuing base of financial support for the national war on poverty. This was most obvious in the case of the Ford Foundation, whose support for projects such as New Haven's was limited to terminal grants, with the expectation that once these grants had been exhausted, the financial burden would be assumed by others. One alternative the Foundation apparently had in mind was the federal government,[9] and, indeed, the enactment of the Juvenile Delinquency and Youth Offenses Control Act, the Manpower Development and Training Act, and the Economic Opportunity Act, afforded a financial base far firmer than anything the Foundation could offer. Even so, financing the national war on poverty remained uncertain. As new ventures, the federal programs lacked what students of the appropriations process have called a "budget base," that is, a firm expectation that their annual appropriations—and in some cases authorizations—would be renewed.[10] Moreover, it was uncertain just how much the nation, and the federal government, was prepared to spend on these programs. The escalation of the war in Vietnam, together with the ambitious commitment to eliminate poverty, promised to make heavy demands on the country's resources. And despite the Johnson administration's assurances, there was some doubt the nation possessed the *will*, if not the resources, to endure the costs of both simultaneously.

There was, finally, uncertainty about the administration and management of the programs, both at the national and the local level. In mounting their attacks on poverty, both the Kennedy and Johnson administrations had followed a common presidential strategy and entrusted their programs to newly created federal agencies. Like most new agencies, however, those created to administer the national war on poverty were untested politically. Presidential support notwithstanding, these new agencies faced the job of forging for themselves a place in the federal hierarchy, in Congress, and what is of particular interest here, at the grass roots.

Grass roots support was especially critical. Neither the federal agencies nor the Ford Foundation had the authority, the manpower, or the intention of doing the job themselves, and, instead, were relying on the cooperation and participation of other groups in the country. Their programs were billed as "comprehensive," and whatever else this term may mean, in these cases it meant simultaneous activities in education, public health, child care, recreation, and numerous other activities designed to eliminate the causes and conditions of poverty. To initiate such activities, however, national officials needed the backing of a wide range of local public and private institutions, among them boards of education, health and welfare councils, civil rights organizations, and police departments. This was a formidable task indeed, especially for agencies without experience in the field and with few established and reliable channels of communications to the grass roots.

To overcome these administrative and political difficulties, federal and Foundation planners encouraged the creation of local "planning and coordinating" bodies or community action agencies as they came to be known under the Economic Opportunity Act. These institutions were central to the reform strategy of the national agencies and were to serve as the local mechanisms for mobilizing community resources in the fight against poverty. Like the national agencies themselves, however, these new local institutions were also untested politically and there were no assurances they would succeed in convincing other local institutions to cooperate with each other or with national and local anti-poverty officials. Indeed, given the historical record of bureaucratic and professional autonomy within local communities, there was considerable doubt key groups in education, law enforcement, or welfare, to cite but three examples, would in fact participate in any meaningful way.

Strategy for Alliances: Bureaucratic
Reciprocity

New Haven: A Partner and an Ally

The uncertainty that marked the early years of the national war on poverty had a direct bearing on the strategy adopted by New Haven's planners in their search for outside financial backing. Acting on the premise that the national agencies needed both assistance and support from the grass roots, the city's planners approached them not as a "beggar with a bushel basket," as one commentator described Lee's relationship with federal urban renewal agencies,[11] nor as just another city looking to benefit from Foundation and federal largesse. New Haven's posture was rather that of an ally. The strategy was to identify and align the local agency with those who controlled funds nationally, to link New Haven's appeal for these funds with the perceived self-interests of national anti-poverty officials. In short, New Haven's planners sought to fashion alliances with the national agencies, alliances in which New Haven would offer something in return for the financial support it was seeking.

A Model Anti-Poverty Project

At the heart of this alliance strategy was the concept of a model anti-poverty project. As Howard Hallman put it in one of the early proposals to the Ford Foundation, the New Haven project would be:

a pioneering effort, aiming at kind of a comprehensive social plan that has never before been prepared. It would not only point the way for future change in New Haven, *but would serve as a point of departure for other cities developing planning along these lines* [emphasis added].[12]

Part of New Haven's contribution to the alliance, then, was to be an operational test of the war on poverty. The New Haven project was to be a pilot project that could be used to promote social innovation on a national scale. If successful, New Haven's experience could be cited as evidence that "a comprehensive social plan that had never before been prepared" was both feasible and desirable. Moreover, New Haven's project could be used as a "point of departure for other cities," as a prototype for those local communities who preferred to innovate by imitation rather than by invention.

The success of this strategy rested in large part, quite obviously, on the ability of New Haven's planners to show concrete results, or, as was the case during the early negotiations with the national agencies, to convince them that the proposed model project was something more than an empty promise. For a less well positioned city, such a commitment would doubtless have been ineffective, or what is perhaps more to the point, in all probability never entertained by its representatives. But New Haven was different, at least in the minds of those who formulated the model project strategy. While the city's problems were "typical of those besetting many American cities, the response to these problems [had] been quite atypical."[13] New Haven had a number of important assets that made it an attractive place to invest anti-poverty funds, and New Haven's planners used these assets to establish the credibility of their commitment to develop a model anti-poverty project.

Chief among these assets was the backing of New Haven's Mayor Richard C. Lee and Lee's national reputation and record. As mayor, Lee had demonstrated a rare degree of political skill and a willingness to use this political skill to further the cause of urban reform. Among his achievements redevelopment stood as the most visible and the most publicized. Lee was responsible, the planners noted in their 1963 application to the Office of Juvenile Delinquency, "for the city's massive attack on the causes of urban decay . . . an attack that is unmatched in the nation today."[14] Under his leadership the city had embarked on an urban renewal program that

on a per capita basis far outstrips any other in the United States and projects now being planned will increase the lead still further. The renewal projects in execution embrace two major downtown projects, an industrial land-reclamation project, and two large neighborhood renewal projects involving approximately 15 percent of the city's population.[15]

Redevelopment was only one of Lee's achievements, however. The process of change begun by the mayor in urban renewal had already penetrated other facets of the community's social and economic life, had already had an effect on *education*, where the city had recently adopted a $20.0 million school construction program that called for replacing 40 percent of the city's total school plant; on *housing*, where the city was engaged in a $6.6 million housing rehabilitation program; and on *industrial and business development*, as a result of which, the planners claimed, "thousands of new jobs would be created to help the city solve its unemployment problems."[16] From all this the message was perfectly clear. Under Lee, the New Haven planners reminded the Office of Juvenile Delinquency, the city "had demonstrated the will, energy, and talent, to carry-out vast programs in urban renewal."[17] In other words, New Haven was not only concerned about the deterioration of the urban center but, more importantly, *it had shown it could do something about it*, and do it, moreover, *in a nationally visible way*.

Lee's support for the project was most critical and relied on most heavily during the early negotiations for the Ford Foundation grant, the first grant to be sought and received by the city. At this point in the project's history, when the anti-poverty agency itself and its programs were still on the drawing board, there was little else the planners could cite by way of achievement, and the Foundation grant was awarded, it seems, largely on the basis of Lee's past performance and his public and private commitments to back the effort.

Even so, the Foundation hedged its investments. If Lee's record and backing provided some basis for sanguine expectations about the fate of the anti-poverty project, still, they were not sufficient to dispel all the uncertainties surrounding this as yet untried and untested venture. Against the mild protests of the local planners, who had initially counted on a six-year grant, the Foundation restricted its commitment to three years. In so doing, however, Foundation officials agreed to consider renewing the grant at the end of this period, provided the planners could produce a workable project.

And produce they did! "It is our conviction," New Haven anti-poverty officials stated in their *Second Annual Report to the Foundation*, "that the project, even though only at the mid-point of the initial grant period, has already had a significant impact on public policy—local, state, and national."[18] This was no idle claim. During the first year and a half, the new agency had moved quickly to establish itself and its programs in the community. More than thirty anti-poverty programs, among them three neighborhood employment centers, ten pre-kindergarten classes, and eight work crews, were already underway, and some twenty others were in various stages of planning and implementation.[19] "This record," the staff concluded, reminding the Foundation of the broader implications of the project, "clearly suggests that the Ford Foundation and CPI can continue to make a contribution of national significance toward the search for solutions to the great domestic problems of the day."[20] Apparently the Foundation agreed. A year later, in 1965, it renewed New Haven's grant for an additional three years.

New Haven's success with the initial Ford Foundation grant served a second and no less important function for the new agency. In addition to providing a base for renewal of the Foundation grant, the early record also served as a resource that the staff used to sell New Haven and its anti-poverty project to various federal agencies. Here, too, the strategy was to fashion alliances, and here, too, part of New Haven's contribution to these alliances was the offer of a prototype anti-poverty project. In this case, however, the local staff could rely on more than promises. It could cite the original Ford Foundation grant as an endorsement of the agency and its efforts, and could point to these efforts as concrete evidence that New Haven could fulfill its commitments.

New Haven's record with the federal grants, which amounted to roughly $11.5 million between 1962 and 1966, was no less impressive than its record with the Foundation. What is more to the point here, this record was recognized and accepted as such. As early as 1964, testimonials to New Haven's success abounded. While many of these were admittedly overdrawn, it is clear that, even discounting for political rhetoric, the city had achieved precisely the status promised by the model anti-poverty project strategy. By the time the Johnson administration embarked on its drive to combat poverty, New Haven and its anti-poverty project had come to be singled out with regularity as one of the foremost examples of what a local community could do to stem the downward spiral of social and economic decay in the central city. As one national news commentator put it when discussing the administration's then-proposed Economic Opportunity Act:

One of the reasons the White House decided to pitch an important part of the program at the local level was the exciting example of progress made in New Haven, Connecticut, in less than ten years. With an extraordinarily tenacious Mayor named Richard C. Lee, help from the Ford Foundation and federal agencies, Yale's home town is now absorbed in what it labels "human conservation" under an agency headed by a young ex-labor leader, Mitchell Sviridoff.[21]

Even more significant endorsements came from two highly placed officials. After a visit to New Haven in February 1964, Secretary of Labor Willard Wirtz wrote Sviridoff thanking him for a "richly rewarding day." "I returned to Washington," Wirtz continued, "with a new sense of what is possible and will have New Haven [very much] in mind as plans are completed here for the new national programs."[22] And two years later the director of the federal Office of Economic Opportunity, Sargent Shriver, testified before the House Subcommittee on the War on Poverty that

I think anyone could go up there [New Haven] from this committee and observe in fact what you describe as being ideal. . . . We certainly don't have 700 New Havens around the country. We haven't had time. But we know where we are going and where we are trying to get to and the mechanism we have is this community action concept at the local level. Where it works it works extremely well.[23]

These testimonials had a twofold significance for the local staff. For one thing, they provided official endorsement for the city's reform effort, recognition that New Haven's was indeed a model anti-poverty project. This provided no small sense of personal gratification for the young, devoted, Kennedyesque staff of the agency. Equally important, the testimonials enhanced considerably New Haven's future bargaining position with the federal agencies. Once the project had been officially defined as a success and as an ideal worth imitating, federal officials had *a stake in its continuing good health.* To have failed to act in ways consistent with that stake would have endangered the reputation and credibility of these federal officials, a risk few administrators would be anxious to undergo. In short, New Haven was a known and proven entity. And rather than spawning the feeling that the city had been overindulged, its success simply served further to legitimate additional infusions of federal largesse.

Promoting New Haven's Model

That New Haven's anti-poverty project was recognized as a prototype was not an entirely fortuitous occurrence, for in addition to developing the model itself, the New Haven staff engaged in an extensive campaign to make the city's project known nationally. This in itself was as much a part of the overall alliance strategy as was the development of the model. If one of the keys to the spread of the national programs was the availability of a model other communities could imitate, another was that these communities be aware of the model to be imitated, and convinced of its relevance and value. In short, a second way in which New Haven came to the support of the national agencies was by helping them to promote the national effort across the country.

Public relations. To promote the national effort, the staff relied in part on traditional public relations techniques. In late 1963 a special Division of Public Information was established within CPI "to stimulate public awareness, both locally and out-of-town, of New Haven's Community Action Program."[24] Operating under Sviridoff's personal supervision, the division disseminated publicity designed to apprise the nation of the project and its accomplishments: press releases to national and local news media; a monthly newsletter with a circulation of 14,500 (1966); general accounts of the project and its history, administration, and programs; reprints of articles, some twenty in all, about the agency and the project, articles often encouraged and sometimes solicited by Sviridoff; and miscellaneous pamphlets and brochures, among them edited copies of the agency's annual reports and applications for grants.[25]

To supplement the written word, the division produced a slide show to illustrate "with drama and accuracy the impact of CPI and CPI-related programs,"[26] a show viewed in one year by an estimated 3,600 people.[27] It also organized a speakers' bureau to schedule appearances of staff members before such groups as the League of Women Voters, Rotary Clubs, temple and church organizations, and labor unions; and, finally, the division conducted guided tours of the city and the city's anti-poverty project.

Guided tours. The technique of guided tours was one of the principal methods used by local staff personnel to promote the city's project nationally. As *The New York Times* reported, "New Haven is a national showcase to which people make pilgrimages to see how it is done."[28] If the members of the House Subcommittee whom Sargent Shriver advised in 1966 to visit the city had not already done so, it would be only a slight overstatement to assert that they were in a minority, at least among those with an active interest in the national war on poverty. Between 1963 and 1966, the New Haven staff hosted an estimated 3,000 visitors, including federal, state, and foundation officials, foreign delegations, and most important of all, local groups planning their own projects.[29]

Each group was carefully and graciously accommodated by a staff conscious of the opportunities such visits provided to extend the agency's influence beyond the boundaries of the city. Tours were fully programmed and elaborately staged, designed to ensure maximum exposure to the virtues of New Haven generally, and, specifically, to the virtues of the anti-poverty project. Typically, a tour included a briefing by central office personnel, frequently by Sviridoff himself, on various facets of the agency's activities, followed by staff-conducted tours to the field—usually routed through urban renewal areas—to view individual programs: a pre-kindergarten class in a low-income housing project, a work crew consisting of five or six school drop-outs clearing a trail in a local park, or a storefront employment center. At each site, visitors were again briefed, this time by the agency's neighborhood staff, and then invited to mingle informally with the agency's clientele.

New Haven's role as a national showcase was at no time more evident than when the staff was hosting groups from other communities. These groups constituted the single largest category of visitors to the project—in 1965 alone, for example, more than fifty community delegations, or *an average of about one delegation a week*, toured the project.[30] For these visitors especially, a tour of New Haven served a number of important functions, functions in many respects not unlike those served by an election campaign.

Principal among these was the information, both general and specific, the New Haven staff disseminated about the national war on poverty. Among those who visited the city—and in this respect there was little difference between local and non-local groups, or between public and private groups—relatively few were informed about the nature and scope of the national war on poverty, and even these few were far from what might be termed highly knowledgeable. Some, for example, were totally unaware of certain aspects of national policy, most commonly the Juvenile Delinquency and Youth Offenses Control Act and the Manpower Development and Training Act, and the opportunities afforded by them to local communities. Others were bewildered by the intricacies of the federal bureaucracy, by the technicalities incumbent upon the development, submission, and pursuit of grant applications. Still others were unfamiliar with techniques used to reach the poor, and many visitors expressed disbelief at New Haven's staff's practice of searching for the unemployed and the school drop-out in bars, poolrooms, and other establishments of "dubious moral character."

All this may sound like an exaggeration, or at least a caricature, of those who visited the city. If so, it is only a slight one. Indeed, as far as can be determined from reports of other agency personnel who travelled extensively throughout the country, and from newspaper accounts, visitors to New Haven were not unique in their ignorance of anti-poverty programs. Nationally, the level of information about the war on poverty seems to have been quite low. All four national programs were new, and, initially, local communities had few guidelines on authorized procedures and practices. Yet planning for the war on poverty, as I indicated earlier, was to be a highly decentralized process, and many communities, faced with the responsibility of developing proposals on their own, found themselves unprepared and unequipped to push ahead. And their efforts to do so were complicated by the fact that at least some of the participants in the planning process had little or no prior experience with social welfare programs, and little or no exposure to conditions in the "other America."

This last point suggests yet a second aspect of New Haven's role as a "national showcase." New Haven was not only a source of information on the national war on poverty but also a source of political support for those struggling in other communities to launch projects. Whether knowingly or not, some visitors to the city were there to be sold on the value of the war on poverty. To be sure, the vast majority of those who came were already favorably disposed to some type of social reform. But the degree of enthusiasm and commitment specifically to the war on poverty varied widely.

In part, these variations were due to the political processes set in motion by the national war on poverty, and specifically by the Economic Opportunity Act. As a prior condition to receiving federal grants, communities were required to establish "broadly based, coordinated programs," which meant, according to regulations eventually issued by the federal Office of Economic Opportunity:

participation in policy-making by major public and private agencies responsible for services and programs concerned with poverty, other elements of the community as a whole, and the population to be served by the community action program.[31]

In other words, anyone who planned to institute a local anti-poverty project was required to fashion a new coalition among community groups: among educators, social workers, religious leaders, civil rights workers, union leaders, the poor, and businessmen. For many local organizers, this occasioned innumerable problems. Not a few of the established groups viewed the war on poverty with suspicion—among other reasons, because they viewed the programs as a threat to their own self-interests (some union leaders, for example, feared that anti-poverty efforts to secure employment for blacks would stir discontent among rank and file members) or because they considered the program an undesirable extension of federal, or, more generally, governmental, power into local community life, a by-no-means novel, yet nonetheless common, concern among visitors to the city.

Viewed in this context, a visit to New Haven can be conceived as a political maneuver in which the New Haven anti-poverty staff joined with organizers from other communities in an effort to dispel anxieties, fears, and misgivings about the war on poverty, and, more positively, to win allies for the program. Tours of the city, discussions with staff members and with representatives from local public and private agencies, including the Department of Education and the Greater New Haven Community Council, all were arranged and conducted with this objective in mind.

To what extent they were successful cannot be determined in any precise way, for there is little information on the subsequent behavior of visitors to the city. That visits had some positive value cannot be doubted, however, at least not if conversations I had with visitors themselves are even partially reliable measures. Clearly, most of these visitors were exceedingly favorably impressed by the New Haven effort. For those already committed to the war on poverty, a visit helped reinforce their enthusiasm and support; for the remainder, it helped demonstrate that a local project could be something more than an expensive utopian venture or a refuge for incompetent party workers, or for unimaginative and tired bureaucrats.

Expertise and Personnel

Closely related to its role as a showcase city was New Haven's contribution to the national effort in the area of personnel and staffing. The passage of the Economic Opportunity Act and the subsequent growth nationally of interest in community action programs resulted in what the federal Office of Economic Opportunity called a "major new demand for able administrators in an area where few experienced managers are available."[32] Here, too, New Haven was to demonstrate its value as an ally.

Given its record and reputation, New Haven was a natural recruiting ground for those searching for anti-poverty administrators, and many communities, as well as the Foundation and the federal government, made frequent demands on the agency for staffing assistance and support. In some cases these amounted to requests for expert advisors who would help organize, reorganize, or evaluate projects in other communities. The most notable example of this was Sviridoff's efforts on behalf of Mayor John Lindsay of New York City. Supported by a $150,000 Ford Foundation grant and a staff of twenty-seven—many of them from New Haven—Sviridoff conducted a five-month investigation of New York City's anti-poverty programs. In June 1966, the Sviridoff Committee recommended a sweeping overhaul of all the city's activities in manpower, welfare, and education, a recommendation the reform-minded *The New York Times* called "the most intelligent approach any metropolitan center has yet developed toward meeting the monumental challenges involved in the war on poverty."[33]

In many cases, staff consulting led to more permanent positions in the anti-poverty agencies of other communities. Sviridoff himself, for example, was later named by Mayor Lindsay to head the Human Resources Administration, a new super-agency whose creation Sviridoff had recommended. In June 1966, George Bennett, the agency's manpower director, was appointed executive director of Action for Boston Community Development, an agency he had previously helped evaluate for the Ford Foundation. Richard Brooks and Andrew Raubeson, both at one time administrative assistants to Sviridoff, helped organize projects in New London and Waterbury, Connecticut, respectively, and then left New Haven to head these projects. In addition to these four, at least six other local staff members accepted high-ranking positions in the anti-poverty agencies of other communities.[34]

Obviously, there were limitations to the amount of consulting and the number of locally apprenticed personnel New Haven could provide the national war on poverty. Although Community Progress, Inc. was a relatively large bureaucratic establishment—by 1966 there were more than 200 full-time staff members—its supply of trained personnel was not inexhaustible. Certainly, it was not sizeable enough to meet the "critical shortage of personnel" that, staff members reminded the federal Office of Economic Opportunity, "posed grave implications for the success of the national effort."[35]

To alleviate this shortage and at the same time to demonstrate further the value of New Haven's support, Sviridoff and his staff embarked on a more systematic training effort for the war on poverty. With a grant from the federal Office of Economic Opportunity, a Community Action Institute (CAI) was established in New Haven during the spring of 1965. Under the grant New Haven was to be a training resource for local communities throughout New England and for New York state outside of New York City. Among other things, the institute was to provide personnel from these communities with an opportunity for on-the-job training in New Haven and to share with them the agency's own experiences in dealing with federal agencies and federal programs, with the poor, and with other community organizations. In addition, the institute staff was to conduct field courses in other communities and prepare instructional materials—pamphlets, films, tapes and manuals—for distribution to individuals and organizations in local communities throughout the region.[36]

In terms of size and growth, the institute's experience to date has been impressive. By spring 1967, for example, CAI had serviced, on an average, more than 1500 individuals annually from communities in the seven-state region. During this same period, 1965 through 1967, the institute's budget rose by some $400,000, from under $100,000 in 1965 to more than $500,000 in 1967.[37]

Whether these gross figures signify success in terms of the institute's stated objectives cannot be determined from the data now available. But whatever the success in these terms, two things are perfectly clear. First, the institute represented a formalization of New Haven's role both as a prototype and promoter for the war on poverty and as a source of expertise and manpower. Second, through the institute, New Haven showed once again that it was a willing, able, and valuable partner in the alliance against poverty.

Organizing a Constituency: The National
Association for Community Development

The formation of the Community Action Institute coincided with two additional moves by the local staff, both designed to strengthen the war on poverty and to enhance New Haven's position nationally. One of these was the creation of the National Association for Community Development, an "educational and charitable organization," chartered in March 1965, "to encourage, promote, and stimulate the Community Development of human resources."[38] This, at least, was how the association was described in its Articles of Incorporation. Translated into political terms, it meant that the association was a professional interest group, an organization of state and local officials—more than 100 of whom attended the March 1965 meeting in Washington, D.C., at which the association was formed—designed to achieve two overall objectives: first, to rally and demonstrate grass-roots support for the then recently passed Economic Opportunity Act, and, second, to provide a formal structure within which those responsible for local anti-poverty projects could develop a common sense of identity, common perspectives, and common norms about the war on poverty.

To a large extent the National Association for Community Development was Sviridoff's handiwork, and his election as the Association's first president was as much a recognition of the part he had played in organizing this new interest group as it was a testimony to his national prominence in the war on poverty. In October 1964, for example, just two months after the passage of the Economic Opportunity Act, he met in Washington with federal and local officials and agreed to head an Ad Hoc Steering Committee that was to explore the prospects for a formal organization to support the war on poverty.[39] Between October and the following March, New Haven's anti-poverty chief devoted a major part of his own time and energies, as well as those of his staff, to laying the foundations for the new association. He took the lead in hiring a professional Washington lobbyist to serve as an interim executive secretary of the yet-to-be-formed association, in drafting the association's constitution, in arranging details for the March conference, and in selecting the slate of candidates that was eventually elected as officers and board members of the new association.

Once established, the National Association for Community Development was quickly endorsed by federal anti-poverty officials—by Sargent Shriver, the director of the Office of Economic Opportunity; by Jack Conway, the acting deputy director; by Stanley Ruttenberg, the manpower administrator in the United States Department of Labor; and by Samuel Ganz, the executive officer of the Manpower Administration. These endorsements were voiced during panel discussions on which federal officials, some sixteen in all, exchanged views and criticisms with their state and local counterparts, and in formal addresses by federal officials to the assembled delegates.

That national officials endorsed the new association was no more surprising than the subsequent decision of the federal Office of Economic Opportunity to permit local agencies to use federal anti-poverty funds to pay for membership in the association. Throughout the entire planning period, Sviridoff had maintained close liaison with his counterparts in the federal government, and from them had received continued support and encouragement. Indeed, according to one New Haven staff member, the original idea for the association had been advanced by federal officials themselves, who suggested in October 1964 that local project directors develop a formal organization to lend support to the national reform effort.

If the suggestion was advanced by federal officials, the leadership was provided largely by Sviridoff, and the National Association for Community Development thus stands as yet another New Haven contribution to the national alliances. In working to establish the association, Sviridoff provided further evidence of his commitment to the alliances, of his willingness to spend his resources—his time, his staff, his knowledge of local projects, and his popularity and prestige across the nation—on behalf of his allies in the federal government.

Mobilizing a Constituency

As president of the new association, Sviridoff's first opportunity to demonstrate his backing for the national war on poverty occurred at the closing session of the March 1965 conference. In an address to the delegates, the Labor Department's manpower administrator, Stanley Ruttenberg, urged the association to join with the federal government in a nationwide campaign to recruit unemployed youths as seasonal farm laborers. Behind this proposal lay the long and bitter debate over the use of foreign farm labor in the United States, a debate marked a year earlier (1964) by congressional refusal to renew legislation permitting the use of imported Mexican and British West Indian laborers. The refusal touched off strong protests among United States growers, who complained that the pool of domestic farm labor was insufficient to meet their needs, and who predicted that crops would go unharvested, bankruptcies would rise, and prices would soar.[40]

Much of the controversy at the time centered on the United States Department of Labor. By statute, the secretary of labor was authorized to relax the ban on imported labor whenever, in his judgment, conditions warranted such a move. Although many growers demanded such a relaxation, Secretary of Labor Willard Wirtz refused, and, instead, initiated a search for alternative ways of satisfying agricultural needs consistent with Labor Department policy.

One such alternative was Ruttenberg's suggestion to use unemployed urban youths as farm hands, a suggestion Sviridoff publicly endorsed at the closing session of the conference. Before the conference adjourned, he secured the passage of a formal resolution agreeing in principle to support the Labor Department's efforts to find alternatives to imported farm labor, and he then returned to New Haven to work out a plan. Within a week he and his staff had drafted a proposal they felt would satisfy both the farmers and the Department of Labor, a proposal to "match the excess supply of unemployed urban youths and the excess seasonal demand for rural agricultural workers."[41]

New Haven's proposal called for organizing unemployed youths into small groups, each with twenty-five to thirty members, headed by a foreman, and modeled on New Haven's Home Town Corps.[42] Since the summer of 1963, New Haven's anti-poverty agency had been experimenting with a combined manual-work-remedial-education program in an effort to reach disaffected teenagers and to counter youthful alienation. In general the work required few skills. This mattered little, however, for the main objective of the program was the inculcation of social norms and work habits in a population that was either unaware of them or unaccustomed to them. The Home Town Corps was a mechanism for acculturation, and for this very reason was well suited to the needs of a seasonal farm program.

As president of the association, Sviridoff assumed responsibility for mobilizing support for the proposal. Although the association had endorsed Ruttenberg's appeal, it had done so only in principle, and without any lengthy debate or discussion. Once back in New Haven, Sviridoff initiated talks with other anti-poverty project directors across the country, outlining for them the proposal he and his staff had prepared and soliciting their comments and their backing. At the same time, he and his staff met in Washington with Labor Department officials, including Ruttenberg, to explain New Havens' proposal and to offer the use of their own agency on a pilot basis.

For Sviridoff, the response to his own appeal for and offer of support was disappointing. Among other association members there was little enthusiasm for the enterprise, and what enthusiasm there was was insufficient to warrant the association's official endorsement of the New Haven plan.[d] This, coupled with the relatively high cost of the proposal, apparently discouraged the Labor Department,[e] and the proposal was never adopted. After several weeks of feverish activity, the agency discontinued its efforts to rally support and quietly but reluctantly shelved its plan.

In attempting to mobilize association backing for the proposal, Sviridoff clearly miscalculated the reaction of other project directors, as well as his own ability to persuade them. Though he miscalculated, there was less risk in the undertaking, in his mind, than some of his staff advisors had thought there would be.[f] He had pressed for the adoption of the Home Town Corps proposal against the urgings of some staff members who correctly anticipated that other project directors would not support him. Sviridoff, however, believed he stood to gain whatever the outcome. Had the proposal been accepted, his stature would have been enhanced considerably; if not, then at least he would have demonstrated his own willingness to support and cooperate with his allies, and in so doing would have demonstrated the credibility of his own commitments.

Sviridoff's efforts on behalf of Ruttenberg and the Labor Department were but part of that broader strategy whereby he and his staff tried to identify themselves with the national war on poverty. The development of a prototype project, the promotion of this project outside New Haven, the use of agency expertise and personnel, the formation of a professional interest group to support the national effort—in all these ways, the staff sought to demonstrate to national anti-poverty officials the value of New Haven's support for the war on

---

[d]Sviridoff never made entirely clear why other local officials turned down his proposal. It is clear, however, that many of them, while supporting Ruttenberg's appeal in principle, were reluctant to do so in practice.

[e]The estimated cost of the proposal for New Haven alone was $108,650, and this did not include the salaries and travel expenses of the 300 inner-city youths the agency planned to recruit. The $108,650 was requested from the U.S. Department of Labor to pay for crew foremen, administrative personnel, staff travel expenses, health examinations, and job-traning classes before and after deployment to the field. Community Progress, Inc., "Proposal for an Out-of-State Work Program," New Haven, March 17, 1965, pp. 13-17, passim.

[f]Staff members who advised against the proposal raised two major objections: first, that most communities were just beginning their anti-poverty projects and would be reluctant to divert energies and resources to the type of program suggested by New Haven; and second, that civil rights organizations would object to the use of black or Chicano teenagers as "stoop laborers," whatever assurances there might be that the teenagers' well-being would be guarded.

poverty. To be sure, there was a strong element of local self interest in all this for Sviridoff, and his staff had a direct stake in perpetuating and protecting the outside sources upon which they were so heavily dependent for money. But this local self interest coincided with the interests of the national agencies themselves, and such coincidences are the stuff from which alliances can be forged.

6

The Politics of the Matching Game

As I indicated at the beginning of the last chapter, New Haven's quest for outside financial support was related to a more general policy objective, namely, the minimization of demands on the local community. Through their alliances with the Ford Foundation and various federal agencies, New Haven's anti-poverty officials qualified politically for this support, and in so doing moved toward the realization of this broader objective. But qualifying *politically* was only part of the job. In addition, the local agency had to qualify *financially* by raising matching funds. How this was done, the techniques developed by the New Haven staff to meet the matching requirements of the national programs, and the implications of these techniques for the city's programs will be examined in this chapter.

Several important considerations are involved in matching, among them the amount, kind, and source of matching funds, and the degree of correspondence or fit between the activities supported by grant and matching funds. The amount of required matching, for example, can range from zero to 100 percent, with the grantee required to pay no money at all or an amount equal to the grant itself; the kind of money to be raised may be new cash outlays, funds reallocated from existing programs, or services-in-kind; the sources may be public or private, local, state, or even national, and grant or matching funds may be used to support the same or different program(s) in the same or different public policy areas. In all these respects, practices can and do vary, and these variations can have a significant bearing on the behavior of grant recipients.

Of the four national programs used by New Haven to support its anti-poverty efforts, three required some type of matching commitment as a precondition for the award of the grant itself. With the exception of the *Manpower Development and Training Act,*[1] each program stipulated that its own grant funds be supplemented with funds from other sources. In each case, however, the amount of matching varied. To qualify for grants under the Juvenile Delinquency and Youth Offenses Control Act,[2] for example, local communities needed to raise one dollar for every dollar they received from the federal government, a ratio set by federal statute. The Economic Opportunity Act was far more generous.[3] Under Title II of the Act, the Office of Economic Opportunity was authorized to fund up to 90 percent of local project costs, as opposed to the 50 percent allowed under the Juvenile Delinquency Act. The Ford Foundation, on the other hand, had no fixed matching formula, at least none that was ever made public. But even the foundation had its price tag, roughly $1.2 million for its three-year grant to New Haven, an amount agreed upon in the January 1962 negotiations between city and Foundation officials.

Matching: Local Policies and Practices

New Haven's approach to matching was guided by the same overriding considerations that led it to seek outside financial support in the first place, namely, the desire to impose as few dollar costs as possible on the local community. Indeed, this objective was an agency norm, accepted as a major premise by the city's anti-poverty staff, and used by them to measure their own performance. And in these terms they were highly successful. As I indicated earlier, between 1962 and 1965 roughly 92 percent of local project costs were paid for by groups outside the city. Of the more than $9.7 million New Haven spent during this period on its reform effort, only *$892,000* was local tax money.[4]

Matching One Source with Another

In large part the agency's success in matching can be accounted for by the practice of using funds from one outside source to supplement those from another. To qualify for the original Ford Foundation grant, for example, New Haven pledged some $1.2 million: $570,000 from the City of New Haven, $330,000 from the New Haven Redevelopment Agency, $160,000 from the New Haven Housing Authority, and the remainder from private sources, such as the New Haven Central Labor Council, the Urban League, and the New Haven Foundation. Both the Redevelopment Agency and the Housing Authority, however, were federally supported agencies, and the funds they contributed to the matching sum were funds they had originally obtained from their federal counterparts. Of the total $1.2 million in Ford-matching funds, then, only $570,000 was actually local tax money. And since this $570,000 was to be allotted over a three-year period, the political and fiscal pressures on the Lee administration were reduced even further.

This same general technique was used to qualify for federal grants under the Economic Opportunity Act and the Juvenile Delinquency and Youth Offenses Control Act. Both these acts required local communities to raise matching funds from non-federal sources, a restriction that ruled out the possibility of using either the grants the agency had received from the Housing Authority or the Redevelopment Agency, or the grants it received under the Manpower Development and Training Act. There were, however, no restrictions of either a statutory or administrative nature on the kinds of non-federal money that could be used, and with the Ford Foundation's grant already in hand, the New Haven staff simply turned to this source to meet a large part of the federal matching requirement. In its 1963 application for a grant under the Juvenile Delinquency Act, for example, the staff requested *$800,000* in federal money, and matched it with \$562,250 from the Ford Foundation and \$241,000 from the City of New Haven.[5][a]

In the short run, the practice of using Ford Foundation funds to match federal grants, and vice versa, proved a highly useful money-saving device. Over the long term, however, the practice had two serious disadvantages, arising, first, from the nature of the Foundation's agreement with the city, and, second, from the projected rise in the cost of federal grants. The Foundation grant, it will be recalled, was awarded originally for a period of three years, a period that was later extended an additional three years. After this second three-year period, Foundation support would end completely, with no second renewal contemplated. By this time, however, the price of federal assistance was scheduled to increase. After June 30, 1968, local projects would be required to shoulder 50 percent of the cost of many of the programs funded under the Economic Opportunity Act, as opposed to the previously required 10 percent.[6] In other words, by 1969 New Haven faced the prospect of life without the Foundation, along with more stringent federal matching requirements. If the agency and its programs were to survive, alternative sources of financing were needed.

One possible source was the City of New Haven. But neither Sviridoff nor other agency officials ever indicated that they were prepared to abandon their policy of minimizing demands on New Haven's taxpayers. To have done so, they felt, would have been to court political trouble, for any request that local taxpayers assume responsibility for the Ford Foundation grant would almost surely have exposed the agency to local partisan conflict. Moreover, even if more local money were allocated, and few agency officials expected it ever would be, it might prove a mixed blessing. More city money might have meant additional local controls on the agency, and, given the uncertainty of the local political context, this was one of the things agency officials were trying to avoid.

Creating a State Matching Program

Instead of creating a local financial base in anticipation of the eventual loss of Foundation backing, staff members continued their practice of looking outside the city for possible sources of money. In early 1965 they found just such a source. In February, a bill was filed in the Connecticut General Assembly calling for financial assistance to communities seeking to "improve and accelerate the

[a]Precise data on the Ford-local ratio of matching for the second Juvenile Delinquency Act grant (\$700,000) and for the first Economic Opportunity Act grant (\$1,100,000) are not available. Staff members informed me, however, that the same practice was followed in these two later grants. For a criticism of this particular matching strategy, see Martin Rein and S.M. Miller, "Social Action on the Installment Plan," *Transaction* 3, No. 2 (January/February, 1966), p. 35. This and other criticisms of the strategy are discussed in chapter 9.

education of children whose educational achievement has been or is being restricted by economic, social, or environmental disadvantages."[7] Two months later the bill passed the legislature, and Connecticut's Governor John Dempsey signed into law a $10,000,000 State Aid to Disadvantaged Children Act under which the City of New Haven stood to gain some $1.4 million biennially in state funds.[8]

For Sviridoff and his staff, the significance of the act lay in the subsidies it provided, albeit indirectly, for their own anti-poverty project. To be sure, under terms of the act, only local boards of education, and not anti-poverty agencies, were made eligible for assistance. But the act also specified that whatever assistance local boards received was to be used for "pre-kindergarten, tutorials, school drop-outs, work study and remedial education programs."[9] Thus, even though the funds were not made available directly to Community Progress, Inc., they were nonetheless earmarked for programs already a part of the city's anti-poverty effort and, as we will see presently, the local staff planned to use them as matching for future federal grants.

That New Haven and its reform effort benefited from the state act was more than accidental good fortune. For one thing, Sviridoff himself had played a major role in organizing support for the act around the state, working closely with and through the Connecticut Association of Boards of Education, of which he was a former member, and the association's Committee of Big City Boards.[10] Moreover, both he and his staff had had a major voice in shaping the content of the act itself. Indeed, in all but one respect, namely, a detailed "maintenance of effort" clause,[b] the bill eventually adopted by the legislature and signed by the governor was the same as the one drafted and circulated by the New Haven staff. This proposal included on the one hand a stipulation that state funds be allocated only for programs such as those noted above, and on the other an allocation formula that ensured an "adequate share" of state money for the larger urban communities in the state.[c]

---

[b]The clause in question required local communities to "maintain existing state and local expenditures at a per pupil rate of annual increase at least equal to the average per pupil rate of increase throughout the state." It was replaced by a clause urging communities to maintain their efforts without indicating what, specifically, would constitute an acceptable annual rate of increase. The change is reported in Community Progress, Inc., "Summary Report of the Meeting of the Special Committee on Categorical Aid for Public Schools," January 6, 1965 (typewritten).

[c]The allocation formula devised by the staff and adopted by the state specified that funds be distributed (a) by multiplying one-half of the total amount appropriated by the average of the percentage representing the ratio of the number of children in the community receiving Aid to Dependent Children to the total number of such children in the state and (b) by multiplying one half of the total amount appropriated by the percentage representing the ratio of the number of families in a community with annual incomes under $4,000 to the total number of such families in the state. New Haven, for example, with 19 percent of all children in the state receiving Aid to Dependent Children and 9.2 percent of the state's families with incomes under $4,000, received $1.4 million under the Act; Hartford, $1.6 million; and Windsor Locks, a small community in the north west central part of the state, $28,000.

Given the limited scope of the state act, it may seem strange that Sviridoff and his staff devoted as much time as they did to its passage. To be sure, education was a major part of the city's anti-poverty effort. But there were other activities as well: manpower and employment programs, recreation, neighborhood services, health, and day-care centers, to mention but a few, and these were not covered by the legislation. How was it, then, that the staff staked so much of the future of the entire enterprise on the availability of new money in education alone?

The explanation for this behavior can be found in the staff's operational definition of matching, a definition they had used throughout the project's history in dealing with the Foundation and federal agencies, and one they intended to use in subsequent transactions with federal officials. Beginning with the original Foundation grant in 1962, the staff had successfully claimed expenditures in one program area as matching those in another. Instead of matching each grant item for item, or activity for activity, they simply allocated non-grant funds to some programs and not to others. Thus, for example, in one application for a grant from the Office of Economic Opportunity, New Haven earmarked matching funds for six project components and charged the remaining eighteen, including some $206,000 in agency administrative costs, exclusively to the federal government.[11] Nor were the funds claimed as matching in this or other grant applications always under the direct control of the anti-poverty agency. Indeed, the $892,000 in city funds used between 1962 and 1965 was money that had been appropriated by the City of New Haven for local public agencies that were participating in the project, not for Community Progress, Inc.

The Use of Small Amounts of Local Seed Money

Although most of the matching funds for the anti-poverty project came from sources outside the city, New Haven *did* contribute some $892,000 between 1962 and 1965. The amount was relatively small and the city's return on its investment rather substantial, *roughly $1,000,000 in outside funds for every $100,000 in local money*. Even so, it represented a demand on the local tax dollar, and in keeping with their overall strategy of avoiding such demands, the staff employed a number of techniques that served to obscure the nature and extent of these demands.

The use of third parties. One such technique was the reliance on third parties to act as the agency's spokesmen in its efforts to raise city money. Anti-poverty officials themselves avoided open participation in New Haven's budgetary process. Neither Sviridoff nor any member of his staff ever appeared before the city's budget-making institutions, and they refrained from openly or publicly urging local tax money for the project. Rather, they worked privately, behind the scenes, to secure the backing and cooperation of other local groups and individuals who in turn agreed to act as spokesmen for city money. Chief among these were the agency's allies in the Lee administration, including Lee himself, Lee's budget director, Dennis Rezendes, and New Haven's superintendent of schools, Lawrence Paquin. These were the individuals whose role it was to propose, explain, and, if necessary, defend the city's share of the matching.

Incomplete accounting. Just how much the City of New Haven actually contributed to the anti-poverty project was, moreover, never fully revealed publicly. An examination of the city's budgets for the years 1962 through 1965, for example, reveals but three explicit references to funds appropriated by the city as matching for the anti-poverty project, and these amounted to only $450,000.[12] This was some *$442,000* less than the *$892,000* in local matching the anti-poverty agency claimed in a *private* staff report it submitted to the Ford Foundation in 1965.[13]

Nor were the anti-poverty agency's *publicly* distributed accounts of its financial activities any more revealing. For one thing, it was not until late 1965 that the agency made public any data on the fiscal structure of the project, and what data it did make public were incomplete.[d] In the "Finances" section of its *1965 Community Action Program Review*, a report circulated widely in the city, the agency reported that some $526,000 in local funds had been used as matching since 1962.[14] This was $76,000 more than the amount listed in the *Municipal Budgets*, but some $366,000 less than what the anti-poverty agency claimed in its private report to the Ford Foundation.[15]

"In-kind services." Two practices, both of which helped New Haven's anti-poverty officials minimize demands on the local tax dollar still further, account for the differences among the public and private figures reported by the agency and the city. One of these was the use of a technique employed widely in matching, namely, "in-kind services." In this case the services were those of local public officials who contributed their time and skills to the project. In all, some $366,000 in staff services was claimed in grant applications, and listed in the agency's private report to the Foundation. This money was not included either in the city's or the agency's public accounts of the project's financing. In other words, the $450,000 reported in the *Municipal Budgets* and the $526,000 reported in the agency's *1965 Community Action Program Review* referred only to that money the anti-poverty agency termed "new local outlays in cash."[16]

Double matching. If both the anti-poverty agency and the city reported only new cash outlays, how does one account for the fact the two did not report the same amounts? As can be seen from the figures in the preceding paragraph, the agency itself claimed $76,000 more than the amount actually appropriated by the city. Admittedly, the difference is slight, but though slight, its explanation is most intriguing.

---

[d]See above, chapter 3.

It is intriguing, because in reality these funds did not exist. Relying on a variation of the old shell game, the city's anti-poverty staff placed the same pea (dollar) under each shell (grant application). To state it somewhat differently, agency officials used the *same* local money to match *different* outside grants. Of the $450,000 actually appropriated by the City of New Haven, $76,000 was claimed twice by the anti-poverty agency, once as matching for the original Ford Foundation grant, and then again as matching for a federal grant.

Matching and Policy Formation

Given the relatively easy terms on which New Haven's anti-poverty staff was able to obtain outside financial support, the question naturally arises as to what, if any, policy costs these terms entailed for New Haven. Grants-in-aid, such as those used in the war on poverty, are instruments of national policy, and over the years have proved effective means of attaining indirectly political objectives that could not be attained directly. The grant-in-aid process, for example, was used by the federal government to help spread civil service reform when, through the Social Security Act amendments of 1939, states desiring federal welfare funds were "compelled . . . to develop state merit systems for employees paid in whole or in part by [federal] funds."[17] More recently, Title VI of the Civil Rights Act of 1964 "barred discrimination under any program or activity receiving federal assistance against any person because of his race, color, or national origin."[18] Conceivably, then, New Haven's relatively easy access to outside funds was more apparent than real, for it is possible that the city's freedom in matching was offset by nationally imposed constraints on the policy discretion of local officials.

If by this is meant that the national agencies imposed their own policy preferences on the city's anti-poverty agency and/or forced the local staff to pursue programs and policies the staff itself deemed unacceptable, then the answer must be an unqualified no. As I have indicated in earlier chapters, between 1962 and 1966 the agency itself, and before it, the unofficial work group headed by Howard Hallman was the prime mover in shaping the content of the city's anti-poverty project. To be sure, those in charge of the national programs occasionally offered suggestions. But these were suggestions only and there is no evidence that these suggestions ever were made prior conditions to the award of a grant or led to conflict between local and national officials. What the evidence does indicate—evidence based on detailed comparison of grant applications and grant receipts, on examinations of internal staff documents, letters, and memoranda, on extensive interviews with staff members, and finally, on observation of some of the actual negotiations between local staff members and national officials—is that during this period the local staff itself was the single most important influence in the area of policy formation as it took the lead in defining and making operational the national anti-poverty program in New Haven.

This is not to say the local staff received everything it requested, either in terms of money or in terms of programs. In some cases, national officials rejected local proposals, but as far as can be judged from the sources just cited, these rejections were for the most part marginal. There were two major exceptions. One, the definition of the Economic Opportunity Act's stipulation that projects be conducted with "maximum feasible participation" of neighborhood residents, was discussed in an earlier chapter. The other, an early proposal to the Foundation, was rejected by the Foundation as not sufficiently action-oriented.[e] Even here, however, the programs eventually funded by the Foundation bore the distinctive mark of local personalities and local concerns. For, while Foundation and federal officials both exercised a veto power over how their money was to be spent, neither openly dictated policy to the local staff. In short, although New Haven's anti-poverty officials did not receive everything they requested, what they did receive was what they themselves had proposed.[f]

---

[e]This was the June, 1961 draft discussed in chapter 2.

[f]What the local staff proposed may, of course, have been proposed in response to subtle cues and signals from the national agencies. In other words, in planning their programs Sviridoff and other agency officials may have been guided by the reactions they anticipated from national anti-poverty officials. That this occurred at a general political level is perfectly clear, for the agency's alliance strategy was rooted in the assumption that the national agencies would respond favorably to the proposed partnership. The evidence is less clear with respect to specific programs. In my conversations with local staff members, I asked whether and to what extent they tried to "read" the specific program interests of the national agencies. Most staff members, including Hallman, who was the agency's chief program planner during these years, claimed the development and choice of programs was the agency's and that they themselves were influenced only slightly by the anticipated response of national officials.

**Part IV
Fashioning a Local
Constituency**

7

A Coalition of Bureaucracies

Strategic Objectives

Important as outside financial backing was for the local project, it was only a part of the overall effort to initiate a reform program in New Haven. As I indicated in an earlier chapter, much of New Haven's bargaining strength nationally turned on its ability to fashion an operating model for the war on poverty. To fashion this model in New Haven, the anti-poverty staff needed the active cooperation and participation of established bureaucracies.[a] The proposals formulated by the city's reform-minded planners, by Logue and, after him, Hallman and Sviridoff, called for changes within existing public and private agencies, *changes that would result in these agencies' becoming more effective instruments of social and economic reform.* Programs such as pre-kindergarten, remedial reading, on-the-job training, neighborhood libraries, and the community school all envisioned an expanded and more self-conscious role for the bureaucracy in alleviating conditions of poverty within the city. They envisioned something more as well, namely, a coalition of agencies active in the area of social welfare.

This objective of working with and through what might be termed the city's established bureaucratic order was one of the distinctive characteristics of New Haven's anti-poverty effort. As we saw earlier, New Haven, unlike some other communities, made little effort to include in the planning or the administration of the project those referred to in the Economic Opportunity Act as the "residents of the areas and members of the groups served." Nor, for that matter, was there much effort to include other community groups, at least not directly. The principal target was the bureaucracy, and rather than working through intermediaries—for example, civil rights organizations, civic groups, political parties, or the general institutions of government—the anti-poverty staff relied largely on direct appeals to the administrators themselves in an effort to win them over to the project.

This concern with the bureaucracy also distinguished the anti-poverty project from previous reform efforts in New Haven during the Lee administration. I have already noted that the project marked the first direct assault on the chronic and

[a]As used here, the terms *bureaucracy* and *bureaucrat* refer simply to public and private agencies and their administrators, exclusive of the elected or appointed boards or commissions legally responsible for them. None of the unflattering connotations commonly associated with the terms is intended by their usage.

stubborn problems of poverty and near poverty in the city, that previously, poverty was dealt with through a variety of standard programs such as AFDC, public assistance, and public health. More to the point here, the anti-poverty effort signalled a significant shift in the role New Haven's established, old-line, public and private agencies were to play in the city's drive to modernize and to cope with the problems of the mid-twentieth century.

The first stage in this drive had been urban renewal, in which existing city agencies had played a relatively minor role. In mounting this program, New Haven's Mayor Richard Lee had for the most part bypassed these agencies by creating a new, largely self-sufficient bureaucracy. The anti-poverty effort was to be different. True, there was a new, and in this case private, non-profit agency. But Community Progress, Inc., unlike the new agencies that were responsible for urban renewal, was to work in conjunction with, rather than apart from, other public and private agencies in the city.

The Bureaucratic Establishment

The Formal Structure

As I noted earlier, New Haven is an old community, and its age is reflected in the institutions under which the city is governed. By this I do not wish to imply that its institutions are antiquated or outdated, though some maintain that such is indeed the case. Rather, I want to note that, since its incorporation in the seventeenth century, the city has been exposed to various political trends that individually and collectively have left distinctive marks on the city's governmental structure.

The most distinctive of these marks and one common to many cities is the formal decentralization of government. Whether from a desire for representativeness, an objective of pre-civil war Jacksonian democracy, or from a desire "to make a city government where no officer should have power enough to do much harm," a goal of post-civil war urban reform, the effect has been much the same.[1] Formal authority has been divided and distributed widely throughout city government, and no single official or governmental institution has been entrusted with control over the entire machinery of municipal government.

This heritage from the past is woven like a bright thread throughout the formal structure of government prescribed by New Haven's City Charter. In the language of textbooks on municipal government, New Haven is governed by a "weak mayor system." There is a single chief executive, elected biennially in partisan elections. But his formal powers are severely curtailed. In addition to other elected administrative officers and a thirty-three member city council, there are a variety of boards and commissions, nineteen in all, that exercise formal authority over roughly 97 percent of the city's full-time municipal employees and 62.5 percent of the city's annual budget. (Table 7-1)

Table 7-1

New Haven Municipal Boards and Commissions

Board/Commission	Members	Number of[a] Professional Staff	Budget as % Overall City Budget
Board of Education	7	1,540	33.5
Board of Police Commissioners	6	478	9.4
Board of Fire Commissioners	5	388	8.6
Welfare Board	5	84	5.8
Board of Park Commissioners	8	144	2.5
Board of Health	6	69	1.4
Board of Library Directors	9	70	1.3
City Plan Commission	6	15	. . .[c]
Board of Airport Commissioners	6	7	. . .
Board of Finance	8	11	. . .
Girls Recreation Guild	5	2	. . .
Board of Zoning Appeals	5	1	. . .
Civil Service Board	3	1	. . .
Board of Tax Review	3	1	. . .
Board of Ethics	3	0	. . .
Building Line Commission	5	0	. . .
Board of Appeals from Decisions of Building Inspector	5	0	. . .
Bureau of Compensation	3	0	. . .
Capitol Projects Committee	9	0	. . .
Totals 19	107	2,801[b]	62.5

Source: City of New Haven, *Municipal Budget, 1961.*

[a]Professional staff are those full-time permanent positions allowed in the 1961 budget. This does not include either temporary or part time employees.

[b]Or 97% of all full-time municipal employees.

[c]Indicates less than 1.0%.

The Rise of a New Bureaucratic Order

This decentralization of New Haven's governmental system has not gone unnoticed or unchallenged. Since the end of World War II, for example, there have been repeated efforts within the community to "modernize" the formal structure of city government by centralizing authority in the hands of a single chief executive. In 1947, a small group of local residents mounted an unsuccessful campaign for a council-manager form of government; in 1954 and again in 1958, Charter Revision Commissions appointed by the mayor recommended strengthening the office of the mayor by providing, among other things, for a four-year rather than two-year term in office and for greater appointment and removal power over the city's administrative officials. Like the earlier 1947 effort, these too were unsuccessful.

Where formal charter revisions failed, informal methods were more successful, for during Lee's administration the office of the mayor became increasingly central to the city's political and governmental life. Lee inherited a city government where, in Robert Dahl's words, "each center of political decision was in a different part of the forest."[2] According to Dahl, the mayor quickly transformed this highly decentralized order into a more centralized one.[3] The transformation was not total, as we shall see presently, and it would be misleading to depict New Haven city government under Lee as a purely hierarchical system. But compared to his predecessors, Lee's interests and influence in municipal affairs were far more extensive and far greater, and his administration has been marked by a degree of executive power that one is hard put to find among the formal legal niceties of the city's charter.

Lee's most impressive achievements have been in urban renewal, the program that brought him into national prominence. It was in this area that his efforts to dominate the city's administrative machinery were most successful. Here the mayor was the single most important influence, the dominant figure in an urban renewal bureaucracy that he had created in his drive to stem physical decay in the city. When Lee first took office in 1954, there was no effective urban renewal bureaucracy. To be sure, a City Plan Department had been established just prior to the outbreak of World War II and since that time had operated with a modest annual budget of less than $20,000. Redevelopment was a more recent creation, 1950, but it too had functioned with little money and few personnel.[4]

Once elected, Lee changed all this. Using a variety of techniques[b] and resources, not the least of which was the ingenious maneuvering that obtained the generous financial backing of the federal government, the mayor quickly built these two agencies into major city departments. In his first budget, for example, he increased the appropriations for City Plan from $21,382 to $102,594. Within three years he had secured a similar increase for Redevelopment, raising its annual budget from $32,414 in 1954 to $122,178 in 1957. These two agencies were soon joined by two others: the Department of Traffic and Parking in 1955 and, in the same year, the Office of the Development Administrator, the latter to oversee and coordinate the activities of all local agencies engaged in the urban renewal program.

Together, these four agencies constituted the core of Lee's urban renewal bureaucracy, *a bureaucracy that was largely self-contained and that operated independent of the city's traditional agencies.* An Office of General Counsel, for

---

[b]One of these, according to Allan Talbot, was the use of Article V, Section 8 of the City Charter which charges the mayor with "responsibility for the efficient government of the city." Under this provision, the mayor issued executive orders modifying the administrative structure of city government. "The only practical limitation to this was the possibility that someone would challenge the order." According to Talbot, no one did. Allan Talbot, *The Mayor's Game* (New York: Harper and Row Publishers, 1967), p. 47.

example, was established within the Redevelopment Agency to handle legal matters pertaining to urban renewal, thus leaving the city's regular legal officer, the corporation counsel, free to tend routine municipal matters. Property assessments and engineering and architectural studies were contracted to private consultants, relieving the city assessor's office and the city engineer of additional responsibility. Housing code enforcement in renewal areas was transferred from the Department of Public Health, an agency more concerned with preventive medicine than environmental sanitation and housing conditions, to a new office within the Redevelopment Agency, the Division of Neighborhood Improvement. The relocation of families within and from renewal areas, a function initially performed by the New Haven Housing Authority under contract to the Redevelopment Agency, was subsequently transferred to yet another new division within the agency, the Office of Family Relocation.

Lee entrusted these agencies and the programs for which they were responsible to individuals he recruited from outside the regular municipal bureaucracy. Edward Logue, the mayor's first development administrator, and one of the leading figures in the program, came to New Haven after serving as administrative assistant to then United States Ambassador to India Chester Bowles. Logue's successor, Thomas Appleby, and Appleby's successor, Melvin Adams, both had had prior service with the federal government. Ralph Taylor, the first executive director of the Redevelopment Agency, was brought to the city from Somerville, Massachusetts; others in this bureaucracy, such as Joel Cogen, Richard Dowdy, Sherman Hasbrouke, George Schuster, Howard Hallman, Robert Hazen, Allan Talbot, Harold Grabino, and Howard Moskoff, to mention but a few, followed a similar route. These "new men" within the Lee administration were outsiders, men in their late twenties or early thirties when they came to the urban renewal bureaucracy, college educated, ambitious, highly competitive, and intensely loyal to the mayor and his programs.

Lee's dual strategy of appointments without regard to local residency or party service and of reliance on new institutions rather than old or existing ones had its costs politically. From both party leaders and party regulars came protests that the organization was being overlooked, and in 1961, led by Democratic Town Committee Chairman Arthur Barbieri, the party reportedly staged a protest against Lee by "sitting out" the mayoralty election. Nor were the Republicans silent. They insisted that the Lee administration return control of the program to local residents, charging at one point that the practice of recruiting from outside the city was an affront to the community, implying as it did that local talent was in short supply.[5]

Despite these attacks, Lee's strategy paid off handsomely, both for the mayor himself and for the new men he had recruited. With the help of these new men and the programs they administered, Lee won elections repeatedly and gained a national reputation as a highly successful and progressive mayor, and were it not for accidents of electoral timing and other political vicissitudes, he undoubtedly would have gone on to higher office. For the new men, service in New Haven also had its rewards and many of these officials rose to national prominence partly as a result of their work in the city. Edward Logue, for example, left New Haven in 1961 to head the Boston Redevelopment Authority and later, in 1968, was chosen by New York's Governor Rockefeller to administer the state's multi-billion dollar Community Development Corporation. H. Ralph Taylor of the Redevelopment Agency was later appointed assistant secretary for inter-governmental affairs in the United States Department of Housing and Urban Development. And Thomas Appleby, Logue's successor as development adminis-trator, departed from the city in the mid-1960s to accept an offer to head the redevelopment program in the nation's capital.

The Traditional Bureaucracies

In the more traditional areas of city administration, Lee's status never matched his status in urban renewal. Unlike urban renewal, which was the focal point of his administration and which was staffed by men recruited by and loyal to him, such areas as education, law enforcement, recreation, and public health were ones that had long histories of independence from the city's chief executive as well as ties with powerful interests within the community. True, during eight consecutive terms in office Lee managed to increase the mayor's voice in these areas, among other things by appointing his own men to various municipal boards and commissions. Even so, his influence over these policy-making bodies and the agencies they ran was limited. Board members, as Robert Dahl observed with respect to the Board of Education, "do not feel particularly beholden to a mayor. . . . The most a mayor can do is to choose people in whom he has confidence and then give them his backing when they call for help."[6] But board members are only one of the groups with which a mayor must contend. Indeed for both board members and mayors alike there are a number of groups—the press, the opposition party, taxpayers' associations, churches, and civic organizations—that compete with them and with each other for a voice in the decision-making process, a fact which, along with time limitations, mitigates against a unilateral power relationship between the mayor and any one group or individual.

No discussion of the city's traditional bureaucracy, obviously, would be complete without mention of the role of the professional administrators themselves. On the surface, it is true, the behavior of the city's some 3,000 public officials during this period would seem to give substance to the old reform axiom that politics and administration are quite distinct from one another. Both individually and as a group, New Haven's appointed public officials normally appeared to have been neutral on public issues. One generally did not find them taking sides publicly in political debates and their activities were seldom mentioned in the rather lively and extensive coverage given local politics in the city's news media. Yet though seemingly uninterested, the administrators counted, and quite heavily, in determining the outcome of public policy.

The nature and extent of administrative influence over policy formation is best illustrated by the pattern of decision-making that prevailed in the Department of Education during the 1950s. Here, according to Nelson Polsby, the key decision-makers were the professional administrators and in particular the superintendent of schools. "The vast preponderance of decisions in the schools," he noted in his companion study to Dahl's *Who Governs?*, "were made more or less according to the prescriptions implied in its organization chart ... [with] the most significant actor in public education [being] the superintendent of schools."[7]

Even this understates the influence of professionals in this the largest—and, in terms of its influence over the values tomorrow's citizens will hold, no doubt the most important—of the city's public agencies. From Polsby's account it might be inferred that decision-making within the department was quite hierarchical, with most of the power concentrated at the top. In fact, there was a good deal less concentration than Polsby's observation would suggest. During the period he studied, the superintendent's role was limited largely to continuing past policies and practices, among them the decentralization of departmental decision-making. Control over such matters as personnel assignments and the placement, testing, grading, and promotion of students lay in the hands of individuals at lower echelons in the educational hierarchy, in the hands of supervisors, principals, guidance counsellors, and even teachers themselves. And while individually these decisions may have been of "little consequence," as Polsby suggests they were,[8] collectively they had a decisive bearing on the overall shape of the city's educational policy.[9]

Elsewhere the pattern was much the same. Although information on other city departments is more limited than it is on education, there is every indication that within such agencies as the Police Department, the Department of Parks and Recreation, and the Department of Welfare, influence over departmental policy was widely shared by individuals scattered throughout the formal structure: by the mayor as the city's chief executive and ex-officio member of the boards and commissions, by board members and commissioners, and finally by the professional administrators themselves throughout the formal organization of the agency. For the most part, however, administrative policy-making in the city's public agencies consisted of lower echelon decisions that were ratified or simply not vetoed by superiors within or beyond the specific agencies. In many cases these decisions were merely a continuation of long-term "common law" practices in the agencies.

Non-Municipal Bureaucracies

In addition to the municipal agencies, those who chartered the city's anti-poverty project maintained weather eyes on yet another group of agencies, those associated with the Greater New Haven Community Council and the State of Connecticut. These agencies were major participants in the life of the city.

Along with the regular municipal departments, they constituted what might be loosely termed New Haven's "social welfare system" and as such were of direct interest to those who mounted the city's reform project.

Within each of these two broad areas there was a varied and diverse collection of institutions. The Community Council, for example, was a loose confederation of some seventy private—and thirty public—agencies active in the areas of health, welfare, and recreation. Dedicated to the objectives of "social planning" and the "promotion of high standards of performance and cooperation among agencies in the area,"[10] the council functioned in a manner similar to the Better Business Bureau. Like the Better Business Bureau, its power to command was minimal.

This limited power to command is understandable, given the composition of the council itself. Among its members were such agencies as the Jewish Family Service, the Boy Scouts, the Red Cross, the Boys Clubs of America, and the Bureau of Social Services of the Roman Catholic Archdiocese of Hartford. While each of these participated formally in the Council, each was highly autonomous, well-established in its own right, with independent sources of financial and political support.[11]

In addition to their autonomy, the private agencies had at least two other important characteristics in common. One of these was specialization. Individually, members of the council were limited in terms of both the problems handled and the services offered. In one case it might be alcoholism, in another tuberculosis, in still others blindness, psychiatric disorders, retarded children, child adoptions, or family counselling. Despite this specialization there had been a relatively high level of inter-agency cooperation, an intricate system of informal referrals from one agency to another that from all indications had worked quite effectively, at least for the clientele served by various agencies.[12]

But this clientele had been quite limited—and this was a second characteristic the private agencies shared. Being for the most part old and well established institutions, each of these agencies had developed a distinctive clientele. And while precise data are not available, information from interviews and from personal observation indicates strongly that this clientele had been drawn primarily from the middle classes and the respectable working classes. For the actual poor at the bottom of society, and especially for the non-white poor who crowded into the city's slums during the 1950s, the resources controlled by these agencies were generally unavailable.[13]

It has been the public and not the private agencies that in recent years have provided care for New Haven's poor. To an extent this has been done by such city agencies as the Departments of Health and Welfare. But caring for the lowest of the social strata increasingly has been a state responsibility, specifically of such agencies as the Department of Welfare, the Department of Labor, the Department of Education, and the state courts. Within the State Department of Welfare, for example, the Division of Public Assistance is responsible for the principal program for income maintenance, Aid to Dependent Children. The Connecticut State Employment Service (Labor Department) and the Division of Vocational Education (Department of Education) each control important access routes to gainful employment as, in a sense, does the juvenile court, whose disposition of cases, many of them involving inner-city residents, has a direct bearing on the life chances and well-being of teen-agers and young adults.

New Haven's "Bureaucratic Order:" Summary

What I referred to earlier as New Haven's "bureaucratic order" was in reality a highly decentralized administrative system. At the time the anti-poverty effort began, the four broad groups of agencies I have been describing all operated independently of one another. Moreover, with the exception of Lee's new bureaucracy in urban renewal, each of these administrative groupings was itself highly fractioned, populated by a highly varied set of agencies that enjoyed considerable autonomy. And it was from these groupings—from the traditional municipal agencies, the private health and welfare agencies, and the state agencies—that New Haven's anti-poverty officials hoped to fashion a social reform coalition.

Rationale For a Commitment

Why the Bureaucracy

Of all the local groups, the agencies comprising the city's "social welfare system" would seem to have been the least likely candidates for membership in the anti-poverty coalition. For one thing the system, being highly decentralized, lacked a single, centralized coordinating mechanism sufficiently influential to dictate bureaucratic policy. This meant that changes in policy could come about only with the approval of individual agencies, each of which was independent and autonomous. At a minimum, dealing with all these agencies in an effort to launch a "comprehensive project" promised to be immensely time-consuming. At maximum, the necessary politicking and coordinating would almost inevitably have doomed the enterprise.

If practical considerations of time did not rule out a coalition with the bureaucracies, then quite possibly the reputation of bureaucracies generally should have led to this negative strategic judgment. Bureaucracies, as more than one observer has asserted, frequently act as the custodians of the status quo and as such represent a major impediment to change. Time has not reduced the force of Robert Michels' observation, based on the history of the German Social Democratic Party, that for new ideas to find expression they must be bureaucratically implemented but that in the process of creating a bureaucratic or administrative apparatus, "New ideas are always renounced in favor of more conservative ones."[14] Similarly, Wallace Sayre and Herbert Kaufman summed up their consideration of the bureaucracies' role in New York City politics with the conclusion that the bureaucrats' "influence is most often exercised against innovations in public policy, in technology, in jurisdictional arrangements, in the organizational structure of department and agencies, and in the administrative procedures of the city government."[15] And within New Haven, Lee showed his appreciation of the wisdom of these academic commentators—if not his familiarity with their actual words—by refusing to risk his urban renewal program to the procrustean ways of an established municipal agency. As we have seen, he created his own, largely self-contained administrative machinery and relied on this new machinery to by-pass existing municipal bureaucracies.

Bureaucratic Resources

If the city's bureaucracies seem an inappropriate choice as partners in reform, still, they were chosen, and not without reason. Like all bureaucracies, those in New Haven controlled important resources, resources the city's reform-minded planners hoped to capitalize on and exploit in behalf of their anti-poverty effort. To begin with, the bureaucracies had information about, and access to, the poor. The public schools alone, for example, had direct daily contact with more than 30 percent of the city's black population, and, indirectly, through pupils to parents and siblings, to a far greater percentage.[16] To a lesser extent the same was true of the Department of Parks and Recreation, whose organized activities in such sports as basketball, baseball, and track and field, brought this agency into frequent contact with the more athletically gifted of the inner-city youth.[17] In addition to information and access, the bureaucracies also possessed important skills: social workers to counsel individuals and families unable to grapple with the demands of contemporary urban society; employment specialists to help evaluate and place the unemployed; health services from the Visiting Nurse Association to care for the homebound or to assist young mothers.

To be sure, these resources were already available to the poor. But their full potential, at least according to anti-poverty authorities, was far from being realized.[18] Under the pressure of administrative responsibilities and heavy case loads, social workers were being forced to forego counselling; employment specialists restricted themselves to serving those who applied for assistance rather than actively seeking out the unemployed; and such few neighborhood facilities as there were, for example, the schools, were usually staffed by non-residents and were open only during regular working hours.[c]

Of no less importance than their information, access, skills, and physical facilities were two additional resources possessed by the bureaucracies. One of

[c]In a few cases, public agencies had exclusive control over services available to the poor. The Public Housing Authority, for example, controlled entry into subsidized low-income housing, excluding, among others, individuals with records of rent delinquency, evictions, or alcoholism, as well as individuals living in concubinage or common-law marriages. Until the U.S. Supreme Court's decision in *Re Application Gault*, 87 S. Ct., 1428 (1967), the Juvenile Court had absolute and exclusive jurisdiction over teenagers charged with offenses.

these was their prestige. As we shall see more fully in the next chapter, anti-poverty officials tried to identify themselves and the project with established public and private agencies as a way of gaining recognition and acceptance from a community that was considered at best uncertain, at worst potentially hostile, toward the new social reform enterprise. Participation by these agencies, it was hoped, would be interpreted as an endorsement of the undertaking, as a signal to the community that the project, though new and unfamiliar, was both legitimate and worthy of support.

The second, and in some respects, the most compelling consideration that led anti-poverty officials to seek bureaucratic alliances was the *staying power* of the bureaucracies themselves. While this characteristic has alarmed and exasperated some advocates of change,[19] anti-poverty officials viewed it as potentially advantageous to their objectives. Community Progress, Inc. itself had an uncertain future, lacking official governmental status and a regularized source of income. If, for any reason, the anti-poverty agency did not survive, if, for example, the national programs upon which this agency was so heavily dependent for support collapsed, or if the agency failed to secure the financial backing of outside groups, it still might be possible to continue the anti-poverty programs themselves, provided, of course, that these programs had a solid institutional sanctuary and base of support in the community.

From the perspective of New Haven's anti-poverty officials, it was critical that, if nothing else, the programs they were proposing survive. As I noted in an earlier chapter, the project was predicated on the assumption that, unless the poor gained skills through such means as education and job training, they would remain ill-equipped to deal with life in urban America. This thinking was at the heart of CPI's theory of reform as was the assumption that few if any of the anti-poverty programs themselves would provide immediate relief for the poor. For New Haven's reformers the war on poverty was a long-term investment, and, facing as they did an uncertain future, they looked elsewhere for ways of ensuring continuing attention to, and support for, the programmatic aspects of their enterprise.[d]

The judgment that the city's public and private agencies were considered best suited in the long run to act as instruments of social reform was rooted as much in anti-poverty officials' estimates of the weaknesses and shortcomings of alternative groups as it was in their estimation of the bureaucracies' strengths. The single most political figure in the city, the mayor, was an elected public official whose future, as I have already noted, was uncertain. So, too, was the future of any given city council (in New Haven the formal name of the council is the Board of Aldermen), a body that in addition to lacking the staying power of the bureaucracies had in the past seldom exercised the immense powers granted it in the City Charter. And while the local political parties had the endurance and the staying power, it was unlikely they could be persuaded to interest themselves in substantive policy questions or pursue such interests without

---

[d]See above, chapter 4.

arousing the suspicions and perhaps the hostility of the state and private agencies or the professional bureaucrats. There remained, of course, the poor themselves, who as much as any other group in the community had a stake in the outcome of the anti-poverty project. But as we have already seen in an earlier chapter, the poor were denied a major voice in the agency on the grounds that the very conditions that necessitated an anti-poverty project precluded effective and meaningful participation. According to anti-poverty officials, sustained political action needed to ensure continuation of reform presupposed a level of social and economic progress the poor had yet to achieve.

Expectations

The strategic commitment to seek bureaucratic alliances was not without its risks. However desirable the administrative and political support of the city's public and private agencies, there was always the danger they would simply refuse to participate and hence seriously damage the reform effort. The entire undertaking was novel and unconventional, outside the ordinary: an agency, Community Progress, Inc., that, while not an official governmental body, nonetheless was not really a private one; an institution staffed by personnel imported from outside the city, newcomers whose avowed purpose was to promote changes in fields where more experienced hands had long toiled. The project was a potential threat to traditional bureaucratic policies, practices, and personnel, and as such, the type of undertaking the bureaucracies might well resist. Indeed, there probably would have been little surprise among "knowledgeable" political observers if the overtures of anti-poverty officials were rejected summarily as presumptuous and unwarranted interference in matters better left to the established agencies and their professional staffs.

Whatever the estimation of knowledgeable observers, anti-poverty officials had sufficient reasons for believing they could persuade the bureaucracies to go along with the reform endeavors. If the new agency's unusual status and innovative role were potential liabilities, they were more than offset by its assets. Community Progress, Inc. was not totally without resources of its own, and although these resources alone hardly assured the success of the project, they at least provided grounds for expecting a positive response from the bureaucracies. In short, here again CPI's strength was that it *had something to offer*.

Not the least of these benefits were the funds controlled by the anti-poverty agency. Unlike other private interest groups, CPI was in a position to couple its demands for change with promises of financial support. This was a rather singular resource, the more so since most of these funds came from sources outside the city, thus allowing anti-poverty officials to pursue their program objectives while at the same time freeing them from the restraints of the local budgetary process.

Important as they were, these funds must be viewed in perspective. Without outside support, there never would have been an anti-poverty project, at least not one of such magnitude, since it is unlikely the requisite funds could have been raised from local sources. But although this support was a necessary condition for reform, it was not a sufficient one. A few agencies, such as the Farnham Neighborhood House, a settlement house that served the Wooster Square and Fair Haven sections of the city, simply refused to participate. Others, for example, the Police Department, the Juvenile Court, and the New Haven Family Services Bureau hesitated, delaying for months their acceptance of grants from the anti-poverty agency. More important, the funds themselves were dependent on prior assurances of some bureaucratic cooperation. As I noted in an earlier chapter, part of New Haven's strategy in dealing with the Ford Foundation and the federal agencies was to convince them of the city's ability to deliver an anti-poverty project and one of the ways used to demonstrate this ability was to secure commitments from at least some local public and private agencies, chief among them the Board of Education and the Community Council. To secure these commitments, anti-poverty officials had to rely on other resources.

One of these resources was the backing of the city's mayor. Although Lee's formal power over the bureaucracies was limited (in the case of the private and state agencies, it was non-existent), and although as far as can be determined he seldom intervened directly in the negotiations between anti-poverty officials and the administrators in the established agencies, his association with the enterprise afforded it an invaluable aura of legitimacy and prestige. Indeed, it is possible, although there can be no conclusive evidence on such a point, that his identification with the project was sufficient to neutralize and sometimes even favorably dispose otherwise "difficult" leaders of administrative agencies.

In addition to Lee, there was Sviridoff, whose appointment as the anti-poverty agency's chief administrative officer gave added strength to the undertaking. Over the years Sviridoff had developed and maintained important alliances throughout the city, the state and, to some extent the nation. These alliances were part of his "bag" of personal capacities, and he was prepared to use them to further the fortunes of the project. As president of the state AFL-CIO, for example, he was reliably reported to have had a voice in the appointment of the incumbent commissioner of labor, whose department included such key agencies as the State Employment Service. As president of the Board of Education he had been instrumental in recruiting New Haven's superintendent of schools, Lawrence Paquin, a professional educator who shared Sviridoff's philosophy that the schools should be one of the major forces for correcting social ills and who was to be a major CPI ally. And while neither of these men, nor for that matter any others who knew him professionally or personally, could be expected to do his bidding automatically, Sviridoff's heading the project insured that it would receive serious and sympathetic consideration—that it would not, as could well have been the case with an executive director of less political stature, simply be ignored and rejected out-of-hand. At CPI, as it is at all levels and categories of government and politics, the *public reputation* as well as the *personal ability* of the official appointed to head the agency was a principal determinant of whether the agency would be taken seriously and would have a serious impact.

There was, finally, something akin to what Robert Dahl once termed "slack resources" within the bureaucracies[20]—in this case, "old time professionals who, according to Sviridoff, "wanted change . . . and had long been nursing good ideas privately for fear of being rebuffed."[21] It would be overstating the case to depict these people as constituting a well-defined progressive or liberal wing of the bureaucracy. The administrators Sviridoff had in mind—May White, an associate superintendent of schools; Mary Dewey, the director of the State Employment Service; Frank Harris, the executive director of the Community Council; Frank Looney, a former director of the New Haven Department of Welfare—were not identified with any common organization or with any publicly articulated program for action. In fact, until the advent of the anti-poverty program, they had worked largely in isolation from one another. As individuals, however, they had already expressed interest in the cause of reform, some of them by assisting Hallman in the preparation of the Ford Foundation proposal. And Sviridoff and other agency officials were counting on them to continue their support for the enterprise, in particular to lend it support inside the bureaucracies and thus serve as key links in the anti-poverty coalition.

Approaches to the Bureaucracies

Agency officials approached the bureaucracies in a manner that can best be characterized as one of utmost caution and circumspection. Despite their resources and despite their ties within the agencies, anti-poverty officials proceeded discreetly, fearing that overly aggressive behavior on their part might arouse opposition and undermine what chances they had for developing a base of support within the agencies. Whether this opposition came from within the agencies themselves or from groups on the outside made little difference. The results would be the same: anti-poverty officials would have to divert their own time and energies to defending the project from attack; administrators with only a marginal interest in the undertaking would have a ready-made excuse for not participating, while those who because of their prior interest had been counted on as allies would be crosspressured and quite possibly less enthusiastic in their support. A publicized squabble or an attack on the agency (no matter how ill-taken) might be fatal at this point.

Circumspection in dealing with established agencies was manifested in a number of ways, among them in the respect that anti-poverty officials evidenced for formal authority. As a matter of policy, the agencies were first approached at the top. Whether the agency in question was headed by a known ally, as was the case with the Department of Education, or by an administrator, for example, the chief of police or a judge of the juvenile court, whose attitude toward the project was unknown or uncertain, the practice was the same. Overtures were made initially to the agency's top official, usually by Sviridoff personally, to determine the general prospects for some type of cooperative venture. Only if the leadership expressed an interest in the undertaking and indicated a willingness to participate were negotiations on possible programs allowed to proceed.

Respect for formal authority was coupled with a recognition of the political realities of administrative life. For most of the established agencies, the reform effort was but a small part of their overall responsibility to the city,[e] and CPI but one of many groups seeking to influence their policies. There were other programs and other clientele, other areas of New Haven besides the inner-city neighborhoods, and all these competed with anti-poverty officials for the attention and energies of administrators. Of course, such competition could not be eliminated entirely, for to have done so would have been tantamount to foregoing all efforts to change the bureaucracies. But it at least could be minimized if one kept informed about conditions within the agencies and avoided those occasions when administrators were likely to be completely preoccupied with other matters.

This was a matter of timing, a tactical consideration that was critical in the thinking of anti-poverty officials and their approach to the city's public and private agencies. If it was known that these agencies were otherwise engaged, anti-poverty officials generally refrained from approaching them. In some cases, such as the annual preparation and defense of agencies' budgets, these engagements were recurring ones and as such, ones the staff could anticipate and program into their planning. Other events were less predictable: a controversy in 1964 over *de facto* segregation in the public schools, a dispute a year later over the removal of a high school principal charged with falsifying school records, or the resignation of a judge of the juvenile court. In cases such as these, it was the staff's practice to postpone contacts with the agency in question, or if already contacted to suspend negotiations until conditions were considered more favorable. That anti-poverty officials did so was in part a matter of personal conviction that administrators should not be set upon in times of stress. But it was also a cautionary strategy, one rooted in the belief that beleaguered administrators, if confronted with a choice between the demands of the old order and those of the new, would ordinarily be more likely to opt for the old.

Caution in dealing with other agencies was also reflected in the staff's recognition of administrative expertise. Although critics later charged CPI with usurping powers that legitimately belonged to others, anti-poverty officials did not dominate or control the other bureaucracies, even within the limited areas of

---

[e]There were a few exceptions, among them the Dixwell Neighborhood House, a settlement house that served the predominantly black Dixwell neighborhood, and the State Welfare Department, whose principal concern was the city's lower classes. Even the Welfare Department, however, was not exclusively concerned with the poor, since it was responsible for such programs as child adoptions and day-care centers for working-class parents.

mutual concern.[f] Nor did they try to do so, since any effort to impose their own preferences in areas of special bureaucratic competence not only would have alienated the bureaucrats themselves, but would have deprived anti-poverty officials of the advantages of existing bureaucratic expertise. Such efforts would have deprived them, moreover, of opportunities to bring more non-CPI administrative personnel into closer contact with the project and to increase their commitment to the enterprise through a sharing in the actual shaping of reform policies.

If the anti-poverty agency did not dominate the other bureaucracies, neither did they dominate it. As should be abundantly clear by now, CPI was far more than a neutral instrument that raised money to finance programs initiated by administrators in other agencies, although this is what Sviridoff once claimed publicly in an effort to disarm his critics.[22] Anti-poverty officials themselves obviously were a remarkably influential force in determining the content of programs the other agencies would administer. But they were a force *along with* the officials of the other agencies. Both sides of these bilateral bureaucratic coalitions participated in the formulation of program proposals and both contributed to their ultimate shape. And the negotiations between the two, between representatives of the old order and the new, were emphatically joint enterprises in which the judgments and interests of the two coincided to the mutual benefit of both.

The specific ways in which anti-poverty officials approached administrators in other agencies was characteristic of their more general approach to the bureaucratic system as a whole. Sviridoff, whose personality and philosophy dominated the agency, defined himself as a reformer, not a revolutionary, one whose role was to modify, not recast, the entire order of things. The goals ascribed by Karl Popper to "utopian social engineers," namely, "to weave an entirely new gown, a really beautiful new world," was not a goal to which he aspired.[23] He was rather a "piecemeal engineer,"[24] to borrow again from Popper, whose responsibility it was to foster marginal or incremental changes in the system.[25]

These marginal changes were of a special sort, additions to, rather than deletions from or alterations in, the bureaucracies. With few exceptions, existing bureaucratic policies, programs, and personnel were left unchallenged and undisturbed. In a sense, anti-poverty officials disregarded what was, by-passing the established order and avoiding direct confrontation with those who

---

[f]This was one of the themes stressed by the Republican candidate for mayor in 1965. Reacting to CPI's success in securing cooperation from the bureaucracies, the candidate, Joseph Einhorn, warned the community that the new agency was taking over functions traditionally under the jurisdiction of the city's public and private agencies. *The New Haven Register*, January 20, 1965, January 25, 1965, and May 12, 1965. Earlier, the New Haven Republican Town Chairman, Henry DeVita, charged that a group of "so-called professionals" had seized control of city government. *The New Haven Register*, October 23, 1964. Einhorn's attacks on the anti-poverty agency are discussed below in chapter 8.

benefited from it.[g] Instead, they concentrated on what was to be, developing new programs within the bureaucracies, using their priceless resource—funds from Ford and the federal government—to *expand* rather than *reallocate* the resources and responsibilities of local agencies.

This distinction between the expansion and the reallocation of bureaucratic resources was more than a matter of semantics. The funds controlled by anti-poverty officials could have been used as leverage to institute what might be termed "non-additive" as well as "additive" changes, that is to say, as inducements to agencies to eliminate certain policies or to remove or transfer certain personnel. In a few cases this was actually done, or at least tried. As part of their drive to expand and revitalize legal services to the poor, for example, anti-poverty officials persuaded the mayor and members of the Legal Aid Commission not to reappoint the incumbent director of municipal legal aid. And in an effort to "prevent drop-outs and raise achievement levels in grades five and six in selected inner-city schools,"[26] agency officials and their allies in the Department of Education proposed, unsuccessfully, to transport pupils from three neighborhood schools to special instructional centers.[h] These, however, were among the few exceptions.[i] In the vast majority of cases, the practice was to avoid direct or indirect confrontations with the programs and personnel of the on-going system, to accept it as given and to build onto, rather than do away with or destroy, what others before them had created and would in all likelihood defend quite vigorously.

Outcomes

Patterns of Cooperation

In most cases the bureaucracies proved cooperative—sometimes enthusiastically so—and the anti-poverty agency's call for a bureaucratic coalition was successful.

[g]This disregard of what was included a refusal to comment publicly on the activities of the bureaucracies. Although staff members considered some administrators to be less-than-competent or reactionary, and some bureaucratic practices to be out-of-date and in fact harmful, they refused to say anything publicly that might be interpreted as criticism of the bureaucracies.

[h]This proposal was vetoed by parents in the neighborhood who objected in general to the busing of children and, as would have been the case with this program, to the busing of children from predominantly white schools to predominantly black ones, and vice versa.

[i]In one case a new program agreed to by the Board of Education, funded by the Ford Foundation, and actually operating in the schools proved more troublesome than had been expected. The program, Joint Education and Training (JET) exempted a small number of junior high school students with disciplinary records from the regular school schedule and assigned them to a special teacher in the same school. The assignment was apparently beyond the capacities of at least some of the special teachers and reports that JET students were roaming noisily around school corridors and disrupting the regular school program led to the program's termination. For two additional illustrations of program proposals that conflicted with existing practices see the discussions below of the manpower and legal programs.[27]

Between 1962 and 1965 more than *twenty-five* agencies, large and small, public and private, state as well as local, joined in New Haven's war on poverty. During this period roughly $15.0 million was invested in some sixty programs that reached, at least according to figures published by the anti-poverty agency, more than 44,000 of the city's 150,000 residents.[28]

Of the agencies that participated, the single most important one in terms of project expenditures, number of programs, and significance in the minds of anti-poverty officials, was the New Haven Board of Education. As I indicated in chapter 4, one of the project's principal objectives was to reach the young and, having reached them, to provide them with the skills necessary to achieve self-sufficiency in a highly competitive society. To this end, more than $3.5 million or 46 percent of the total spent in 1965 alone was invested in the schools. Beginning with pre-kindergarten, continuing through the early years of elementary school, and into the junior high schools, programs were instituted in an effort to strengthen the educational process. There was no assurance these programs would work: no assurance, for example, that the city's sixteen pre-kindergarten centers would help counter the presumed shortcomings of early family life in the slums; that the expansion in the number of special reading teachers from three (1963) to twelve (1964) would help overcome the literacy problems that so handicapped many of New Haven's inner-city children; or finally that a work-study program for first year high school students combining regular classroom instruction with part-time, in-school jobs as clerks, teachers' assistants, custodians, and librarians, would actually help reduce the school drop-out rate by inducing a more positive attitude toward the schools, toward learning, and toward educational achievement. Despite these uncertainties, the schools were one of the chief focal points of the reform effort and education one of the chief ways anti-poverty officials and their backers in the bureaucracies tried to counter the "cycle of poverty."

Compared to the New Haven Board of Education the participation of other bureaucracies was modest. Individually, none of them had a clientele as large and as important as the schools and none of them received as large a share (Table 7-2) of the anti-poverty budget. Still, each of these agencies played a part in the reform scheme, both in terms of the services they provided directly to the poor and in terms of their support for the overall project.

In the project design originally developed for the Ford Foundation, most of these agencies were to be part of what Hallman termed "coordinated community services." In each of New Haven's six inner-city neighborhoods, there was to be an effort to "pull together" the services offered by social workers, sanitarians, public health nurses, homemaking advisors, police youth workers, and recreation workers, an effort, in short, "to coordinate and integrate" the energies and expertise of various public and private agencies. In each neighborhood, moreover, an intermediate school was to be designated a "community school" and as such to function as the center of social service activity.[j]

---

jSee above, chapter 4.[29]

Table 7-2

Distribution of New Haven Anti-Poverty Project Funds by Agency

Agency	Percentage[a]
New Haven Board of Education	47.6
Community Progress, Inc.	24.9
Connecticut State Employment Service	6.2
New Haven Library	4.2
Connecticut State Welfare Department	3.6
New Haven Legal Assistance Association	1.9
New Haven Housing Authority	1.3
New Haven Department of Parks and Recreation	1.3
Yale New Haven Hospital	1.8
Greater New Haven Community Council	.8
New Haven Family Services Bureau	.1
St. Martin de Porres Parochial School	.7
St. Rose Parochial School	.4
St. John's Parochial School	.4
St. Stanislaus Parochial School	.4
Clifford Beers Psychiatric Clinic	.1
New Haven Police Department	.5
Juvenile Court	.4
YM-YWCA	.2
Connecticut Co-operative Extension Service	.03
New Haven Council of Boy Scouts	.08
New Haven Wider City Parish	.3
Leila Day Nursery	.7
New Haven Department of Public Health	.7
Dixwell Neighborhood House	.2

Source: Compiled from: Community Progress, Inc., "Community Action Summary," New Haven, December 1, 1965. CPI File, Folder I, Item 10. This is the only agency document that provides a breakdown of expenditures by agencies.

[a]Figures reported in the *Community Action Summary* are annual expenditures averaged over the four year period 1962-1965, and not actual expenditures for 1965. This explains why the total amount listed in the *Summary*, $7.6 million, is somewhat lower than the actual amount spent in 1965, $7.9 million. The summary, it should be noted, includes, but does not differentiate between, money that local agencies received from Community Progress, Inc. and money these agencies received from other sources. In the latter case, only those funds the anti-poverty agency was instrumental in obtaining—for example, the funds received by the Board of Education under the State Aid to Disadvantaged Children Act—are included.

A number of obstacles stood in the way of realization of this ambitious objective. For one thing, only a few agencies, among them the schools, were physically located in the inner-city neighborhoods. New Haven is a relatively compact city of 17.9 square miles, and most public and private agencies maintained only a central office and employed a few field workers. For the inner-city resident who wanted or needed assistance it was usually a matter of his seeking out the relevant agency rather than that agency's seeking out him.

Whether an inner-city resident actually sought out these services depended on a number of factors, not the least of which was his awareness of their availability. This awareness could not always be assumed, and informing residents about the project was no easy task, the less so because anti-poverty officials believed that the poor should not only be informed but also individually identified and contacted. True, some agencies, particularly the schools, maintained some ties with the lower class neighborhoods and could assist agency officials in their efforts to reach the poor. This, as I noted earlier, was one of the reasons the reformers had sought alliances with them. But, increasingly, these ties were being weakened. In the decade just prior to the start of the anti-poverty project, there had been considerable change in the social composition of the inner-city areas, and these changes threatened the formal and informal social life of the neighborhoods. The trend had been away from a sense of community in the neighborhoods, and existing institutions, both public and private, were finding it more and more difficult to communicate with neighborhood residents. Moreover, as in many cities, New Haven's poor, and especially its black poor, frequently changed residences. Whatever the various reasons—evictions, dislike of landlords, efforts to avoid rents, dislocation by the city's extensive urban renewal program, or the sheer high rate of in-and-out-migration—the poor were continually on the move, thus complicating further plans to contact them personally.[30]

It would be overstating the case to claim these obstacles were overcome entirely or that the original design of "coordinated neighborhood services" was realized completely. At least one agency rejected the overtures of anti-poverty officials; others delayed final decisions for months. None participated fully in the sense of being involved in CPI programs in all six poverty neighborhoods. Even so, the neighborhood program *did* become operational, and if even the ideal Hallman had originally envisioned never fully materialized, there was nevertheless a reasonable approximation of the ideal and an extraordinary advance over the previous state of affairs. By 1965, Community Progress itself had opened offices in each of the six neighborhoods. Out of these offices more than 100 full-time agency workers operated throughout the inner city neighborhoods, searching out the poor—on street corners, in barrooms, in poolhalls, and in other locations that eluded the more conventional social welfare agencies—to apprise them of the project and its programs, and to persuade them to participate.[k] Moreover, there were programs the poor could

[k]This in-house capability was part of the original design of the anti-poverty project and as such the only direct service the reform agency planned to offer the poor. As we will see presently, other direct services were later added.

avail themselves of, programs administered in the neighborhoods by the established bureaucracies; for example, expanded recreational activities run by the Department of Parks and Recreation, the Boys Club, the YM-YWCA, and the Boy Scouts, and four neighborhood libraries, one in a converted supermarket, whose programs, like those of the group work agencies, were both an end and a means. The libraries and the group work agencies tried to attract neighborhood residents, the libraries through such leisure-time activities as folk music, talent shows, creative dance classes, and booklending, and to use these contacts to apprise neighborhood residents of other project programs. Among these others were homemaking classes conducted in the community schools by the Connecticut Co-operative Extension Service (4H) and day-care centers for working mothers. In addition, there were the professional services of nurses from the Visiting Nurses Association, of social workers and counsellors from the Family Services of New Haven, of probation officers from the Juvenile Court, and of lawyers from the newly formed Legal Assistance Association.[1] In each case, the services were available in the neighborhoods, either in the community schools, or in storefront offices supported by funds from the anti-poverty agency.

Rejection and Adaptation: Two Cases

Impressive as was the extent of bureaucratic cooperation, there were exceptions, occasions on which established agencies and their allies resisted the efforts of anti-poverty officials. Two instances of resistance are of particular interest: one was in the area of manpower, which along with education, was at the heart of the reform endeavor; the other involved the Legal Assistance Association. In both these cases program proposals presented by anti-poverty officials encountered serious opposition and were rejected by those whom CPI officials first approached. That these rejections were not fatal to the agency's broad social objectives was in no small part due to the ability of anti-poverty officials to exploit the fragmented nature of the political and administrative systems within which they worked. When rejected by one group, Sviridoff and his staff looked for and found others who proved to be more willing partners in reform.

The Manpower Program. In manpower, as in other program areas, New Haven's anti-poverty officials planned originally on the support of existing public and private agencies. Working with such agencies as the State Division of Vocational Education, the State Employment Service, the New Haven Board of Education, and the New Haven Central Labor Council, AFL-CIO, as well as with representatives of various business firms, the staff hoped to fashion a manpower

---

[1]The development of the legal assistance program is discussed below. As will be seen, the development of this program as well as programs in job-training and employment entailed substantial departures from the original reform strategy of working through existing institutions.

system that would help alleviate unemployment in the inner city. As a first step a new institution, the Mayor's Committee on Manpower Resources and Employment, was created in November, 1962, the same month the anti-poverty agency became operational.[m] This "top level working committee," as it was officially described, with representatives from state and city government, labor, and management, was to serve as the "instrument for a cooperative effort in the manpower field."[31]

The cooperative manpower system that agency officials had originally counted on never fully materialized. During the agency's first year in operation, Sviridoff, his manpower director George Bennett, and other staff members struggled to rally the interests involved behind jointly sponsored job-training programs, programs in which the unemployed would be recruited, tested, trained, and then placed in jobs that employers had informally agreed to provide. Publicly, the venture was hailed a success, and indeed, a few local residents did benefit from the combined effort of the various groups.[32] Privately, however, anti-poverty officials admitted that what appeared as a working alliance of public and private, state and local interests was in reality no alliance at all, but rather a fragile working arrangement beset internally by jurisdictional disputes and practical problems.

The chief practical problem was posed by the State Division of Vocational Education, which exhibited what to CPI officials must have seemed to be a paradigmatic example of passive resistance and footdragging by an entrenched bureaucracy. By law, this agency had a major vote in the administration of the federal Manpower Development and Training Act programs in Connecticut. In the area of job training and re-training, this responsibility included the development of program curriculum, the assignment of instructors, the selection of training sites and training equipments, the scheduling of classes, and the admission of trainees. And the division used this authority, if not to block entirely, then at least to hamper efforts to inaugurate those job training program in New Haven being promoted by CPI and its allies on the Mayor's Committee. On several occasions programs were delayed: a tractor-trailer driver program for twelve months; an oil-burner and air conditioning serviceman program for seventeen months; an auto-body straightening program for ten months, during which the division "inspected and rejected four New Haven training sites . . ., one because it was in an area scheduled for redevelopment by the City, despite guarantees from the City the shop would remain intact for at least a year." In other cases the division unilaterally modified program components, for example, by including courses in the curriculum that neither labor, management, or anti-poverty officials considered necessary and felt would only prolong the training and/or discourage trainees, or by failing to include the unemployed in training programs despite commitments from management and labor to hire them once trained.[33]

---

[m]Actually the committee, then known as the Mayor's Committee on Employment Opportunity, had been created a year earlier, in September, 1961, at Sviridoff's suggestion. With the formation of the anti-poverty agency, the name of the committee was changed and its membership enlarged to include staff members from CPI.

This last factor, the inclusion of the unemployed, reportedly accounted for a large part of the division's opposition to programs sponsored by the anti-poverty agency. The division was not uninterested in training, but it wanted to provide it on its own terms. The division had a tradition of excellence. It accepted roughly one out of four (270 out of 1,000) applicants to Eli Whitney Regional Technical School, which served nineteen New Haven area towns, and few of those accepted (approximately 4 percent in 1962) were blacks.[34] Degrees from this school were valuable, since its graduates were widely recognized as highly skilled workers, tool and die makers, mechanical draftsmen, printers, plumbers, electricians, and they readily moved into the ranks of America's affluent working class. The anti-poverty project was a challenge to this tradition. In urging the division to expand and increase its training of inner-city residents, the anti-poverty agency was asking it to relax its academic standards and assume greater responsibility for high risk trainees.

If there were to be programs for the unemployed, and Sviridoff and other staff members considered these essential, it was clear that neither he nor his staff could rely on the Division of Vocational Education. During its first year in operation, relations between the anti-poverty agency and the division became increasingly strained, and agency officials all but abandoned their efforts to fashion an alliance or even a *modus vivendi* with the state agency. There never was a public break between the two; they simply went their own ways, the division maintaining its control over institutional training programs under the Manpower Development and Training Act, the anti-poverty agency searching for alternative means for developing an employment program for inner-city residents.

For the anti-poverty agency, the search proved highly rewarding. By 1966, CPI had opened four Neighborhood Employment Centers where agency staff members recruited, counselled, and tested inner-city residents, close to 4,000 according to its own figures (Table 7-3) between October 1963 and March 1966. In place of the institutional or in-class training programs controlled by the Division of Vocational Education, on-the-job training programs were administered by the anti-poverty agency, through which local employers contracted to provide up to twenty-six weeks of occupational training for inner-city residents, and to pay a minimum of $1.50 per hour, and to be reimbursed to a maximum of $30 a week for training expenses. In addition, there were several other procedures:[35]

1. work-crews that were modified public works programs for "those youths who were not ready for assignment to high skill training programs or direct placement on the job"[36]
2. basic or remedial education classes run by the New Haven Board of Education for the chronically unemployed
3. a pre-vocational training center in a warehouse rented and renovated by CPI where elementary skills training was offered in such fields as auto mechanics, typing, woodwork, sewing, and drafting
4. and after 1964, the federal Job Corps.

Table 7-3

Training and Employment Placements: October, 1963 through March, 1966

Program	Number	Percent
Direct Placement	2,183	46.5
On-the-job Training	670	14.4
Work Crews (Basic)	641	13.6
Work Crews (Summer)	377	8.3
Work Crews (Intermediate)	187	4.1
Institutional Training	429	9.3
Other, including Federal Job Corps	222	3.8
Total	4,709[a]	100.0

Source: Community Progress, Inc., *The Human Story* (New Haven: Community Progress, Inc., 1966), p. 25.

[a]The total number of *persons* placed or trained was 3,841. The above table reflects the fact that some were placed more than once.

All these programs cost money, quite obviously, money that anti-poverty officials obtained by capitalizing on opportunities afforded by the diversity of interests and institutions in the manpower and employment field. The principal opportunity resulted from the struggle nationally within the United States Department of Labor between the United States Employment Service and the Office of Manpower, Automation and Training. OMAT, as the latter agency was more commonly known, had been established in 1962 by the Kennedy Administration pursuant to the Manpower Development and Training Act. According to the official description contained in the *Government Organization Manual*, this new federal office "coordinated Labor Department programs and operations relating to manpower planning, development, utilization, distribution and administration in order to improve the effectiveness of the Department's overall manpower programs."[37] In less measured terms, this meant the Office of Manpower, Automation and Training was a *counter-bureaucracy*, a new institution designed to challenge the Labor Department's well-entrenched bureaucratic establishment, including the highly conservative and highly autonomous United States Employment Service.[38]

OMAT's design in underwriting CPI's employment programs was sufficiently clear. By underwriting these programs and others like them throughout the country, the office tried to win grass-roots support in its struggle with the employment service. Relying on demonstration or pilot projects—and as we have seen CPI had shown a special capacity for selling itself as a vehicle for this type of project—the office hoped to show what could be done if manpower programs were used as an instrument of social reform.

This policy of using manpower programs as an instrument of social reform was at the heart of the dispute between the two agencies. Over the years the employment service had come to identify with the interests of employers and employer groups, more concerned about filling job orders submitted by employers than in locating jobs for the unemployed, and little inclined to service the needs of the poor. As an alternative, the Kennedy administration and OMAT sponsored a number of projects like New Haven's, hoping these would stimulate interest and ultimately force the service either to change its policies or face possible dissolution.[39]

Not unexpectedly, the employment service resisted. Both OMAT and the projects it sponsored constituted a threat to the service's hegemony in the employment field and it responded by trying to mobilize its own allies to counter the intrusions of the new agencies. Among these allies were—and continue to be—the state employment services, the counterparts of the federal office in each of the state governments.

If, as a general rule, the state employment services worked closely with their federal counterpart, they were—and are—nonetheless independent political forces, capable of resisting, either individually or collectively, demands emanating from Washington. This independence was made clear in the Connecticut State Employment Service's response to the federal agency's opposition to OMAT sponsored projects. Despite USES objections, the state service supported the manpower programs administered by New Haven's anti-poverty agency. Initially, this support was hesitant, at least at the district level. CPI's recruitment of inner-city residents for the early institutional training programs, as well as its opening of Neighborhood Employment Centers, was by implication a criticism of the way the New Haven District Office was handling its job and the office at first refused overtures from the agency to share information about clientele and jobs. At the state level, however, the anti-poverty agency found strong backing in the person of Mrs. Mary Dewey, the director of the State Employment Service. At her direction, the District Office released employment service tests and test scores to the agency's Neighborhood Employment Centers, as well as information on job orders filed with the service by employers, and files on individual registrants.[40] With her support CSES personnel were outstationed at the agency's employment centers;[41] a USES proposal to establish federally financed, state administered job opportunity centers in New Haven to undercut CPI's own Neighborhood Employment Centers was thwarted;[42] and the opposition of the director of the State Office of Economic Opportunity, who himself was a former deputy director of the State Employment Service, to the designation of Community Progress rather than CSES as the chief recruiter in New Haven for the federal Job Corps, was effectively overcome.[43]

The Legal Assistance Association. The development of New Haven's Legal Assistance Association, one of the first such associations in the country, reflects much the same pattern as did the agency's manpower and employment program. At first the association was rejected, in this case by the New Haven Bar

Association, and rejected with heated public denunciations of its activities. But the rejection was only temporary, and the association's backers managed to offset the bar's opposition by rallying other groups within the legal profession.

Although independent, New Haven's Legal Assistance Association was closely identified with the anti-poverty agency. In fact, the association had its beginnings in an earlier unsuccessful effort to include an experimental socio-legal program within the structure of CPI's own neighborhood program.[44]

In the fall of 1962, two attorneys, both recent Yale Law School graduates, were hired by the anti-poverty agency and assigned to work in the Dixwell and Wooster Square sections of the city. As part of what Hallman called "CPI's neighborhood team," the lawyers were to "study and recommend changes in the legal and commercial institutions and to promote citizen education in the law."[45] Conspicuously missing from this mandate was litigation. The lawyers maintained that this was an essential part of their professional role; Sviridoff and other staff members demurred, insisting that their efforts to win support from such established agencies as the Juvenile Court and the Police Department would be jeopardized if the lawyers were allowed to proceed against them.

This tension between the professional dictates of the lawyers and the strategic concerns of the agency's executive director was never fully resolved to the complete satisfaction of either. Although Sviridoff normally prevailed, on at least three occasions the lawyers disregarded his political counsel and acted according to their own professional norms. Two of these were challenges by one neighborhood lawyer to practices of the Juvenile Court, the third a bitter public criticism by the second neighborhood lawyer of the handling of an interracial rape case, criticism directed at the mayor, the prosecuting attorney and the courts just six months prior to a municipal election. In all three cases, Sviridoff reacted angrily, in the last case dismissing the lawyer involved.[46]

Despite these incidents and Sviridoff's own reservations, the program survived. He himself never totally opposed it, and he recognized that his own policy was denying the poor the benefit of an aggressive legal service system. Besides, there was strong support for litigation, and not only from the neighborhood lawyers. One of his closest staff advisors, Richard Brooks, like the neighborhood lawyers a recent Yale Law School graduate, pressed him continually to lift the restrictions he had placed on the lawyers. If this were not enough, influential individuals outside the agency advocated a similar change: Professor Joseph Goldstein of the Yale Law School; Attorney Charles Parker, chairman of the Board of Legal Aid Commissioners in New Haven; and Mr. Junius Allison of the National Legal Aid and Defender Association, whose organization was interested in sponsoring a model legal-social program in the city. This backing, plus his own sense of what the poor needed, was sufficient to overcome Sviridoff's hesitancy. Unable to encompass the lawyers as professionals in CPI's chain of command, frustrated in his efforts to orchestrate their activities into his own larger purposes, and impelled by his personal liberal inclinations, Sviridoff ultimately, albeit grudgingly, agreed to support a modified legal program. His support was contingent upon one proviso, however, namely, that the legal program be made independent of CPI. By so doing, it was expected, the reform agency would avoid embarrassing and controversial incidents arising from legal challenges to the activities of public and private agencies in the city, some of which were members of the anti-poverty coalition.

New Haven's Legal Assistance Association was formally incorporated as a private, non-profit corporation in April 1964, but it received little public notice until the following autumn. In October 1964, the association presented its plans for a model legal program—including its plans to establish neighborhood law offices and to represent clients for a minimal fee of fifty cents in both civil and criminal proceedings[47]—to the New Haven County Bar Association. The bar heatedly rejected it. A former director of the Legal Aid Bureau denounced the program as a hoax, maintaining it was not really a legal assistance program for the poor but a social research experiment.[48] The Republican town chairman, a lawyer by profession, charged that the program was the handiwork of a group of "social theorists at Community Progress, Inc. . . . who showed little confidence in the community's traditional legal institutions."[49] Not unexpectedly, some raised the spectre of socialized law, while others voiced concern that inexpensive legal services would encourage frivolous litigation and burden still further an already overburdened judicial system.

To counter the opposition, the association's backers called upon the mayor and Democratic Party town chairman Arthur Barbieri for support. Both men reportedly worked behind the scenes to mobilize administration and party forces on behalf of the program, but to no avail. Despite their efforts and the endless maneuverings of friendly members of the legal profession as well as those of anti-poverty officials themselves, the local bar association formally went on record in opposition to the proposed program. By an estimated vote of 165 to 119 the bar passed a resolution approving the program in principle but opposing it in its specific form.[n] At the same time the bar recommended the proposal be submitted to the state bar association's Committee on Unauthorized Practices for a ruling.[o]

The county bar association's action proved to be only a temporary setback. Backers of the new legal program carried their case to the state level and in March 1965, the state bar association's Committee on Unauthorized Practices

[n]The resolution to disapprove the legal program was adopted on November 16, 1964 during a bar association meeting closed to the press and the public. The staff of the anti-poverty agency subsequently conducted an informal follow-up study of the vote, and while the data are, as the staff admitted, somewhat crude, they do provide some insights into the bar association's action. Backers of the program suspected, for example, that much of the opposition was at base economic and the data seem to bear this out. Seventy-eight percent (N=144) of the lawyers in single member firms voted against the proposal compared to 11 percent (N=47) in firms with five members or more. "Analysis of the New Haven County Bar Association Vote on Legal Services Program Sponsored by the Legal Assistance Association" (New Haven, March 1965) (mimeographed), p. 7, Table VII.

[o]Opponents based their *formal* objection on the technicality that the Legal Assistance Association was a corporation, and as such prevented [from practicing law] under the bar association's Code of Ethics.

ruled that the proposed programs did not violate any canons of professional ethics. The president of the state bar association went even further and openly praised the New Haven effort, asserting that "the Legal Assistance Association and plans of this type are in the best interest of both the Bar and the Public."[50] Two months later, the association received further moral and political support from another prominent figure in the legal profession, then Associate Justice Arthur Goldberg of the United States Supreme Court, who lauded the program while presiding at the formal opening of one of the association's Neighborhood Legal Offices.[51]

The Bureaucratic Coalition in Perspective

For New Haven's anti-poverty officials, the bureaucracies proved to be less conservative than might have been expected, given the oft asserted undifferentiated claim that these institutions serve as the custodians of the status quo. Most public and private agencies seemed quite willing to participate, and between 1962 and 1966 more than twenty-five of them joined with the new agency in launching the city's attack on poverty. Nor was the bureaucracy's non-hierarchical and fragmented nature any more troublesome. While some have viewed the existence of numerous independent and autonomous agencies as an obstacle to change,[52] in this case their existence worked *to the advantage* of *a strikingly innovative* anti-poverty project.

When opposition from one agency threatened key elements in the project, as it did in the case of manpower, anti-poverty officials were able to turn to other agencies and to use these agencies to attain essentially the same ends. To be sure, had the bureaucracies not been fragmented, had there been instead a single, centralized coordinating mechanism sufficiently influential to dictate all bureaucratic policy, as some critics of municipal government have urged there should be, the work of anti-poverty officials would have been simplified considerably. But of course there was no such mechanism—and even if there had been, it could have vetoed as well as approved the entire enterprise.

8

The Project and the Community

A Salient Reference Group

While preoccupied chiefly with winning support from public and private agencies in the city, CPI officials were well aware that the remainder of the community could not be disregarded. Their concern about community reaction was voiced repeatedly, in staff meetings, for example, and in informal conversations. In some cases, the references were to readily identifiable groups—among others, to the city's two newspapers, to the Republican Party, and to various ethnic groups such as the Italians, the largest in the city; in other cases, the references were to less well defined, amorphous groupings such as "the electorate," "public opinion," or "community sentiment." In both the sub-group and the "at large" senses, the "community" was a continually salient, significant reference group, and its response weighed heavily in the minds of the backers of the reform effort.

Concern with the community was, however, largely *anticipatory* and *defensive*, a strategic posture rooted in the fear that the anti-poverty project would become embroiled in political controversy and fail to accomplish its purposes. There were several possible community responses to be avoided. Hallman, among others, feared the project might fall victim to *destructive stereotyping*, that it would be perceived as "just another welfare scheme" and as such become the target of fiscal and social conservatives within the city. Others, including staff officials at the Ford Foundation, raised the possibility that the enterprise would stir *racial antagonisms* and expose CPI and the Lee Administration to the charge of racial favoritism. Still others suggested the project would serve to *attract the poor, blacks, and other minority groups to New Haven, thus accelerating further the deterioration of the city's social and economic life.*[1]

On the foregoing and other[a] grounds, the project was considered potentially controversial, and controversy was above all something that anti-poverty officials were determined to avoid. To this end, a good offense was the best defense, and they tried to promote a positive, favorable image of the project by defining it in ways they believed to be congruent with community norms and by identifying it with established and reputable institutions. These efforts to win support in the community—or at least to neutralize whatever opposition there might be—were additional elements in the strategies described earlier of proceeding cautiously,

---

[a]Among them the fear that the agency, staffed largely by outsiders, would be attacked as a collection of "carpetbagging do-gooders."

119

seeking points of low resistance, and contributing the lion's share in CPI's many bilateral alliances in the city.

Linkages with the Community

Why the Community?

That New Haven's anti-poverty officials should be sensitized to the community may seem somewhat puzzling, given what has already been said about the formation and control of the agency. As we saw earlier, this new agency was deliberately located outside the formal structure of municipal government in an effort to insulate it from the vagaries and uncertainties of the electoral process and the civil service. This independence was furthered by the practices employed by the staff. The public was given little information of political value. Key decisions, including the decision to inaugurate the project, were made without prior public knowledge, let alone consultation. Indeed, from what has been said it may have been inferred that the project was controlled by a rather imperious set of leaders, intent on telling the community what to do and devoid of interest in community reaction to its activities.

Nothing could be further from the truth, for there were considerations that made the community's response to the project a matter of no small moment to CPI officials. These considerations provided key links to the community. How the community responded to its activities had a major bearing on the agency's overall reform strategy—on its efforts, for example, to promote the city as a model project and on its efforts to maintain favorable relations with the Lee administration.

The Demands of a Model City

One consideration that sensitized anti-poverty officials to community reaction was the model project strategy. In their quest for outside financial backing, agency officials had presented New Haven as an ideal context for fashioning an operational model for the national war on poverty. In so doing they had committed themselves to developing, among other things, what they termed a "broad coalition of community interests."

Given this commitment, the last thing agency officials could afford was to have their project troubled by local political controversy! Whatever the fate of projects in other communities, New Haven's was to be harmonious. Otherwise, the agency's credibility would be undermined and the enthusiasm of the crucial public and private outside investors dampened. To be sure, the mere absence of controversy would be only that; it would not demonstrate that agency officials had in fact developed widespread community *support* for the project. But as long as the anti-poverty project was free of open political conflict, agency officials could construe this in terms most favorable to themselves.

Ties with the Lee Administration

The linkage between the community and the agency was reinforced in a direct and immediate way by the pattern of the agency's local alliances, and most especially by its alliance with the Lee administration. Although the mayor did not formally control the agency, in a broad political sense he was responsible for it in that he was publicly identified with the project. Both he and anti-poverty officials expected that whatever the agency did would have a bearing on his political fortunes, and it was a standing order within the agency that nothing be done to damage these fortunes or in any way embarrass the administration.

This standing order was rooted in part in personal considerations, in Sviridoff's long association with Lee and his recognition and admiration for what the mayor had accomplished. But personal considerations aside, Lee was an established political force in the community, the major figure in what Dahl felicitously described as New Haven's executive-centered coalition. As long as Lee benefited, or at least did not suffer, from his association with the reform effort, his continued backing could be expected. It was less clear, however, how he would react if the project became a political issue, particularly in a municipal election. Any substantial opposition to Lee at the polls, even if not sufficient to defeat him and even if not clearly attributable to the anti-poverty project, might well give the mayor pause.[b] And a hostile or even an uneasy major would have been a serious liability. It would have cost the agency not only its most valuable ally, but also other allies in that it probably would have jeopardized the agency's standing with other public and private agencies in the city as well as with the national funders. As we have seen, the mayor's support for the project, while not sufficient to convince any of these groups to cooperate, was nonetheless a necessary pre-condition for the cooperation of many of them.

An Alternative Fiscal Base

A third factor in the agency's concern about the community's response was the uncertainty of its own financial base. The anti-poverty project was supported principally by outside funds, and while this support was of major significance to the local effort, it lacked one important quality—namely, permanency. The backing of the Ford Foundation was to be available, at most, for six years; and the federal grants and contracts, while renewable annually, were continually subject to curtailment either by congressional or executive action.

If outside support were discontinued or reduced, alternate funds would be needed to ensure the survival of the agency, or at least some, if not all, of its programs. One alternative source was the local community, whether through

---

[b]If an unexplained decline had occurred in Lee's margin of victory—in six out of eight elections between 1953 and 1967, he won 60 or more percent of the vote—the burden of proof might well have fallen to the new and unorthodox CPI to demonstrate that it was *not* the cause of the decline.

voluntary contributions or through the tax rolls, And while anti-poverty officials refrained from making a direct appeal for local financial support, they were nonetheless careful not to alienate potential local sources of support. Sviridoff outlined this policy in an early discussion of the reform effort. In a speech explaining the anti-poverty project to the Community Council of Greater New Haven, the area's consortium of private (and public) charity agencies, he cautioned:

We must be careful, henceforth, to present our program goals and program reports in a way that will permit this community to make balanced and objective judgments, at the appropriate time, of whether specific programs are worthy of continued support.[2]

In short, the community was a potential ally, one to be cultivated and prepared for future contingencies. If, for the time being, it had no direct say in the project, it was not to be ignored but carefully nurtured as a hedge against future eventualities.

Promoting an Image

Preemption and Prevention

As I noted, a major goal in the agency's dealings with the community was to ensure that the project enjoyed a positive image. There was no effort, as there had been in the case of the bureaucracies, to fashion an active coalition with others in the city. Here the strategic objective was to avoid, or at least minimize, the likelihood of opposition. If, as its backers believed, the project was vulnerable on several counts, if, for example, some community members believed that the project would exacerbate the racial or class cleavages in the community, ways had to be devised to counter such negative reactions. Ideally, it would be possible to cultivate an initial positive image rather than to wait and then fight to live down negative attributions. The project was new, without an established tradition or reputation beyond its avowed purpose of helping the poor, and it would be some time before critics could fully comprehend its implications, relate these to their own self-interests, and rally others to the opposition cause. This afforded agency officials an opportunity to present themselves and the project in their own terms, in terms designed to preempt potential critics and forestall potential opponents.

Defining the Project

As part of their effort to promote a positive image, CPI officials relied on a definition and interpretation of the project that related it to community norms.

By stressing selective features of the reform effort,[c] the staff tried to locate the project within the prevailing ideological framework in the city and tried to demonstrate that the undertaking not only was compatible with community norms, but, indeed, was rooted in and supportive of them.

How the agency would define the project was suggested by the *names* selected to denote the project itself (Opening Opportunities) and the anti-poverty agency (Community Progress, Inc.). Of course, names alone were not sufficient; nor did anti-poverty officials think they were.[3] But the names chosen symbolized the norms to which the agency appealed, and summarized the major themes, three in all, used to explain and justify the reform effort to the community.[4]

1. One of these themes appealed to the venerable American norm of *individual responsibility*, to the social imperative that a man ought to care for his own needs and those of his family or dependents. Agency officials stressed this repeatedly—in their formal and informal discussions of the project, in their addresses to community groups, in their publications, and in their news releases—as the goal they had set for the project. The objective was to help transform individuals who had hitherto been dependent on society into self-sufficient and productive citizens.

   Had the appeal been limited to a reaffirmation of this norm, there would have been little justification for the agency's own undertaking. If individualism was what counted, there was no reason for outside intervention, no warrant for specially organized and designed efforts to aid the poor. Logically, at least, these would be in violation of the norm. But logic was not the concern. As agency officials well realized, any move to help the poor, and especially the black poor, in a community with a substantial immigrant stock[5] was an invitation to compare the plight of these newcomers with the immigrants' own heritage of hardship and an invitation to ask the emotionally charged question: "We made it on our own; why can't they?"

   Anticipating such objections, agency officials developed an elaborate rationale, epitomized by the project's name, Opening Opportunities. It was a rationale that stressed the *changed nature of poverty*, distinguishing the plight of the poor in the 1960s from that of an earlier era. Previous generations, so the argument ran, had benefited from the functioning of the private market place, from the workings of what Sviridoff once termed the "natural law of upward movement."[6] This was no longer the case. If poverty was once a "way station on the way up . . . [it was now] producing generation after generation of families dependent on public and private sources of welfare."[7]

   The difference was not so much in the character of the poor—the initiative of the immigrant as opposed to the inertia of the blacks—as it was in the structure of the environment. To be sure, the black's inability to disguise his

---

[c]The selective nature of CPI's public information campaign—for example, regarding its finances—is discussed in chapter 3 above, in "The Strategic Use of Information Dissemination."

minority status was a liability earlier immigrants had not faced. But in addition to this factor was the changing nature of the job market—and here agency officials introduced what has come to be a frequently made, but no less accurate for its familiarity, analysis of the changing American economy. During the great waves of European immigration, there were jobs, however undesirable, for the unskilled worker, jobs that afforded him a degree of self-sufficiency and self-esteem, and a toe-hold on upward social mobility. For the contemporary black, even these jobs—involving only brawn and sweat—were in short supply. The economy had changed and provided greatly reduced demand for the services of those who lacked educational pre-requisites or occupational skill, like most blacks. Stating this somewhat differently, the opportunity to be self-sufficient was being *denied* the new urban poor, and providing this opportunity was what CPI was all about.[8]

By defining poverty as "lack of opportunity," agency officials cast themselves in a special role—namely, as a source of *temporary* assistance for those unable to make it on their own. By the same token, they differentiated themselves and their programs from existing social welfare efforts, most especially from income maintenance programs. This does not mean that CPI officials aligned themselves against such programs as Aid to Dependent Children, or that they refused to believe that there would not always be some citizens dependent on society for sustenance. In the long run, however, they argued that the *amount* of dependency could be reduced and that programs such as the ones they were sponsoring could help eliminate much of the need for public and private welfare programs.

2. *Reducing the costs of dependency* was a second theme stressed by anti-poverty officials, in this case with a special view to appealing to local self-interest. As the agency's name, *Community* Progress, Inc., indicated, there were collective benefits to be derived from the project. The poor, clearly, would be the most direct beneficiaries; but indirectly there would be others, since the entire community stood to gain by sharing in the positive side-effects associated with the project.

The most obvious of these were the savings in the costs of public welfare, in public assistance, for example, or in low income public housing. Less obvious were the hidden or indirect costs of dependency. "In addition to the burden of dependency the public at large must bear," agency officials noted in support of their proposed legislation for disadvantaged children,

the public also loses the human resources that go undeveloped. The poverty population is truly an untapped national resource; an extra investment in education will yield dividends in more productive citizens, many of whom will enter such critical occupations as medicine, engineering, technology and management.[9]

There were other costs as well, specifically that unless something was done, conditions would continue to deteriorate. The costs of public assistance would continue to rise, as would the costs of other public services such as law enforcement, the administration of justice, public health, and fire services. Worse still, there was a threat of social unrest, the chance, and it was more than mere chance, that the poor and especially the black poor would turn to extreme measures unless society met their legitimate demands and aspirations. Speaking in April 1964, some three months before the outbreak of the country's first "long, hot summer," of rioting[10] and some three years before New Haven's own disorders [disorders which, although not the direct concern of this work, will come in for brief attention in the next chapter], Sviridoff warned:

There is a real and present danger that society's failure to permit the achievement of legitimate goals invites extreme and often times irresponsible action. To be more explicit, to the extent we fail to stimulate constructive public and private policy which will make it possible for the Negro to achieve social, economic, and political breakthroughs accomplished by the earlier immigrants to the city, to that extent, too, we strengthen irresponsible, irrational, and intemperate leadership in the Negro community.[11]

3. Thus conceived, New Haven's anti-poverty project stood as an alternative to the high costs of poverty, to the rise in public welfare budgets—and to desperate, destructive attempts by elements of the poor to take justice into their own hands. It was an alternative, moreover, that appealed to yet another community norm, namely a *belief in progress*, a belief once again symbolized in the agency's name, Community *Progress* Inc. Agency officials were quite explicit in their support for existing institutions and processes, in their belief that poverty could be alleviated by reform rather than revolution. And implicit in this, indeed, in their entire behavior, was an affirmation that at base contemporary American institutions were both benign and susceptible to intelligent influence and guidance—that evils could be managed by altering rather than destroying all that was familiar and traditional in the community.[12]

A complacent agency leadership might well have limited its community relations effort to explaining and justifying the project in terms of deeply held local norms. But CPI officials did not propose to be so complacent. Instead, they tried to reinforce the favorable image they were promoting on the verbal plane in two additional ways: first, by identifying the project with local institutions and local personalities; and second, by stressing propaganda of the deed as well as of the word.

Identifying the Project

How the community responded depended as much on how the project was *identified* as on how the project was *defined*. At least this is what agency leaders assumed, for in addition to appealing for community acceptance in terms of the three themes just discussed, they tried to identify the effort with widely recognized symbols of community influence and status. The principal of these, as has been noted on several occasions, was Mayor Lee. But Lee's endorsement had its costs. After all, he was a partisan politician, and CPI was a private, non-profit corporation, and, in form at least, "non-partisan." Since in addition to Lee's own partisanship CPI was headed by an identifiable "Lee man," criticism could be expected from the city's two newspapers—both of them right-of-center in orientation—as well as from the Republicans, if CPI's base of support did not extend considerably beyond Lee. Besides, as we have seen, Lee's support could not be relied on for the long haul.

To an extent, these broader ties with the community were provided by the appointment of "leading members of the New Haven community"[13] to the governing board of Community Progress, Inc. Its nine members included two bankers, a senior partner in one of New Haven's most prestigious law firms, the secretary of a local manufacturing firm, the president of another local firm, two highly respected Protestant ministers (one an Episcopalian, the other a Congregationalist), the secretary of Yale University, and a former president of the New Haven Junior League. This was a group of unquestionable credentials, and of known stature and reputation, individuals who could hardly be expected to endorse, let alone associate with, an enterprise of questionable value.

As a legitimating device this board was similar to the Citizens Action Commission that Lee had created to win acceptance for his urban renewal program. But it differed from Lee's CAC in several respects. The board was a formal governing body and Lee's commission was not. Further, Lee's commission was larger—with more than 400 members on its top level committees and its various action committees—and more broadly representative. Among its members were representatives from labor, education, social work, religion, and health, thus providing Lee and his urban renewal program with a "broad and heterogeneous set of sub-leaders."[14] By contrast, the anti-poverty board was a highly selective group, dominated by what Robert Dahl termed the city's "social and economic notables."[15] Only two of its members, one an Italian, the other a black, had roots among the city's ethnic and racial minorities, and both these men were conspicuous successes—the Italian, president of a local manufacturing firm, and the black, a Congregationalist minister with a doctorate in sociology. Thus, although the board was respectable, it was unlikely to provide the anti-poverty project with the diverse set of sub-leaders and ties to the community that Lee's Citizen Action Commission had.

What the board lacked, the agency could have obtained in other ways—for example, by following Lee's lead and actually creating a citizens' advisory committee like the commission. Indeed, a move to use the commission itself was advocated prior to the agency's formation by those who feared the selective nature of the board would be a political liability. The plan was rejected, as we saw in chapter 3, on the grounds that Lee's use of the CAC had, for the time being at least, rendered this and similar citizens' advisory groups politically suspect.[d]

---

[d]The CAC was rejected, among other things, because of its reputation as a "rubber stamp," a reputation the planners feared would reflect poorly on the new project.

Agency officials did rely on an alternative technique to identify the project with a diverse set of local institutions and personalities. The desire for such identification was one of the strategic objectives in seeking a bureaucratic coalition. The endorsements such identifications would bring were not the only reasons CPI's leaders sought to align themselves with these agencies. There were other advantages to these alliances, discussed earlier, including access already developed to clienteles within lower class neighborhoods. Endorsements were an important consideration, however. As well established institutions, these agencies had access to important constituents—individuals and groups that were not served directly by the agencies but who nonetheless approved of, supported, and even contributed to their work. This was the case, for example, with St. Martin de Porres, an elementary parochial school that served the predominantly black Dixwell section of the city. A grant to this school was awarded with not only the city's black, but also its Catholic, population very much in mind. The grant itself would serve as a gesture of good will toward the city's substantial (estimated at 75 percent) Catholic population, and the elementary school's participation in the anti-poverty project suggested that the reform effort had the recognition and the endorsement of both blacks and Catholics. It was simply "good politics," one staff member explained to those who expressed concern over the diversion of funds from the public schools.[16] This, along with grants to other on-going agencies, would help identify the project with established institutions and quiet possible community uneasiness about a new and somewhat unfamiliar enterprise.

Establishing a Record

Analysis or Advocacy. However useful the endorsements of other city institutions or the agency's own protestations of support for community norms, neither would have been of much value had the anti-poverty project failed to show results. True, agency officials were careful to moderate their claims, citing the complexities of the urban crisis in an effort to avoid "raising the expectations of the community beyond what is realistic."[17] Complexities notwithstanding, the community would have to be shown *some* concrete results. Otherwise, why the expenditure of so many millions?

Demonstrating results of the project could be difficult and hazardous. For one thing, most of the agency's investments were in long-term programs such as pre-kindergarten, remedial reading, and work crews, whose *full* impact would not be realized for years. For another, many of the desired outcomes, even if they did materialize, were not easily discernible by means readily available to the ordinary citizen. Changed attitudes among school drop-outs, juvenile delinquents, welfare mothers, or the unemployed would be far less visible than, for example, a new office building or hotel erected in an urban renewal project area. If such changes did occur, it would require subtle and sophisticated analyses to determine the precise influence of the anti-poverty project itself, as distinguished from the effects of a larger social environment that included changes in the condition of the national economy and the mounting influence of the civil rights and black nationalism drives that were simultaneously bearing on the lives of the inner-city poor.

Such analyses were not forthcoming from CPI, for the agency followed the virtually universal social reform practice of not building into its operation what social scientists would consider adequate evaluation procedures. Admittedly, there was an effort to do so early in the agency's history. As part of a grant from the federal Office of Juvenile Delinquency, the agency established a Research Division and staffed it principally with social scientists, specifically sociologists. But throughout its brief history—by the end of 1965, most of its professional staff had left—the division was a marginal part of the agency. More to the point here, the division's *major research undertaking*, a systematic evaluation of CPI's youth development programs, *was never completed.*[18]

The fate of the Research Division, and especially its uncompleted evaluation project, resulted from lack of support within the agency. This lack of support stemmed partly from differences in personality and in personal styles, differences that were particularly marked between the head of the Research Division and Sviridoff;[e] and partly from what many in the agency considered the division's chronic inability to deliver results in a reasonable time. Moreover, as the agency's public claims of success went unchallenged, and as the favorable image it was promoting in other ways became accepted, there was little the Research Division could contribute to the overall image of the project. Indeed, *agency officials had everything to lose and nothing to gain from systematic analysis*, either by their own researchers or by others, *since such an analysis might reveal that project programs were less effective than agency officials were claiming.*

To promote a favorable image of their accomplishments, agency officials relied on advocacy rather than analysis. As members of an agency that had no past record or established standards of performance, an agency, furthermore, about which information was not readily available, the agency was in a position to define success in its own terms. This was done in a persistent stream of news releases, brochures, and reports in which sucess was defined largely in terms of the size and extent of the project. The comprehensive nature of the project, its numerous clientele, participating agencies, and programs—all these, agency officials maintained, "represented significant innovations in New Haven's response to the needs of the urban poor,"[19] and proved that the urban crisis could be met by other than "revolutionary means . . . without overturning the existing system of urban agencies and institutions."[20]

---

[e]The status of the Research Division, along with the status of another professional group, the neighborhood lawyers, stands as the notable exception to Sviridoff's control of agency personnel (see chapter 3 above). Doubtless in part because the division's work was less public in nature than that of the lawyers, Sviridoff was less active in directing its behavior. Still, it was an open secret within the agency that he was unhappy with the division's performance, and his toleration of the division was a continuing puzzle to many staff members. One possible explanation for the toleration was that Sviridoff respected academics and feared negative reaction from the outside academic world, especially from the Yale community, if he took action against the division.

"Creaming." The record presented to the community was not, however, a purely quantitative one. Although agency officials relied heavily on the extensive nature of the project to demonstrate what they claimed were significant inroads into the problem of poverty, they were mindful of the need to show qualitative changes in the actual conditions of the city's lower classes. It was one thing to cite the large number of programs and program participants, quite another to establish that the poor were in fact benefiting, that the programs themselves were effective, and also that the poor were, as agency officials insisted they were, capable of being helped.

As a means of ensuring that at least some qualitative change was associated with the project, the agency, in Sviridoff's words, "deliberately and unashamedly courted success in the early stages of the program."[21] This was done, in part, by selectively recruiting clientele. Like many political actors operating with imperfect information, Sviridoff imputed a structure to conditions among those he was acting upon (in this case the poor) and whatever the empirical validity of this structure, it at least provided a guideline for his own behavior. Part of this structure was that the poor, like other groups in the community, were of varying kinds. Some were more likely to succeed than others and it was the former—the saveable poor—not the latter that he considered the project's chief concern. This was known as "creaming," the recruitment of low-risk clientele as opposed to those who, because of the complexity of their personal or familial problems, were unlikely to succeed however extensive or intensive the services provided them.

Apart from relying on the testimony of agency officials, it is difficult to document this practice precisely, since detailed information on agency clientele during these years is not available. There is one partial exception, however—namely, the AVCO and Olin-Mathieson job-training programs, and although even here the data are imperfect, they do provide some insight into the practice.

These training programs were among the earliest sponsored by the anti-poverty agency as part of its overall manpower effort and ones frequently cited as evidence that "it was possible for the long-term unemployed to make it . . . in terms of status jobs and 'real good salaries.' "[22] Through these programs fifty men participated in job training designed to prepare them as draftsmen, X-ray technicians, laboratory technicians, and pilot plant technicians. Of the fifty who participated, forty-two completed the training and of these thirty-two moved directly into jobs with the AVCO and Olin-Mathieson manufacturing firms.[23]

Whether or not one accepts the agency's claim that these training programs were a striking success is less important here than the fact that agency officials had helped to predetermine the outcome. As agency officials saw it, the training programs were a "calculated risk,"[24] for if they failed, it would be a mark against the agency and the project both in the community at large and in the lower-class neighborhoods. Since there was no advantage to stacking the deck against success, the agency hedged its bet by careful selective recruitment of trainees. The fifty who participated in the training program were the best qualified of those who had applied. The better educated the applicant—and to a lesser extent the better his employment and police records—the better were his chances of being accepted into the program.[25]

Conflict avoidance. In recruiting largely qualified trainees for its training programs, the agency gave notice that it would not make unreasonable demands on other community groups and institutions. This was part of the agency's more general strategy of conflict avoidance. Like other agency strategies—that of defining the project in terms of community norms and that of identifying the project with established public and private agencies—this, too, was designed to promote a favorable image, in this case by lending substance to the agency's oft-repeated claim that its intentions were peaceful and its activities in harmony with existing community norms and institutions.

Of all the agency's policies, "conflict avoidance" was the one that created the most tension within the staff. This tension was most noticeable in the relations between the central office and the neighborhood workers. For the latter, poverty was highly personalized; direct, daily exposure to the ugly realities of the slums, along with the initial belief systems that led them to seek such employment, was likely to generate a sense of urgency and indignation about the system in which the slum dweller was enmeshed. Out of this indignation grew demands that the agency adopt more militant and aggressive tactics in dealing with the "system"—with landlords, money-lenders, the police, schools, the courts, the welfare agencies—and that it abandon or at least modify its policy of moderation, and follow, as it were, Mary Elizabeth Lease's advice to nineteenth century farmers "to raise less corn and more hell."

But Sviridoff controlled both agency policy and agency personnel and he insisted that staff members scrupulously observe the strategy of conflict avoidance. For non-agency personnel, protest of the sort advocated by some neighborhood workers might be legitimate, perhaps even desirable, since these more extreme tactics would help define the anti-poverty project as a moderate enterprise. For CPI personnel to employ such methods, however, was something New Haven's anti-poverty chief refused to permit. And those few staff members who defied his policy were quickly sanctioned in ways that were meant both to deal with the specific deviation and to deter future challenges to his own authority and to the project's reputation in the community.[26]

Community Reaction

General Response: 1959-1966

To the extent that community reaction can be measured without polls and surveys, it would seem to have been favorable; certainly there is no evidence that it was generally negative. Between 1959 and 1966—an inclusive period of eight remarkable years—New Haven's planners were, with few exceptions, able to pursue their programs for social and economic reform untroubled by public criticisms and controversies. The local press, especially *The New Haven Register*, which agency officials feared might follow its stolidly conservative and rather contentious instincts and launch a public crusade against the project, reacted with surprising moderation. Despite some initial reservations, for example, about whether the taxpayers would have to pay for the Ford-launched programs,[27] and despite intermittent subsequent barbs,[28] both *The New Haven Register* and *The New Haven Journal-Courier* were, on balance, restrained in their treatment of the project;[29] on one occasion *The Register* was even laudatory.[30]

In general, there were few open and prolonged attacks on the agency. All told, there were four between 1959 and 1966 and only two of these originated in the non-inner-city community.[f] One was the dispute with the New Haven County Bar Association described in chapter 7; the other was with a group known as the Better Education Committee. The former centered on the proposed activities of the New Haven Legal Assistance Association and it was limited to this specific question, never broadening to include other facets of the anti-poverty project. The dispute with the Better Education Committee was radically different. This group's attacks were more broad-gauged and sweeping, more explicitly partisan than the bar association's, and as such, the first serious challenge to the agency and the reform program it was sponsoring.

Partisan Conflict: The Better
Education Committee

The dispute with New Haven's Better Education Committee began some two and a half years after the announcement of the original Ford Foundation grant. In a sense, this marked the discovery of the city's anti-poverty agency, for at the heart of the dispute was the agency's role in city government. Prior to this the issue had not arisen, at least not in any public debate. Despite the fact that CPI was a political institution, an institution that spent federal and foundation funds to influence local public policy, no one had openly questioned its existence and no one had fought for control of it.

Like CPI, the Better Education Committee was a newcomer to the city's political life. The committee was formed during the summer of 1964 to oppose school busing proposed by the New Haven Board of Education to deal with *de facto* school segregation. The committee's subsequent history followed a familiar pattern.[31] With the implementation of the busing program in September of the same year, the committee gradually shifted focus, first to educational questions in general, and eventually, in January 1965, to the city's anti-poverty project.

The committee's attack on the new agency contained a number of themes, some familiar, others unfamiliar, not all of them consistent. According to the committee's chief public spokesman, Joseph Einhorn, the anti-poverty project was, among other things, "a massive program of colonial welfarism," "wasting

---

[f]The agency's promotional activities discussed in this chapter were addressed to primarily non-inner-city residents. CPI's difficulties with inner-city groups are examined in chapter 3.

millions of taxpayers' dollars" on programs that dealt with "symptoms rather than causes." For this he partly blamed Sviridoff and his staff whom he characterized as a "group of omnipotent social theorists" interested in their "own personal aggrandizement." But Mayor Lee was also at fault. Had it not been for the failure of the Lee administration, the new agency would not have been necessary in the first place. In Einhorn's words: "The federal government [felt] that Mayor Lee and his long entrenched administration [were] not qualified to spend . . . federal funds wisely and, therefore . . . turned control over to a private agency." With these funds, CPI had usurped many municipal functions and Einhorn urged the mayor to reclaim these for the city.[32]

By summer's end, Einhorn's attacks had become more intense, and decidedly more partisan in tone. In August 1965, he received the Republican Party's nomination to oppose Lee in the November elections. A Democrat who reportedly had shifted parties in 1964, Einhorn's claim to political prominence was chiefly his public opposition to school busing and to the anti-poverty project.

For Einhorn, for the Better Education Committee, and for the Republican Party, the 1965 municipal elections were a disaster. The Democrats swept the city. For the first time in history the Republicans were left without representation on the thirty-three-member Board of Aldermen. Einhorn himself fared badly; he was soundly defeated by Lee, who polled some 66 percent of the total vote, his second largest in eight elections. For their part, anti-poverty officials were elated. They had defined the election as a test of their own programs and they interpreted the outcome as a resounding demonstration of support for the project they had been fashioning during the preceding five years.

The Project and the Community:
Summary

In dealing with the community at large, New Haven anti-poverty officials tried to promote a favorable image of their project—among other ways, by defining it in terms compatible with local norms, by identifying it with established community institutions, and by amassing a record of achievement. Whether these strategies were a success, whether individually or collectively they help account for the relative calm that prevailed during the project's formative years, cannot be established definitively without systematic data on public opinion. That there was little controversy, and that what controversy there was was more strident than effective, lends credence to the agency officials' own beliefs (expressed in the wake of the 1965 municipal election) that the community was behind their effort. But the evidence is not clear-cut. Einhorn's poor showing in 1965 was an ambiguous demonstration of support for the anti-poverty effort. Like most elections, this one focused on many issues—Lee's long tenure in office (twelve years), his record in urban renewal, his association with the anti-poverty effort, and on personalities and parties as well. Still, the election was rich with meaning for the project. If it was not a clear mandate for reform, the election nevertheless revealed that whatever opposition there was to the project was not as yet sufficiently intense or widespread to make much difference at the polls. It is little wonder that the anti-poverty staff was more than encouraged by the outcome.

In effect, the 1965 municipal election brought to a close what I have referred to throughout the study as the formative years of New Haven's anti-poverty project. As I indicated at the outset, this time period spanned the years during which the project was planned (1959-1962), and the tenure of CPI's first executive director, Mitchell Sviridoff (1962-1966). Sviridoff, who was selected to head the new agency in 1962, continued as its director until October, 1966. By the end of 1965, however, his reputation as an anti-poverty administrator was firmly established and his expertise was much in demand throughout the country. Between the 1965 election and his resignation ten months later, he became increasingly preoccupied with assignments outside the city, principally his assignment as a consultant to New York City's newly-elected mayor, John Lindsay.

What happened between the point at which this narrative stops and the time of writing, 1970, may be briefly noted. In 1966, after four years of sustained growth and expansion, the agency entered a stage of consolidation and retrenchment. Most of the original staff left the agency and were replaced by personnel who were characterized more for their deliberate administrative style and less for their driving entrepeneurial quality than the men who had dominated the agency during its formative years. To be sure, new policies and new programs continued to be adopted. But compared to the formative years, the rate of innovation declined markedly.

Politically, the agency's fortunes varied; indeed, events since 1966 tarnished New Haven's reputation as a model city, leading to some of the almost gloating negative publicity that occurs on the occasion of falls from grace of the once-favored. One instance of difficulty for the agency occurred in June, 1968, when the New Haven Board of Aldermen voted to designate itself, rather than CPI, as the city's official community action agency under the Economic Opportunity Act.[33] The vote was in large part a reflection of the growing split within the local Democratic Party, between Lee on the one hand, and the city's Democratic town chairman, Arthur Barbieri, on the other.[34] Closely allied with Lee, the agency was caught in the crossfire of intraparty politics.[35] With support from the mayor, however, who vetoed the board's action, and support from the federal Office of Economic Opportunity, which sided with the mayor, CPI retained its status and continued to serve as the city's official anti-poverty agency. But the time of low visibility and freedom from political sniping was clearly past.

The board's action was probably less damaging to CPI's reputation than events that occurred during the previous summer. On the evening of August 19, 1967, any hope that a reform-minded New Haven would avoid the fate of other communities was shattered when racial disorders erupted in the Hill section of the city. The disorders were sparked by what the National Advisory Commission on Civil Disorders classified as a nonracial incident, the shooting of a Puerto Rican by a white,[36] and more especially by rumors regarding this incident.[37] Initially, the outbursts were sporadic, limited to bottle and rock attacks on vehicular traffic in the neighborhood. By late evening, however, the disturbances had intensified and over the next four days a section of this and one other neighborhood were plagued by rock throwing, window breaking, occasional looting, and arson, and some sniping.

Compared to disorders in such communities as Newark, Detroit, and Minneapolis, New Haven's riots were relatively mild, with no deaths and only three reported injuries.[38] But for all its mildness, the strife that ended New Haven's dream of a community untroubled by civic or racial disorders was no less jarring politically, casting doubt as it did on New Haven's reputation generally, including Lee's political genius, the value of his redevelopment program, and CPI and its strategies. For CPI, the blow was especially great, since, correctly or incorrectly, the accusation has been made that the disorders were a paradoxical offshoot of its very programs to help blacks and the poor. While these disorders and their causes are not the direct concern of this study, they will be addressed briefly, in the next chapter in a concluding discussion of the political strategies CPI employed during the formative years of the project.

Part V
Conclusion

Policy Innovations and Political Strategies

In this study I have examined the evolution of one of the country's first and most prominent anti-poverty efforts, New Haven's Community Progress, Inc. Of special interest have been the forces that shaped this new enterprise during its formative years, 1959-1966, the individuals responsible for initiating and directing it, the resources they possessed and developed, and the ways they used these resources to promote social reform both locally and nationally. What remains to be done, by way of conclusion, is to summarize the principal themes that emerge from my analysis of CPI's early history, and in particular to highlight what this story tells us about the strategies of policy innovation.

The Strategies of Reform

General Characteristics of New Haven Politics

In the midst of the drama of innovation and change that marked the formative years of New Haven's anti-poverty project much remained that was familiar. In the 1965 mayoralty campaign, Republicans charged that New Haven was characterized by "politics as usual and the usual politics." The observation was intended as a criticism of Mayor Lee and his programs, including the anti-poverty project. Nonetheless, the observation was quite fitting, for the political process that characterized the formative years of the project was fundamentally similar to the process described in the now-classic studies of the city by Dahl and his associates during a somewhat earlier period, when redevelopment was the central issue, but when anti-poverty had not yet surfaced as a concern in its own right.[1]

The reform was initiated and directed throughout the formative years by individuals who were distinguished by their political and administrative roles and not by their economic power or social status. In fact, the city's social and economic notables, a group that has been so conspicuous in the often-roiled literature on community politics,[2] played a relatively small part in this area of public policy. They neither initiated nor vetoed proposals, either openly or behind the scenes. A few of them did help legitimate the effort by serving on the agency's board of directors or by publicly endorsing the project and its goals. But even as legitimators the role of the social and economic notables was minor compared to that of New Haven's major political figure, the mayor, and that of the professional administrators who ran the city's established public and private agencies.

The reformers were a small, intense minority, a group whose members were distinguished, in Dahl's terms, "by the rate and skill with which they used their political resources"[3] to achieve their political and policy objectives. Among these resources were the backing of the mayor, Sviridoff's public reputation and personal ability, the fragmented nature of the political system, the latent energies of the bureaucrats, and the time, skill, knowledge, and dedication of the CPI staff. These, and not social prestige, economic power, sheer numbers, or electoral strength, were the principal resources available to and used by the city's anti-poverty team in its drive to promote the reform enterprise.

Organizing the Reform

Those close to the project during the planning years had a preview of the resourcefulness of the city's reformers, which was evident from the very first in such matters as Hallman's skill and determination in drafting a saleable reform proposal, in cultivating friendly administrators, and in nurturing the beginnings of the reform coalition. Later evidence of the reformers' resourcefulness and strategic ingenuity were two critically important decisions calculated to create an organizational base for reform: the decision to establish a new, private non-profit corporation; and the decision to appoint an individual of Sviridoff's political stature and personal ability to head this corporation.

These two decisions about institutional form and institutional control were complementary. Sviridoff provided the agency with a scarce, vital resource: creative, politically sophisticated, executive leadership capacity, wielded by a man of recognized stature who had the mayor's respect; the agency provided Sviridoff the institutional framework within which he could demonstrate his capacity and willingness to act decisively.

The critical interplay between the institution and the man was manifest throughout Sviridoff's tenure as executive director, and especially in the ways he fashioned the further desideratum of a successful organization, a talented, loyal, energetic staff. CPI's institutional form freed Sviridoff from many of the organizational restraints of public bureaucracies, such as established staff traditions and expectations, and civil service regulations, and he used this freedom in developing his anti-poverty team. He recruited individuals from diverse professional backgrounds, individuals who shared his reform philosophy and, remarkable for an urban agency, individuals who came from outside the city and whose ties were thus to CPI and to Sviridoff, not to some other local center of power. Through these and other means, Sviridoff created a highly centralized agency and organized its resources and energies toward the single, paramount goal of mounting a dramatic and effective reform project.

*Political Fragmentation and Political
Opportunities*

While Sviridoff's CPI was a highly centralized organization, the political world of which it was a part was not. It was a world in which power and influence were extraordinarily fragmented—widely distributed among various individuals, groups, and institutions, including the mayor, federal and Foundation officials, and the professional administrators who controlled the city's public and private agencies.

It has long been a tenet among reformers that a political system so divided impedes innovation and change.[4] *The New Haven experience was just the opposite*; the decentralization of power was a positive advantage, particularly in the agency's efforts to weld a bureaucratic coalition. The availability of numerous independent agencies, some of them engaged in similar or identical tasks, afforded CPI's leadership with a rich and variegated arena within which to maneuver. For CPI, a decentralized political system was a flexible system, one that permitted them to avoid administrators known to be unsympathetic and to discontinue negotiations with those who proved to be recalcitrant. With some effort, CPI officials doubtless could have persuaded, or perhaps pressured, some recalcitrant administrators to participate; could have "dragged them kicking and screaming," so to speak, into the reform coalition. But once in the coalition, this "kicking and screaming" would have continued and would have served only to disrupt an otherwise untroubled process of reform. Further, since cavilling tends to beget cavilling, the entire tone of the early CPI success might well have been radically altered.

Anti-poverty officials had no need for such reluctant allies and were, in fact, better off without them. And New Haven's decentralized political system did provide realistic alternatives in the form of administrators who shared Sviridoff's and Hallman's belief that reform was needed. Thus there were no costs, at least in the short run, to the strategy of avoiding recalcitrant and reluctant administrators, a strategy which contributed to the dramatic, unruffled pace of program innovation and program adoption during the early years of the project.

The decentralization of power was advantageous in another way as well: *it facilitated CPI's use of the demonstration effect*. With numerous independent centers of administrative decision-making, the staff was able to approach first those officials who were already favorably disposed to reform. The record CPI established with these officials later served to demonstrate to less favorably disposed or uncertain administrators what the new and unfamiliar enterprise was all about, or not about.

In dealing with officials from other agencies, the staff tried to demonstrate that CPI was an organization committed to a "positive approach to change," and to limited program objectives. In practice, this meant, first, that negotiations centered on specific program proposals, backed by well-reasoned arguments and presentations that were devoid of discourses on the inequities and injustices of "the system," or on the shortcomings of the specific agency. It meant, second, assurances that the new reform organization was not a "super-agency" commissioned by the mayor, the Ford Foundation, or the federal government to undermine the authority of existing agencies; that, on the contrary, CPI had no intention or desire to squander its resources by expanding the scope of its activities beyond the specific reform programs it was sponsoring.

Equally important, anti-poverty officials sought to demonstrate that they were prepared to shift a large measure of the burden of cooperation from the participating agencies onto CPI itself. This they did in part by providing much of the staff work needed for new programs, for example by developing program proposals and by articulating justifications for these proposals that cooperating officials could employ in shepherding them through their own administrative hierarchies. They did so in an even more convincing fashion by assuming responsibility for funding the programs, thus relieving administrators of the initial financial burden of participation.

The Art of Pyramiding

Much of CPI's success locally, including its successful courting of the city's bureaucracies, rested on the agency's unusual and important resource base, the joint financial backing of the Ford Foundation and the federal government. Obtaining outside funds was one of the agency's "distinctive areas of competence."[5] A sketch of how CPI practiced grantsmanship provides further illustration of the agency's enterprising use of resources.

CPI developed the financial support that was so crucial to its success through a skillful application of the "art of pyramiding."[6] When initially conceived, the proposed project must have struck some as a grand and visionary utopian scheme. Its conceivers had few initial resources other than their own dedication, knowledge, and imagination, and an enduring hope they would, as they eventually did, gain the active support of the mayor. Lee's backing for the effort was essential; his influence in the city was unparalleled and his record in urban renewal had gained him recognition as one of the country's foremost and most progressive urban leaders, thus enormously enhancing the city's visibility to granting agencies.

While New Haven's planners had few initial resources, they were able to use these resources to obtain the first grant from the Ford Foundation. This grant constituted an additional resource which, together with those already in hand, was used to create yet other resources, among them the agency's highly talented staff and numerous operating programs that could be used as part of the model project strategy. These were used to expand still further the agency's resource base—to secure the backing of federal agencies, for example, to win renewal of the Foundation grant, and to establish the agency's reputation and standing among local anti-poverty officials elsewhere in the country.

All these resources, finally, were used by the New Haven staff to increase its influence nationally and to strengthen its ties with federal administrators by helping them to organize and to mobilize political support for the national war on poverty, which in turn helped consolidate the agency's base of support in New Haven. In short, New Haven officials obtained the funding necessary for their project through a systematic, step-by-step multiplication of resources.

Social Reform and Political Constraints

Like entrepreneurs generally, the bureaucratic entrepreneurs who ran New Haven's anti-poverty project were limited in what they could do. They operated under both internal and external constraints, and while they were able to avoid or overcome many of these, others directly or indirectly influenced their behavior and the shape of the project.[a] In a few cases, these constraints deterred agency officials altogether.

Of particular interest here are the constraints associated with what the literature on control of local politics often calls "indirect power," and what the CPI experience reveals about the constraining influence of anticipated reactions and community norms and values. Such phenomena are of interest, since in the continuing dialectic about who rules, and how they rule, in local communities, it is often asserted that "powerful interests" consisting of prosperous social and economic elites influence the outcome of local policy through their domination of the "non-decision making process." Through either their control of community norms, or through the anticipated reactions of others—that is, through the action or inaction of others dictated by fear of elite opposition—power elites of social and economic notables are said to restrain public officials by restricting the public agenda to "relatively non-controversial issues, notwithstanding that there are serious but latent power conflicts within the community."[8]

Agency officials *were* constrained by community norms and anticipated reactions, *but not by a social and economic elite.* One advantage of long-term participant observation is the advantage it gives observers (like the present writer) in sensing officials' day to day thoughts, preoccupations, and fears. The powerful interests that most concerned agency officials were not the city's social and economic notables but, as should be amply clear by now, such political figures as the mayor, the administrative heads of agencies, and, more generally, the New Haven electorate. For the CPI staff, these were the salient reference

[a]Among these were the staff's persisting faith in the system, and its belief that existing institutions and processes were sufficiently benign and flexible to meet the challenges of poverty. This belief caused the staff to stop considerably short of, and, indeed, to reject even the milder forms of confrontation politics. Similarly, the agency's assumptions about poverty, that it was in large measure rooted in the lack of educational and employment opportunities, led the agency to stress programs in these areas and contributed partly to the agency's early opposition to resident participation.[7]

points—in about the order listed. They were the individuals and groups most frequently cited in staff meetings and in informal conversations, and the ones whose predicted reactions to specific policy alternatives deterred agency officials from adopting these alternatives.

It was the electorate, for example, that stood in the way of increasing local tax money for the project. To be sure, the electorate included individual businessmen, retailers, bankers, manufacturers, and socialites who might qualify as members of an upper-class elite. But expected reactions of these groups were less important to the reformers than the expected reactions of the city's middle- and working-class homeowners. It was the electorate also, or at least middle- and working-class parents, whose expected reactions prevented agency leaders from openly pressing for or publicly endorsing public school integration. And it was members of the general electorate, in this case the city's substantial Roman Catholic population and some black militants, who deterred the staff from including birth control among its programs. Finally, and in a more positive sense, it was the electorate, and, in particular, the residents of the neighborhoods most directly affected by relocation from urban renewal areas, whose expected response was an initial stimulus to the city's anti-poverty effort.

While a factor in agency decisions, fear of negative community reaction was far from an immobilizing influence on agency officials. For one thing, some of the potentially most troublesome community norms are cast at an exceedingly high level of abstraction, and therefore no automatic, unambiguous inference can be made from them whether an individual should be for or against the project. This was the case, for example, with the norm of individual responsibility and its corollary, anti-welfarism. The generally inconclusive nature of these norms afforded agency officials the opportunity to define the project in terms compatible with them, by stressing among other things the ultimate savings in welfare the community would realize. In a sense, the CPI staff exploited anti-welfare sentiment to promote a welfare program, in much the same way federal officials a number of years later convinced the stolidly conservative chairman of the House Ways and Means Committee to support the Nixon administration's welfare reform proposals.[9]

Second, while fear of negative community reaction deterred agency officials in specific instances, numerous program alternatives remained, and numerous opportunities to implement these alternatives. If specific programs such as birth control or busing to integrate public schools were rejected because they were considered offensive to community sentiment or because they were potentially controversial, other programs *could* be adopted—among them pre-kindergarten, work-crews, on-the-job training, remedial reading, the community school, and the skill center. In fact, the alternatives were sufficiently numerous that the agency was able to launch a reform project of considerable magnitude. Between 1962 and 1966, CPI sponsored more than *sixty* reform programs, programs that were no less effective simply because they were inoffensive and non-controversial.

The New Haven Reform Coalition:
An Assessment

The broad, comprehensive reform effort mounted in New Haven was based on a political coalition carefully nurtured and maintained by CPI officials. This coalition was crucial to the success of the New Haven enterprise and its development stands as one of the agency's principal achievements during the formative years of the project.

While this coalition was of unquestionable value to New Haven in the short run, some of the agency's coalition strategies may have occasioned long-term difficulties for the project. Both prior to and especially after Sviridoff's resignation from the agency, the wisdom of CPI's coalition strategies was questioned. Three strategies in particular were challenged by critics of CPI and hence warrant special consideration here: (1) CPI's reliance on outside funding; (2) its alliances with local public and private agencies; and (3) its discouragement of citizen participation.

CPI's Reliance on Outside Funding

The relationship between local and national officials in New Haven's war on poverty illustrates what the late Morton Grodzins meant when he compared American federalism to a "marble cake" rather than a "layer cake."[10] The relationship was a partnership, and to look upon the war on poverty, at least as it was waged in New Haven during these years, as a program marked by conflicting and competing interests is to miss the point. In this case, national and local officials were not part of opposing political subsystems. They were members of a vertical alliance, an administrative coalition that cut across both public and private spheres as well as all levels of government. It was a coalition, moreover, consisting of individuals who shared a common outlook regarding the nature of what Grodzins termed the "federal bargain," and who shared a common outlook regarding the necessity of vigorous joint local-national action to meet the critical problems of mid-twentieth-century America.

As we have seen, New Haven benefited handsomely from this coalition and demonstrated once again that its renown at grantsmanship was well deserved. From 1954 through 1969, the years of the Lee administration, the city continually exploited outside funds, first in urban renewal and then, as we have seen, in anti-poverty. And it did so at little financial cost to the city itself. In anti-poverty alone, for example, more than *90 percent* of the some $16.3 million spent between 1962 and 1966 came from sources outside the city.

In an important sense, the key to New Haven's success in obtaining anti-poverty funds was its past success, first with federal urban renewal money and later with the initial Ford Foundation grant. The record established with these monies by Lee, Logue, Hallman, and Sviridoff, far from spawning the feeling that New Haven had been overindulged,[11] simply served further to legitimate additional infusions of federal and Foundation largesse. Moreover, there was some overall social rationale in so favoring New Haven. In effect, the city was a known and proven entity for investing in a concentrated way funds that would be spread thin if invested evenly among other cities. By investing heavily in New Haven, the Foundation and the federal government considerably enhanced the chances of a viable demonstration program, a fact New Haven's planners recognized and exploited fully in their bid for outside financial support.

But New Haven's model project strategy had its limitations. For one thing, the Foundation limited its support to a maximum of six years. For another, by demonstrating the value of anti-poverty projects, New Haven helped increase the overall demand for federal anti-poverty funds. And there were no assurances these scarce federal funds would be sufficient to meet this growing demand, or that CPI would continue to be supported in the manner to which it had become accustomed.

Concern over the future funding of the project was voiced early in its history. *The New Haven Register*, it will be recalled, greeted the announcement of the initial Foundation grant warily, asking who would pay eventually for the programs and warning, by implication, that the burden might ultimately fall on the New Haven taxpayer.[12] Others expressed precisely the opposite concern, pointing to the failure of CPI to use early Ford Foundation and Office of Juvenile Delinquency grants as leverage for developing regularized local budgetary support. Martin Rein and S.M. Miller, in a slightly veiled allusion to New Haven's matching of Ford and federal Juvenile Delinquency funds against each other, concluded that "such fiscal participation was unlikely to yield a deep commitment" in the community. And lacking this commitment, they asked, "who would keep the project going?"[13]

The New Haven project *has* in fact been kept going. Yet at the time of this writing, some four and a half years since the publication of the Rein and Martin article, CPI's future remains uncertain. As a private, non-profit corporation, located outside the formal structure of government, the agency is still dependent on annual grants and contracts from sources outside the city. Since the termination of grants from the federal Office of Juvenile Delinquency (1966) and from the Ford Foundation (1969), most of this support has come from the federal Office of Economic Opportunity and from the United States Department of Labor.

Neither of these agencies, however, can be reliably counted on as continuing sources of funding for CPI. The status of the Office of Economic Opportunity itself as a granting agency is much in doubt. And while the Department of Labor is a safely established political institution, the programs it helped sponsor in New Haven (such as the Neighborhood Employment Centers, on-the-job training, and the Neighborhood Youth Corps) could be abolished, transferred to other, less hospitable agencies, or replaced by entirely new programs such as the National Alliance of Businessmen's JOBS, programs whose sponsors might choose not to work through CPI.

The Institutionalization of Reform

Yet even if CPI's future remains uncertain, there is a strong likelihood many of the programs it helped institute will continue. One of the principal objectives in CPI's overall reform strategy was to win cooperation and support of city agencies. The staying power of these agencies, it was hoped, would provide insurance against CPI's own uncertain future.

This strategy has been quite successful. In the area of public policy to which anti-poverty officials devoted the single largest share of project money—education—such programs as pre-kindergarten, adult basic education, remedial reading, work-study, and the community school seem almost certain to continue, and quite possibly will expand. Elsewhere the prospects are equally hopeful; the expectation is that neighborhood libraries, police neighborhood centers, day-care centers, legal assistance, expanded recreation programs, and the use of para-professionals by private health and welfare agencies will continue.

What makes the prospects for these programs hopeful is that they have been institutionalized. They are formally administered by such established agencies as the New Haven Department of Education and the New Haven Department of Parks and Recreation. Significantly, the programs are no longer dependent on funds channeled through CPI. In some cases (for example, the neighborhood libraries), the programs are funded almost fully by the city. For the most part, however, these programs continue to be supported by so-called "soft money"— outside funds such as those provided nationally under the Elementary and Secondary Education Act and the Safe Streets Act, and, within Connecticut, under the Community Development Act and under the CPI-initiated and -encouraged State Aid to Disadvantaged Children Act.

Admittedly, there are no guarantees that these state and national programs themselves will survive, or that the administering agencies will continue their level of funding in New Haven. But the willingness of established local agencies to pursue outside funding for CPI-initiated programs is an indication that these programs have the type of institutional support envisioned in the anti-poverty agency's reform strategy. It is an indication, moreover, that in addition to instituting reform programs, CPI taught the city bureaucrats, in the words of one observer, "to have the moxie to raise more federal and state funds on their own."

Resident Participation and
Resident Protest

Along with the mayor and federal and Foundation officials, the city's bureaucracies were the principal participants in CPI's reform coalition. Between 1959 and 1965, agency officials devoted themselves almost exclusively to winning and maintaining the active support of these allies. Equally important, they did little to encourage expanded participation in this coalition. Indeed, prior to the passage of the Economic Opportunity Act in 1964 there was no incentive to do so, for the backing of these allies was all that CPI needed to mount its reform effort. Had additional participation been encouraged—and encouraging more participation would have been costly in and of itself—the generally successful and conflict-free process of social reform might well have been disrupted.

CPI's early strategy of limiting participation in the reform coalition may, however, have been something of a mixed blessing. A *limited coalition* was doubtless one of the factors that allowed CPI to move so rapidly to the forefront of the national war on poverty, for reducing the number of participants has obvious tactical advantages from the standpoint of organizational effectiveness. But the agency's early disregard of other groups, and especially other groups in New Haven, may have cost the project important allies. More to the point here, it may have occasioned hostility toward the agency, with serious consequences for its future history.

By far the most serious and most widely publicized of these possible consequences were the 1967 New Haven riots. In the aftermath of the riots, it was suggested that to a significant extent they were an outgrowth of CPI's early discouragement of resident participation.[14] The most notable of these suggestions is found in the *Report* of the National Advisory Commission on Civil Disorders (the Kerner commission). According to the commission, one major cause of the riots nationally was that

ghetto residents increasingly believe that they are excluded from the decision-making process which affects their lives and community. This feeling of exclusion, intensified by the bitter legacy of racial discrimination, has engendered a deep seated hostility toward the institutions of government. It has severely compromised the effectiveness of programs intended to provide improved services to ghetto residents.[15]

To illustrate its point, the commission cited New Haven, where, the commission charged,

well intentioned programs designed to respond to the needs of ghetto residents were not worked out and implemented sufficiently in cooperation with the intended beneficiaries.[16]

It is, to understate the point, at best difficult to unravel the causes of the New Haven riots of 1967. Like those in other communities, they were complex, and much is unknown about them. The Kerner commission's findings were based on "evidence presented [the] Commission in hearings, field reports, and research analyses of the 1967 riot cities."[17] But the dimensions of this evidence are not specified—for example, whose testimony was received, what facts were considered, and whether this testimony or these facts were entirely consistent with one another and with the commission's sweeping observations about New Haven, "its well intentioned programs," and the disorders. As a result, there is little basis for an independent assessment of the commission's hypothesis. Moreover, given the controversy that attends even the most rigorous historical reconstruction of complex events—and here one is reminded of the Warren Commission—it becomes clear almost by definition that the commission's undefended assertion has little probative force.

A number of unresolved issues—questions not raised, and events overlooked or unexplained in the commission's report—must be considered in appraising the effects of CPI's resident-participation policy on the 1967 disorders. For one thing, the disorders were quite localized, limited principally to sections of two of the seven neighborhoods served by the anti-poverty project. What distinguished these sections from the remaining ones is unclear. Conceivably, the hostility of which the commission spoke was, for some as yet unexplained reason, limited to these sections. If so, one wonders why? If not, then one wonders what else besides hostility was involved and whether there is any evidence that active membership in the anti-poverty coalition would have made a difference.[18]

Second, prior to the disorders, there had in fact been changes in the agency's policy toward resident participation, changes that were not cited by the commission. In 1965, for example, a Resident Advisory Commission had been established consisting of twenty-one members, three from each of the seven project neighborhoods. In November of the same year, the membership of the agency's governing body, its board of directors, was expanded from nine to sixteen, to include *seven elected representatives*, one from each of the project neighborhoods.[b]

In point of fact, only a miniscule proportion of project neighborhood residents availed themselves of the opportunity to choose board members. In the neighborhood elections held in the fall of 1965, for example, only 909 residents, or less than *1 percent* of those eligible to vote did so. By 1967, voter participation had increased, but only slightly, to 1,661, or less than *6 percent* of those eligible.[19] These data, coupled with the further evidence that residents were active in taking advantage of specific CPI-provided opportunities, make it clear that most residents were more interested in the tangible services provided by the project than in the abstract issue of who was to control the project.

Of course, one cannot always make valid inferences about attitudes from behavior, and doubtless the low turnout was rooted in other factors as well—for example, in a lack of awareness of the elections and a disbelief that they would materially affect the course of agency policy. Whatever the explanations, the point to be stressed here is that nearly two years prior to the disorders, participatory concessions were won for neighborhood residents and—formally at least—they had an opportunity to voice their preferences in the agency's councils.

---

[b]Expanding the board's membership had a twofold significance. On the one hand it constituted official recognition and acceptance of the policy of resident participation. Equally important, given the CPI's public resistance to this policy, it demonstrated the efficacy of neighborhood pressure on the agency.

Whether or not the 1967 disorders were an outgrowth of CPI's early non-participation policy, the agency was clearly vulnerable politically on this issue. For one thing, its initial resistance and subsequent reluctant compliance with the Economic Opportunity Act's provisions for resident participation brought the New Haven agency into conflict with one of its principal allies, the United States Office of Economic Opportunity. Second, this resistance occurred in the face of rising militancy among the poor, and CPI simply failed to adjust with sufficient grace and speed to this new political force.

By 1965, the poor were no longer as politically inactive—or as invisible—as they had been when the project began.[c] New groups were forming in the city, such as the Hill Neighborhood Union which sparked the 1965 attack on CPI's resident participation policy. Like all emerging groups, they were searching for issues and for constituents. By resisting resident participation, anti-poverty officials gave them an exploitable issue, and the opportunity to undermine the agency's prestige and credibility among neighborhood residents. Finally, and no less significantly, the agency's early policy weakened its overall reputation. Whether or not this policy actually contributed to the 1967 disorders, critics and commentators later *asserted* that it did and by so doing helped obscure the important achievements of the city's anti-poverty agency.

The New Haven Achievement

To understand these achievements, one must look beyond the disorders, and indeed beyond New Haven itself, for the significance of the city's anti-poverty project rests largely on its national implications. Community Progress, Inc. was locally initiated and locally controlled. But it was initiated and controlled by individuals with an enduring sense of national purpose, and with a conviction that their contribution to social reform would benefit more than just New Haven.

The extent of this contribution in terms of the actual alleviation of poverty in New Haven is an as yet incomplete story. During the tortured decade of the 1960s there was a striking decline *nationally* in the number of "poor people," from 39.4 million in 1959 to 24.2 million in 1969, a decline, curiously, that was not widely acknowledged during this time when poverty became more and more a political issue. The decline was especially striking between 1963 and 1967—a period marked by the beginnings of the national war on poverty—when the

[c]CPI may in fact have contributed to the rise of political activism in New Haven. Its widely publicized success in obtaining financial backing for the project gave the poor, or at least those claiming to speak for the poor, an objective worth fighting for, an objective, it will be recalled, that was previously missing in the city. Moreover, CPI was essentially a clientele agency, and in this respect similar to such federal agencies as the Veterans Administration and the Department of Agriculture. Like these and other clientele agencies, it was almost inevitable that the clients themselves would demand a major voice in running the agency's affairs.

annual rate of decline was some four times greater than during the previous four years.[20]

The extent of this decline in New Haven is unknown. But even if the trends in New Haven were similar to those nationally, one could not conclude that CPI had been the cause, tempting and comforting though such a conclusion would be. Given the nature of the project, CPI's contribution to whatever decline there was can at best have been marginal and indirect. Its programs were long-range in nature, stressing the *prevention* of poverty through programs in education and occupational training, rather than the *immediate alleviation* of poverty through direct transfer of funds to the poor. CPI's principal social welfare objective was to improve the life chances of a new generation of poor, and its major welfare premise was that programmatic reform of the type instituted in New Haven was the most efficient and effective way known to redistribute income eventually and at the same time ensure the self-sufficiency and self-respect of a hitherto dependent and disinherited population.

The New Haven project cannot, however, be assessed solely on its contribution to the actual alleviation of poverty, for it was something more than just a social welfare policy. It was also part of a political process concerned as much, if not more, with the redistribution of power as it was with the redistribution of income and the reduction of dependency. As I indicated above, the New Haven project was dominated by individuals with a sense of national purpose, and part of this purpose was to convince society to devote a greater share of its resources to the range of problems associated with poverty and near poverty.

This goal was partially realized during the 1960s, for these were the years when the country discovered rock-bottom poverty. Throughout the decade an increasing number of both old and new public and private institutions—government agencies and legislative bodies, the newsmedia, churches and temples, businesses, unions, and industries—began to divert resources to the problems of poverty. Admittedly, the resources diverted are as yet inadequate to the task.[d] But the search for solutions is under way, in ways that contrast dramatically with the general complacency of the previous decade.

CPI was an important factor, albeit one among many, in stimulating social concern about poverty. As model project,[22] prototype, and promoter for the

[d]It is difficult to provide even "within the park" estimates of the amount that would be adequate, since adequacy in this regard is a relative value that is and will be defined through the political process and hence will vary over time. To the extent that the New Haven experience is pertinent, it suggests that the amount needed to combat poverty may be far higher than previously thought. As we saw in chapter 5, New Haven's expenditure per family with an income of under $4,000 was roughly $7,700 for a peak year (1965). If this per-poor-family expenditure is projected nationally and without qualification, the *annual* cost alone of duplicating the New Haven effort would be roughly $88.4 billion, or approximately 42.9 percent of the total federal, state, and local expenditure for that year. As crude as this estimate is, it suggests the fiscal implications of the national action urged by, among others, the Kerner Commission (see below, note 23), and the political challenge that would confront the nation's policy makers if they were to take these urgings seriously.[21]

Johnson administration's war on poverty, the New Haven agency helped articulate and publicize the thesis that poverty is not an ordained and immutable condition of human existence. And it did so at a time when many people had concluded that poverty was ordained, or what is even more likely, simply had not given the proposition much thought.

Of course, many people helped publicize poverty, among them Michael Harrington, whose celebrated work, *The Other America*, was published the same year (1962) the New Haven project began. The distinctive service of CPI is that it also demonstrated that efforts to improve the well-being of the poor not only *should* but actually *could* be instituted—and instituted in ways that have positive political and popular appeal.[23] Finally, CPI demonstrated that existing political alignments and political issues are not permanent aspects of the social structure, the suggestions of some observers of American politics to the contrary notwithstanding. New Haven's anti-poverty project gave rise to a new political coalition, a coalition that helped politicize conditions among the poor and ensure that these conditions would have a prominent place on the country's public agenda. Now that they are so located, it seems unlikely that they can be disregarded with impunity, as they have been so frequently in the past.

Appendix A: First Board of Directors of Community Progress, Inc., of New Haven, Connecticut

Chester A. Barrett. Executive Vice President and Director, the Second National Bank of New Haven

Current Memberships:[a] Treasurer and Director of the American Red Cross; Corporator of the Family Service; Director of the Better Business; Director of Junior Achievement; Budget Committee of the United Fund; Member of the Board of Directors and Executive Committee of the United Fund; Trustee of the Connecticut Savings Bank; New Haven Screening Committee of the Connecticut Development Credit Corporation; Credit Committee Commission of the Bankers' Association; Robert Morris Associates; Manufacturers' Association.

Rev. Gerald Gilmore. Rector of Saint Paul's Church

Current Memberships: Member of the New Haven Redevelopment Agency; Vice President of the New Haven Council of Churches; Member of the Citizens' Action Commission (Subcommittees: Youth Problems; Wooster Square); Organizer of the St. Paul's Counselling Service; Convener of the Episcopal Clergy Group in New Haven; Member of the Episcopal Church and City Conference; Member of the Episcopal Society for Racial and Cultural Unity.

Mrs. Angus Gordon. Vice President of the Community Council

Current Memberships: Vice President and Treasurer of the Women's Association of the United Church; Chairman of the Nursing School Advisory Committee of Grace-New Haven Hospital; Member of the Council on Hospital Auxiliaries of the Connecticut Hospital Association.

Henry H. Pierce, Jr. Executive Vice President, Union and New Haven Trust Company

Current Memberships: Member, Clinton Board of Education; Vestryman and Warden, Clinton Episcopal Church; Member, Board of Directors, New Haven Citizens' Action Commission; Member, Board of Directors, United Fund of Greater New Haven; Member, Board of Directors, Clinton National Bank;

Source: City of New Haven, Press Release, April 12, 1962.

[a]Memberships as of the date of appointment.

151

Member, Board of Directors, New Haven Savings Bank; Chairman, Mayor's Downtown Landscaping Committee.

Reuben A. Holden. Secretary of Yale University

Current Memberships: Member, Board of Directors, New Haven Y.M.C.A.; Member, Board of Directors, Quinnipiac Council of the Boy Scouts; Member, Board of Directors, Grace-Haven Community Hospital; Member, New Haven Redevelopment Agency; Member, Board of Managers, Jane Coffin Childs Memorial Fund for Medical Research; Trustee, Hopkins Grammar School; Trustee, The Asheville School; Trustee, The Connecticut Savings Bank; Trustee, Yale-in-China Association.

Mrs. Fenmore Seton. Secretary of the Seton Name Plate Co. Incorporated

Current Memberships: Member, New Haven Board of Education; Member, New Haven Citizens' Action Commission; Member, New Haven Citizens' Action Commission Committee on Education; Member, Executive Board, Englewood School P.T.A.

Dr. Edwin R. Edmonds. Minister, Dixwell Congregational Church

Current Memberships: Member, Human Relations Council; Member, Mayor's Advisory Committee on Housing; Member, Board of the Red Cross; Member, Board of the NAACP; Member, Steering Committee for the Formation of the Urban League.

Philip Paolella. President, Plasticrete Corporation

Current Memberships: Director, The New Haven Foundation; Director, Second National Bank and Trust; Director, New Haven Savings Bank; Director, Quinnipiac Council of the Boy Scouts; Director, New Haven Boys' Club; Member, Blessed Martin Center Advisory Board; Member, Sacred Heart Academy Advisory Board; New Haven Citizens' Action Commission: Member, Board of Directors; Member, Finance Committee; Vice President.

James Wayne Cooper. Partner, Gumbart, Corbin, Tyler and Cooper

Current Memberships: Secretary, Greist Manufacturing Co. of New Haven; Secretary and Director, Whitney Blake Company; Director, Second National Bank; Secretary, New Haven Foundation; Counsel, Ann Fuller Fund.

Notes

Chapter 1

1. To date, only one book has been published that deals exclusively with New Haven's anti-poverty project, namely, Gregory Farrell's *A Climate of Change* (Brunswick, New Jersey: Rutgers University Press, 1965). Farrell, a newspaper reporter from Trenton, New Jersey, compiled a brief, popular account of the project that agency officials used to help publicize the project and its programs. In addition to Farrell's book there have been numerous references to the New Haven project in other books, in magazine, journal, and newspaper articles. These are noted in the bibliography.

2. Nelson W. Polsby, *Community Power and Political Theory* (New Haven: Yale University Press, 1963), p. 134. See also James Q. Wilson, "Innovation in Organization: Notes Toward a Theory," paper prepared for delivery at the Annual Meeting of the American Political Science Association, New York, New York, September 3-6, 1963. Jack L. Walker, "A Critique of the Elitist Theory of Democracy," *The American Political Science Review* 60, No. 2 (June, 1966), pp. 285-295.

3. Wallace Sayre and Herbert Kaufman, *Governing New York City: Politics in the Metropolis* (New York: Russell Sage Foundation, 1960), p. 717.

4. Niccolo Machiavelli, *The Prince and the Discourses*, Modern Library Edition (New York: Random House, 1940), pp. 21-22.

5. For an extended discussion of these constraints on innovation see, among others: Anthony Downs, *Inside Bureaucracy* (Boston: Little, Brown and Company, 1967); James March and Herbert Simon, *Organizations* (New York: John Wiley and Sons, 1961); James M. Buchanan and Gordon Tulloch, *The Calculus of Consent* (Ann Arbor: The University of Michigan Press, 1962); and Charles Lindblom and David Braybrooke, *A Strategy of Decision: Policy Evaluation as a Social Process* (New York: The Free Press of Glencoe, A Division of the Macmillan Co., 1963).

6. Wallace Sayre and Herbert Kaufman, op. cit., p. 719.

7. James March and Herbert Simon, op. cit., pp. 172-199.

8. Robert Dahl, *Who Governs? Democracy and Power in an American City* (New Haven: Yale University Press, 1961); Nelson W. Polsby, op. cit.; Raymond Wolfinger, *The Politics of Progress* (Englewood Cliffs, New Jersey: Prentice-Hall, Inc., forthcoming).

9. Nelson W. Polsby, op. cit., p. 117.

10. H. Douglas Price, review of *Who Governs?* by Robert Dahl, *Yale Law Journal* 71 (1962), p. 1593.

11. Decisions in three general issue areas were examined in these studies: (1) political nominations (1941-1957); (2) public schools (1950-1959); and (3) redevelopment (1950-1959). For a list of the individual decisions and the

methods employed for selecting them, see Robert Dahl, op. cit., pp. 332-337 and Nelson Polsby, op. cit., pp. 95-97.

12. The observation is attributed to Norton Long by James Q. Wilson in his "Problems in the Study of Urban Politics," paper prepared for a Conference in Commemoration of the 50th Anniversary of the Department of Government, Indiana University (Bloomington, Indiana, November 5-7, 1964), p. 9.

13. V.O. Key, *Public Opinion and American Democracy* (New York: Alfred A. Knopf, 1963), p. 536.

14. William L. Miller, *The Fifteenth Ward and the Great Society* (Boston: Houghton Mifflin Company, 1966). At the time of his writing, Miller was a professor of social ethics at the Yale University Divinity School and a former city alderman from New Haven's fifteenth ward.

15. Allan Talbot, *The Mayor's Game: Richard Lee of New Haven and the Politics of Change* (New York: Harper and Row Publishers, 1967). Talbot is a former administrative assistant to New Haven's Mayor Lee.

Chapter 2

1. City of New Haven, Press Release (New Haven, April 12, 1962).

2. League of Women Voters of New Haven, *New Haven, A Handbook of Local Government* (New Haven: League of Women Voters, 1963), p. 2.

3. City of New Haven, New Haven Board of Finance, *Budget of the City of New Haven: General Fund, Bond Fund, Capital Budget* (New Haven, October 1965), p. III and p. D.1.

4. Community Progress, Inc., "Categorical State Aid to Education," New Haven, January, 1965, pp. 8-9 (mimeographed).

5. Community Progress, Inc., *New Haven Youth Development Program*, Part 1 ("The Setting"), Chapter I, "The New Haven Community" (New Haven: Community Progress, Inc., 1963), pp. 6-7. The trend has continued throughout the 1960s. According to U.S. Census figures, the proportion of blacks in New Haven had risen to 22.3 percent by 1967. U.S. Bureau of the Census, *Current Population Reports*, Series P-28, No. 1476, "Negro Population of Selected Areas of the United States in Which Special Censuses Have Been Taken January 1, 1965, to June 30, 1968" (Washington: U.S. Government Printing Office, December 6, 1968).

6. Yale University, Political Science Research Library, *New Haven Community Study, Survey No. 2, 1959*. This survey was conducted for Robert Dahl's study of New Haven. While the data suggest that the problems of poverty were not uppermost in the minds of city residents, they are ambiguous. It is unclear, for example, whether redevelopment symbolized and summarized all the problems of the slums, including those mentioned in the text, or whether it signified only the physical decline of the city.

7. For a critical appraisal of the response of private health and welfare agencies to the changing conditions in New Haven's inner-city neighborhoods, see Paul F. Nagel, "What is the Place of Social Welfare in the Kind of Community We Want?," paper read before the meeting of the Pinewoods Institute, Plymouth, Massachusetts, July 26, 1963. Frank W. Harris, "Let's Fish or Cut Bait," paper read before the meeting of the Pinewoods Institute, Plymouth, Massachusetts, July 26, 1963. Nagel was the executive director of the United Fund and Community Council of New Haven; Harris the executive director of the Community Council of Greater New Haven, Inc.

8. Robert Dahl, *Who Governs?*, pp. 115-140. For the mayor's own account of his reaction to this early encounters with poverty in the Oak Street neighborhood, see ibid., p. 120.

9. Paul F. Nagel, op. cit. and Frank W. Harris, op. cit. To be sure, there were occasional departures from established methods, but these are noteworthy principally for their uniqueness. All of them were limited in terms of resources and clientele, including the two most notable ones, an after-hours school program instituted by Isadore Wexler, principal of the predominantly black Winchester Elementary School, and a social services program instituted in one of the city's public housing projects, Farnham Courts. For an account of Wexler's activities, see Lester Velie, "Stepping Stones from the Slums," *Readers Digest* (October, 1963), pp. 175-180. The Farnham Courts project is discussed in Ludwig Geismar and Jane Krisberg, *The Forgotten Neighborhood: Site of an Early Skirmish in the War on Poverty* (Metuchen, New Jersey: The Scarecrow Press, 1967).

10. For a convincing and moving description of Oak Street's history see Raymond Wolfinger, *The Politics of Progress*, Chapter VII, pp. 1-5.

11. Ibid., Chapter VII, p. 3.

12. Letter, Hallman Files.

13. Memorandum, Hallman Files.

14. Letter, Hallman Files.

15. Memorandum, Hallman Files.

16. Memorandum, Hallman Files.

17. "Prospectus for a Problem Family Study in New Haven, Conn.," June 5, 1959, p. 3 (mimeographed).

18. Memorandum, Hallman Files.

19. Memorandum, Hallman Files.

20. Memorandum, Hallman Files.

21. Paul F. Nagel, op. cit., p. 3.

22. Letter, Hallman Files.

23. "A Program for Community Improvement in New Haven," January, 1960 (mimeographed).

24. Ford Foundation, "Urban and Regional Program Grants, 1955 through February 28, 1961" (mimeographed).

25. Dwight Macdonald, *The Ford Foundation: The Men and the Millions* (New York: Reynal and Company, 1956).

26. For example, Allan Talbot in his book *The Mayor's Game* mentions Hallman only in passing. Not unexpectedly, Talbot, a former administrative assistant to the mayor, stresses Lee's role, though he does so in highly measured terms.

27. Interview, Mitchell Sviridoff. Sviridoff repeated his remarks publicly at a February, 1965, staff party honoring Hallman, who had resigned from the agency.

28. Howard Hallman, Letter to Isadore Wexler, December 6, 1960.

29. Minutes of Meeting of Special Group organized to discuss a "Program for Human Development in New Haven," New Haven, February 23, 1961 (mimeographed).

30. "A Program for Educational Improvement and Human Development," New Haven, June, 1961, pp. 17-18 (mimeographed).

31. "A Comprehensive Program for New Haven's Gray Areas," New Haven, October, 1961 (mimeographed).

32. Howard Hallman, Memorandum to the Files, November 20, 1961 (typewritten).

33. Howard Hallman, Memorandum to Thomas Appleby, Frank Harris, and Harold Grabino, December 8, 1961 (typewritten).

34. Memorandum, Hallman Files.

35. Floyd Hunter, *Community Power Structure* (Chapel Hill: University of North Carolina Press, 1953).

36. This is the impression one obtains from Allan Talbot, op. cit.; from Gregory Farrell, *A Climate of Change*; as well as from documents made public by the anti-poverty agency itself. See, for example, Community Progress, Inc., *Community Action Program Review* (New Haven: Community Progress, Inc., 1965) and Community Progress, Inc., *The Human Story* (New Haven: Community Progress, Inc., 1966).

37. Allan Talbot, op. cit., pp. 148-149.

38. Ibid., p. 176.

39. Ibid., p. 126.

40. Interview, Frank Harris.

41. Most of the participants in this conference were individuals who had either worked with Hallman in the small group I described earlier, or who had been contacted by him during the planning period. The participants are listed in "Conference on New Haven's Comprehensive Program for the Gray Area, January 9 and 10, 1962" (mimeographed).

42. Robert Dahl, op. cit., p. 62.

Chapter 3

1. City of New Haven, Press Release, April 12, 1962.

2. U.S. Internal Revenue Code, Section 501 (c) (3).

3. Herbert Simon, Donald Smithburg, and Victor Thompson, *Public Administration* (New York: Alfred A. Knopf, Inc., 1952), p. 44.

4. *The New Haven Register*, January 20, 1965.

5. Memorandum, Hallman File, January 24, 1962.

6. Herbert Kaufman, *Politics and Policies in State and Local Governments* (Englewood Cliffs, New Jersey: Prentice-Hall, 1963), pp. 33-64.

7. In fact, the suggestion appears in the earliest draft proposal. See "A Program for Community Improvement in New Haven," New Haven, January, 1960, p. 6.

8. Robert Dahl, *Who Governs?*, pp. 130-137.

9. Memorandum, Hallman File, January 25, 1962.

10. Memorandum, Hallman File, January 24, 1962.

11. Raymond Wolfinger, *The Politics of Progress*, Chapter VI, p. 2.

12. Memorandum, Hallman File, January 24, 1962.

13. Ibid.

14. Ibid.

15. "A Program for Community Improvement in New Haven," New Haven, January, 1960, p. 6.

16. Memorandum, Hallman Files, January 24, 1962.

17. City of New Haven, Press Release, April 12, 1962.

18. Community Progress, Inc., Minutes of the Meeting of the Board of Directors, April 16, 1962.

19. Herbert Kaufman, op. cit., p. 93.

20. For a discussion of the political implications of "localism" and "professionalism" in administrative agencies, see, among others, E.E. Schattschneider, *Political Parties* (New York: Holt, Rinehart and Winston, 1942), Chapter VI, pp. 129-158 especially; James E. Fesler, "The Political Role of Field Administration," in *Papers in Comparative Public Administration*, Ferrel Heady and Sibyl L. Stokes (eds.) (Ann Arbor: Institute of Public Administration, University of Michigan, 1962), pp. 117-143; Herbert Simon, Donald Smithburg, and Victor Thompson, op. cit., pp. 40-41; 116-117.

21. Richard Goodwin, "Reflections on Vietnam," *The New Yorker Magazine* (April 16, 1966), p. 103.

22. Community Progress, Inc., *1964 Program Report* (New Haven: Community Progress, Inc., Spring, 1964).

23. E.E. Schattschneider, *The Semisovereign People* (New York: Holt, Rinehart and Winston, 1960), p. 15.

24. U.S. Public Law 88-452, Section 202 (a) (3).

25. *The New York Times*, November 9, 1965.

26. Community Progress, Inc., *The Human Story* (New Haven: Community Progress, Inc., 1966), p. 7.

27. Community Progress, Inc., *The Human Story* (New Haven: Community Progress, Inc., 1966), p. 7.

28. Hill Neighborhood Union, "Complaint to the Office of Economic Opportunity Regarding the Failure of Community Progress, Inc. to Comply with the Requirements of the Economic Opportunity Act and the Community Action Progress Guide," New Haven, July 23, 1965.

29. Ibid., p. 1.

30. Howard Hallman, "Planning with the Poor," New Haven, 1965, p. 6 (mimeographed).

31. Ibid., p. 8.

32. For a discussion of the "new left" in New Haven, see Edward Jasek, "The New Left in New Haven," *The New Haven Register*, January 1, 1966. My own observations are based on this article as well as on conversations with individuals associated with the "new left" in New Haven and elsewhere.

33. This interpretation of "maximum feasible participation" was outlined in a report submitted by the agency to the federal Office of Economic Opportunity. Community Progress, Inc., "Special Report: Involvement of the Poor in New Haven's Community Action Program," New Haven, 1965.

34. Federal officials themselves were not all of one mind on this question. Joseph Loftus (*The New York Times* November 5, 1965) reported that officials in the Bureau of the Budget interpreted the "maximum feasible participation" requirement as referring to jobs at the operating level in local anti-poverty projects, an interpretation, we have just seen, that New Haven officials had advanced.

35. William Buchanan and Gordon Tulloch, *The Calculus of Consent: The Logical Foundations of Constitutional Democracy* (Ann Arbor: Ann Arbor Paperbacks, The University of Michigan Press, 1965), pp. 68-84 especially.

Chapter 4

1. Mitchell Sviridoff, "CPI: Window Dressing or a Program with a Meaning," Remarks to the Dixwell Renewal Forum, New Haven, November 12, 1963, p. 1 (mimeographed). The following account of New Haven's anti-poverty project summarizes the major themes in a number of agency documents, especially those documents prepared in connection with the agency's grant applications to the Ford Foundation and various federal agencies. These applications are listed in the bibliography. References on specific themes are presented in the relevant footnotes.

2. For a discussion and analysis of recently proposed redistributive public policies, see Christopher Green, *Negative Taxes and the Poverty Problem* (Washington: The Brookings Institution, 1967).

3. Community Progress, Inc., "Community Action Summary," New Haven, December 1, 1965 (mimeographed).

4. Community Progress, Inc., *Opening Opportunities* (New Haven: Community Progress, Inc., 1962), p. 7.

5. Community Progress, Inc., *The Human Story* (New Haven, Community Progress, Inc., 1966), p. 27.

6. Samuel Lubell, *The Future of American Politics* (New York: Doubleday and Company, 1956), p. 65.

7. Community Progress, Inc., *Opening Opportunities* (New Haven: Community Progress, Inc., 1962), p. 5.

8. Ibid., p. 5.

9. Ibid., p. 5.

10. Community Progress, Inc., *New Haven Youth Development Program*, Part 2 ("Programs"), Chapter IV, "Rationale" (New Haven: Community Progress, Inc., 1963), pp. 2-4.

11. Community Progress, Inc., *New Haven Youth Development Program*, Part 1 ("The Setting"), Chapter II, "The Inner City," pp. 1-21, passim.

12. Oscar Handlin, *The Uprooted: The Epic Story of the Great Migrations that Made the American People* (Boston: Little, Brown and Company, 1951).

13. Franklin Frazier, *Black Bourgeoisie* (New York: The Free Press of Glencoe, 1965).

14. Franklin Frazier, *The Negro Family in the United States* (New York: The Dryden Press, 1948). The Moynihan Report and the political reaction it occasioned are discussed in Lee Rainwater and William Yancy, *The Moynihan Report and the Politics of Controversy* (Cambridge: MIT Press, 1967).

15. Morton and Lucia White, *The Intellectual Versus the City* (Cambridge: MIT Press, 1962). For a recent statement about social disorganization in the slums and the public policy implications of this disorganization, see The President's Commission on Law Enforcement and the Administration of Justice, *The Challenge of Crime in a Free Society* (Washington: U.S. Government Printing Office, 1967), p. 6.

16. For a contemporary defense of small neighborhood communities see Jane Jacobs, *The Death and Life of Great American Cities*, 1st ed. (New York: Alfred A. Knopf, Inc. and Random House, Inc., Vintage Books, 1963).

Chapter 5

1. These figures were compiled from data in the following sources: (a) Community Progress, Inc., *1965 Community Action Program Review* (New

160

Haven: Community Progress, Inc., 1965); (b) Community Progress, Inc., *The Human Story* (New Haven: Community Progress, Inc., 1966); (c) Community Progress, Inc., "1965 Annual Report to the Ford Foundation: Financial Supplement," New Haven, 1965; and (d) Community Progress, Inc., "Community Action Summary," New Haven, 1965.

2. U.S. Public Law 87-274.

3. U.S. Public Law 87-145.

4. U.S. Public Law 88-452.

5. U.S. Public Law 81-171.

6. The Council of Economic Advisors, *The Annual Report of the Council of Economic Advisors* (Washington: Government Printing Office, 1964).

7. Ibid.

8. Michael Harrington, *The Other America* (Penguin Books, Inc.; Baltimore, Maryland, 1963), p. 26.

9. Paul N. Ylvisaker, "The Approach of the Ford Foundation to the Problems of American Cities," Address to the 29th Annual Conference of the National Association of Housing and Redevelopment Officials, Seattle, Washington, October 1, 1963.

10. Aaron Wildavsky, *The Politics of the Budgetary Process* (Boston: Little, Brown, and Company, Inc., 1964). Richard Fenno, *The Power of the Purse: Appropriations Politics in Congress* (Boston: Little, Brown, and Company, Inc., 1966).

11. Allan Talbot, *The Mayor's Game*, pp. 150-161, passim.

12. "A Program for New Haven's Grey Areas," New Haven, October 27, 1961, p. 24 (mimeographed).

13. "A Program for Educational Improvement and Human Development in New Haven," New Haven, June, 1961, p. iv (mimeographed).

14. Community Progress, Inc., *New Haven Youth Development Program*, Part 1 ("The Setting"), Chapter I, "The New Haven Community." (New Haven: Community Progress, Inc., 1963), p. 1.

15. Ibid., p. iii.

16. Ibid., pp. 1-5.

17. Ibid., p. 12.

18. Community Progress, Inc., "Second Annual Report to the Ford Foundation," New Haven, 1964, p. 5 (mimeographed and bound).

19. Ibid., pp. 1-5. As classified by the agency, pre-kindergarten, neighborhood employment centers, and work crews constituted three separate programs. Besides these three there were twenty-seven other programs, some operating at more than one location in the city.

20. Ibid., p. 5. While New Haven was advancing with its project, another Ford Foundation Grey Area Project, the Philadelphia Council for Community Advancement, was coming to an unhappy end. See Warren Eisenberg, "Bungle in

the Jungle," *Greater Philadelphia Magazine* (December, 1964), p. 39 ff. However unfortunate this failure for Philadelphia, it made the achievements of the New Haven staff appear all the more dramatic and significant.

21. Edward P. Morgan, "Edward P. Morgan and the News," News broadcast, The American Broadcasting System, March 17, 1964.

22. Willard Wirtz, Letter to Mitchell Sviridoff, February 27, 1964.

23. U.S. House of Representatives, Subcommittee on the War on Poverty Program, *Hearings on the 1966 Amendments to the Economic Opportunity Act of 1964*, Part 1 (89th Cong., 2nd Session, 1966), p. 263.

24. Community Progress, Inc., 1965 Community Action Program Review (New Haven: Community Progress, Inc., 1965), p. 86.

25. Ibid., pp. 86-89, passim.

26. Ibid., p. 89.

27. Community Progress, Inc., *The Human Story* (New Haven: Community Progress, Inc., 1966), p. 97.

28. *The New York Times*, June 14, 1966.

29. Community Progress, Inc., *1965 Community Action Program Review* (New Haven: Community Progress, Inc., 1965), p. 87. Community Progress, Inc., *The Human Story* (New Haven: Community Progress, Inc., 1966), p. 97.

30. Community Progress, Inc., *The Human Story* (New Haven: Community Progress, Inc., 1966), p. 97.

31. U.S. Office of Economic Opportunity, *Community Action Program Guide*, Vol. 1 (Washington: Government Printing Office, 1965), p. 17.

32. U.S. House of Representatives, Subcommittee on the War on Poverty Program, *Hearings on the 1966 Amendments to the Economic Opportunity Act of 1964*, Part I (89th Cong., 2nd Session, 1966), p. 164.

33. *The New York Times*, June 6, 1966. The study was conducted under the auspices of the Institute of Public Administration. See: Institute of Public Administration, *Developing New York City's Human Resources: Report of a Study Group of the Institute of Public Administration to Mayor John Lindsay* (New York: Institute of Public Administration, June, 1966). In addition to his publicized efforts on behalf of Mayor Lindsay, Sviridoff was often called upon to assist discreetly in evaluating local projects. In the early fall of 1965, for example, he made a quiet trip to Los Angeles at the request of the federal Office of Economic Opportunity to examine and report on conditions in that city in the aftermath of the summer riots. Prior to this Sviridoff, along with his deputy Howard Hallman, had worked with the President's Task Force on Poverty that had helped draft the Economic Opportunity Act.

34. Among them Thomas Seessel, New Jersey State Department of Community Affairs, a department headed by Dr. Paul Ylvisaker, the former director of the Ford Foundation's Public Affairs Division; Arthur Solomon, United Planning Organization, Washington, D.C.; Lawrence Shobe, Community Action

for Greater Middlesex County, Middlesex County, Connecticut; and Bernard Shiffman, Human Resources Commission, New York City.

35. Community Progress, Inc., "A Proposal to Establish a Regional Staff Development Institute for Community Action Programs," New Haven, January 11, 1965, p. 1.

36. Ibid., See also Community Progress, Inc., *The Human Story* (New Haven: Community Progress, Inc., 1966), pp. 93-94.

37. Community Progress, Inc., *Community Progress*, Vol. 4, No. 3 (May-June, 1967) and Vol. 5, No. 1 (February-March, 1968).

38. National Association for Community Development, Articles of Incorporation Washington, D.C., March 10, 1965.

39. Summary Minutes of Conference of Economic Opportunity Program Directors, Washington, D.C., October 26, 1964.

40. Congressional Quarterly Service, *Congress and the Nation* (Washington: Congressional Quarterly Service, 1965), pp. 762-767, passim.

41. Community Progress, Inc., "Proposal for an Out-of-State Work Program," New Haven, March 17, 1965, p. 1. In true bureaucratic fashion, one New Haven staff member quickly dubbed the proposal SWEAT, an acronym for Social Work Experiment in Agricultural Training.

42. Ibid., pp. 5-12, passim.

Chapter 6

1. U.S. Public Law 87-415. Under this Act the secretary of labor (Office of Manpower Automation and Training) was authorized to fund in full local demonstration projects. Between 1962 and 1965 New Haven received some $2.2 million under this Act. See: Community Progress, Inc., "1965 Annual Report to the Ford Foundation: Financial Supplement," New Haven, 1965 (mimeographed).

2. U.S. Public Law 87-274.

3. U.S. Public Law 88-452. Title I of this Act authorized the funding in full of "work training programs," including the neighborhood youth corps. In 1965 New Haven received Title I grants amounting to $443,000. See: Community Progress, Inc., "1965 Annual Report to the Ford Foundation: Financial Supplement," New Haven, 1965 (mimeographed).

4. Ibid.

5. Community Progress, Inc., *New Haven Youth Development Program*, Part 4 ("'Administration and Budget"), Chapter XII, "Budget" (New Haven: Community Progress, Inc., 1963), p. 5.

6. U.S. Public Law 88-452, Sec. 208(a). The originally scheduled rise in the cost of federal funds was later modified. As amended in 1967, the Economic

Opportunity Act set local costs at 20 percent, as opposed to the original 10 percent and the projected 50 percent. Congressional Quarterly Service, *Congressional Quarterly Weekly Service*, Vol. XXV, No. 50 (Washington: Congressional Quarterly Service, December 15, 1967), p. 2584.

7. State of Connecticut, "An Act Concerning State Aid for Disadvantaged Children," Bill no. 242, Sec. (1), Connecticut General Assembly, Special January Session, 1965.

8. State of Connecticut, Public Act 523, Connecticut General Assembly, Special January Session, 1965.

9. Ibid., Sec. (2).

10. Sviridoff began organizing support for the legislation a year earlier. In a "Memo on Aid for Special School Programs for Towns and Cities Which Have Large Concentrations of Poverty Population," dated March 12, 1964, he outlined his recommendations and urged the formation of a special committee "consisting of representatives of boards of education from around the state, as well as superintendents, mayors and other lay leaders interested in the advancement of education as well as the solution of social problems." Ibid., p. 2. Sviridoff circulated the memorandum, among others, to John Hersey of the National Citizens Committee for Public Schools, Victor Macdonald, the executive director of the Connecticut Association of Boards of Education, and Bice Clemow, editor of *Connecticut Life*. Clemow, a resident of the Hartford area, worked closely with Sviridoff throughout the year and reportedly was instrumental in mobilizing support from bankers and insurance executives in the state capital.

11. Community Progress, Inc., *Application for Community Action Grant Renewal* (New Haven: Community Progress, Inc., May 20, 1965).

12. City of New Haven, Municipal Budget, 1962-1965. The 1964 Municipal Budget, pp. C-6 and C-7, contains two entries on the city anti-poverty project: one under the budget for the Department of Parks and Recreation for $88,000, the other under the Department of Education for $67,000. The 1965 Municipal Budget, p. C-6 contains one entry under the Department of Education for $140,000. The $155,000 appropriated in 1964 was re-appropriated in 1965 for a two year total of $310,000. This $310,000 added to the $140,000 in new funds appropriated in 1965 accounts for the $450,000 reported in the text.

13. Community Progress, Inc., "1965 Annual Report to the Ford Foundation: Financial Supplement," New Haven, 1965, p. 6, Table 4.

14. Community Progress, Inc., *1965 Community Action Program Review* (New Haven: Community Progress, Inc., 1965), pp. 93-95.

15. Community Progress, Inc., "1965 Annual Report to the Ford Foundation: Financial Supplement," New Haven, 1965.

16. Ibid., p. 6, Table 4.

17. Paul P. Van Riper, *The History of the United States Civil Service* (Evanston, Illinois: Row, Peterson and Company, 1958), p. 343.

18. Congressional Quarterly Service, *Congress and The Nation, 1945-1964* (Washington: Congressional Quarterly Service, 1965), p. 1639.

Chapter 7

1. Seth Low, "An American View of Municipal Government in the United States," in James Bryce, *The American Commonwealth*, 2d ed. rev. (New York: The Macmillan Company, 1891), p. 625. Herbert Kaufman, *Politics and Policies in State and Local Government* (Englewood Cliffs, New Jersey: Prentice-Hall, Inc., 1963).

2. Robert Dahl, *Who Governs?*, p. 200.

3. Ibid., p. 200.

4. Ibid., pp. 115-119.

5. *The New Haven Register*, October 23, 1964.

6. Robert Dahl, op. cit., p. 100.

7. Nelson Polsby, *Community Power and Political Theory*, p. 76.

8. Ibid., p. 77.

9. The implications of decentralization within the New Haven school system are discussed in several reports issued in the early 1960s, among them: A.D. Little, Inc., *The Administrative Organization of the School System in New Haven, Conn.* (New Haven, August, 1961); New Haven Department of Education, *Blueprint for Better Education* (New Haven, 1961); New Haven Board of Education, *Proposals for Promoting Equality of Educational Opportunity and Dealing with the Problems of Racial Imbalance* (New Haven, 1964).

10. Community Council of Greater New Haven, Inc., *Directory of Community Resources for Health, Welfare and Recreation* (New Haven: Community Council of Greater New Haven, Inc., 1962), p. 1.

11. Community Progress, Inc., *New Haven Youth Development Program*, Part 2 ("Programs"), Chapter VIIIB, "Family Welfare" (New Haven: Community Progress, Inc., 1963).

12. For an analysis of this inter-agency cooperation, see United Community Funds and Councils of America, Inc., *Inter-agency Communication in New Haven, Connecticut* (New York: United Community Funds and Councils of America, Inc., 1958).

13. For criticisms (by Council members) of the private health and welfare agencies' response, or lack of response, to the changing conditions in New Haven, see Frank Harris, "Let's Fish or Cut Bait," and Paul Nagel, "What is the Place of Social Welfare in the Kind of Community We Want?"

14. Robert Michels, *Political Parties* (New York: Collier Publishing Company, 1962), pp. 61-62.

15. Wallace Sayre and Herbert Kaufman, *Governing New York City*, p. 446.

16. Community Progress, Inc., *New Haven Youth Development Program*, Part 2 ("Programs"), Chapter V, "Education" (New Haven: Community Progress, Inc., 1963).

17. Ibid., Chapter VIII, "Leisure Times."

18. These and other facets of local agencies' activities are evaluated by anti-poverty officials in Community Progress, Inc., *New Haven Youth Development Program*, Part 2 ("Programs"), Chapters V-IX (New Haven: Community Progress, Inc., 1963).

19. Max Weber, *Essays on Sociology*, H.H. Gerth and C. Wright Mills, eds. (New York: Oxford University Press, 1958), p. 230. Seymour Martin Lipset, "Bureaucracy and Social Change," in Robert Merton, et al., *Reader in Bureaucracy* (Glencoe, Illinois: Free Press of Glencoe, 1960), p. 222, footnote 3. Marx and Lenin, according to Lipset, insisted that no reform could succeed unless existing bureaucratic institutions were destroyed and entirely new ones created.

20. Robert Dahl, op. cit., p. 309.

21. Mitchell Sviridoff, "The Strategy of Change in New Haven," Remarks before the annual meeting of the American Orthopsychiatric Association, New York City, March 18, 1965.

22. Mitchell Sviridoff, "Relationship of CPI to the Board of Education," Letter to the Editors of *The New Haven Register* and *The New Haven Journal-Courier*, February 18, 1965, p. 3.

23. Karl Popper, *The Open Society and its Enemies*, Vol. 1, *The Spell of Plato* (4th ed. rev.; London: George Routledge and Sons, Ltd., 1962), p. 165.

24. Ibid., p. 158.

25. This description of Sviridoff's reform philosophy is based on numerous conversations with him as well as on observations of his behavior and an analysis of his public addresses. A list of these addresses appears in Section 1(b) of the bibliography. See also: Community Progress, Inc., "Reflections on a Reform Movement," New Haven, 1964.

26. Community Progress, Inc., *New Haven Youth Development Program*, Part 2 ("Programs"), Chapter V, "Education" (New Haven: Community Progress, Inc., 1963), p. 27.

27. The JET program is discussed in Community Progress, Inc., *1965 Community Action Program Review* (New Haven: Community Progress, Inc., 1965), p. 40.

28. Community Progress, Inc., *1965 Community Action Program Review* (New Haven: Community Progress, Inc., 1965). Participation figures are agency estimates and may well be inflated, for example, by the inclusion of multiple contacts. In any case, the figures do not differentiate the contacts by individuals, by programs, by duration, or by quality.

29. Detailed descriptions of the "coordinated social services program" are contained in: Community Progress, Inc., *New Haven Youth Development*

Program, Part 2 ("Programs"), Chapter IX, "The Neighborhood Base" (New Haven: Community Progress, Inc., 1963); and in Community Progress, Inc., *Opening Opportunities* (New Haven: Community Progress, Inc., 1962), pp. 26-29.

30. For a detailed discussion of social organization in New Haven's inner city neighborhoods, including the problems of reaching the poor, see Community Progress, Inc., *New Haven Youth Development Program*, Part 1 ("The Setting"), Chapter II, "The Inner City" (New Haven: Community Progress, Inc., 1963). Community Progress, Inc., "Activities of the Neighborhood Services Staff, September 7, 1963 to October 31, 1964," New Haven, November 1, 1964; Community Progress, Inc., "Neighborhood Services for Wooster Square and Dixwell Neighborhoods," New Haven, August 15, 1963.

31. Community Progress, Inc., "First Annual Report and Program Review for the Ford Foundation, 1962-1963," Chapter V, New Haven, 1963, p. 5-7. In addition to the mayor, committee members included the manager of the New Haven Office of the Connecticut State Employment Service, the New Haven superintendent of schools, the president of the New Haven Central Labor Council, the president of the New Haven Chamber of Commerce, the executive director of Community Progress, Inc., the director of field services of the State Department of Education, and the director of manpower programs, Community Progress, Inc., who served as secretary for the committee.

32. Community Progress, Inc., *1965 Community Action Program Review* (New Haven: Community Progress, Inc., 1965), pp. 14-21.

33. Community Progress, Inc., "Report on the Relationship between Community Progress, Inc. and the State Division of Vocational Education," New Haven, 1965 (typewritten).

34. Community Progress, Inc., Manpower Division, "General Information Memorandum," January 25, 1963.

35. These programs are detailed in the following grant applications to the Office of Manpower, Automation and Training: Community Progress, Inc., *Special Training Project for New Haven, Conn.* (New Haven: Community Progress, Inc., February 5, 1963). Community Progress, Inc., "The Final Report of a One Year CPI-OMAT Contract Dated January 29, 1963," New Haven, February, 1964. Community Progress, Inc., *CPI II* (New Haven: Community Progress, Inc., July 27, 1964). Community Progress, Inc., *CPI III* (New Haven: Community Progress, Inc., 1964). Community Progress, Inc., *Proposal for an Extension of the OMAT-CPI Demonstration Employment Programs in New Haven, Connecticut* (New Haven: Community Progress, Inc., May, 1965).

36. Community Progress, Inc., *1965 Community Action Program Review* (New Haven: Community Progress, Inc., 1965), p. 17.

37. General Service Administration, *U.S. Government Organization Manual, 1962-1963* (Washington: Government Printing Office, 1962), pp. 306-307.

38. Edward T. Chase, "The Job-Finding Machine: How to Crank It Up," *Harper's Magazine* (July, 1964), pp. 31-36. Jonathan Spivak, "Manpower Morass," *The Wall Street Journal*, July 13, 1967.

167

39. Jonathan Spivak, op. cit.

40. Mrs. Mary Dewey, director, Connecticut State Employment Service, Memorandum to manager, State Employment Service District Office, New Haven, April 9, 1964.

41. Mrs. Mary Dewey, Letter to Seymour Wolfbein, U.S. Office of Manpower, Automation and Training, April 23, 1964.

42. Mitchell Sviridoff, Letter to Richard Boone, acting director, Community Action Programs, U.S. Office of Economic Opportunity, January 21, 1965.

43. *The New Haven Register*, December 10, 1964.

44. Richard O. Brooks, "History of the Development of the Legal Services Program by Community Progress, Inc., of New Haven Connecticut," New Haven, undated (circa January, 1965).

45. Ibid., p. 4.

46. Ibid., pp. 4-5.

47. Community Progress, Inc., "Legal Services Program," New Haven, January 24, 1964. For a discussion of the New Haven program and its contribution to the national effort to provide legal services to the poor, see *The Wall Street Journal*, September 13, 1965.

48. *The New Haven Register*, November 27, 1964.

49. Ibid., October 16, 1964.

50. *The New Haven Register*, March 16, 1965.

51. Arthur J. Goldberg, Address at the Official Opening of the Neighborhood Law Offices of the New Haven Legal Assistance Association, New Haven, May 1, 1965. See also, Arthur J. Goldberg, "Equal Justice for the Poor, Too." *The New York Times Magazine*, March 15, 1964. Goldberg's endorsement had a twofold significance. In addition to being an associate justice of the U.S. Supreme Court, Goldberg was Jewish, and according to the staff analysis, Jewish lawyers, who constituted the single largest ethnic group present at the bar association's meeting, were also the most opposed to the proposal. Sixty-seven percent of the Jewish lawyers (N=103) voted in opposition. "Analysis of the New Haven County Bar Association's Vote on the Legal Services Program sponsored by the Legal Assistance Association, Inc." (New Haven, March 20, 1965) (mimeographed), p. 6, Table IV. Of course, Justice Goldberg was not invited because of his ethnic background. But in a community (and in a state) where ethnic identities are highly salient politically, the justice's ethnic background was an added bonus to the supporters of the association.

52. The negative consequences of decentralization for innovation are discussed in Jack Walker, "A Critique of the Elitist Theory of Democracy," *The American Political Science Review* 60, No. 2 (June, 1966), pp. 285-295. Discussions of its implications for city government specifically are contained in Wallace Sayre and Herbert Kaufman, op. cit., p. 717; Daniel R. Grant, "Urban and Suburban Nashville," *Journal of Politics* 17 (February, 1955), pp. 82-99. For early commentaries on the structure of municipal government and the dysfunctions that flow(ed) from the widespread distribution of power, see among others Frank Goodnow, *City Government in the United States* (New

York: The Century Co., 1906), p. 80; W.B. Munro, *Principles and Methods of Municipal Administration* (New York: The Macmillan Co., 1915).

Chapter 8

1. The observations are based on staff interviews and on minutes of various meetings held to plan the project. The fears of Ford Foundation staff members are recorded in: "Minutes of meeting of Ford Foundation staff and New Haven officials," January 10, 1962 (handwritten). The objection that the project would attract more poor to the city is reported in: "Minutes of meeting held February 23, 1961, at the New Haven Redevelopment Offices to discuss a 'Program for Human Development in New Haven,' " February 23, 1961 (mimeographed), p. 4.

2. Mitchell Sviridoff, "First Annual Report of Program, Progress, Problems, and Possibilities," Address to the Annual Meeting of the Community Council of Greater New Haven, May 27, 1963 (mimeographed).

3. The importance New Haven's planners attached to names is reflected in Hallman's two-page memorandum of December 27, 1961, which he circulated among his colleagues on the Redevelopment Agency staff. The much annotated memorandum concerned the "importance of having the right name for the new, non-profit agency which will administer the Ford Program." After rejecting such names as Community Service Association (it "suggests a social work type of agency") and Community Action Program, the name Community Progress, Inc. was chosen.

4. These themes are stressed, among other places, in: Community Progress, Inc., *Opening Opportunities* (New Haven: Community Progress, Inc., 1962), pp. 1-6 especially; Mitchell Sviridoff, "CPI: Window Dressing or a Program with a Meaning?" Address before the Dixwell Renewal Forum, New Haven, Connecticut, November 12, 1963; Howard Hallman, "New Haven's Attack on Poverty," New Haven, March 3, 1964 (mimeographed).

5. The U.S. Census reported that 42.2 percent of New Haven's population (1960) was foreign born, or native of foreign or mixed parentage. United States Bureau of the Census, *County and City Data Book, 1962* (Washington, D.C.: U.S. Government Printing Office, 1962).

6. Mitchell Sviridoff, "CPI: Window Dressing or Program with Meaning?" Address before the Dixwell Renewal Forum, New Haven, Connecticut, November 12, 1963, p. 4 (mimeographed).

7. Mitchell Sviridoff, "The Urban Crisis in America," Remarks at William Hall High School, West Hartford, Connecticut, April 16, 1964, p. 6 (mimeographed).

8. Ibid., p. 5.

9. Community Progress, Inc., "Categorical State Aid to Education," New Haven, January, 1965, p. 1 (mimeographed).

10. Dated here with the outbreak of violence, July 18, 1964, in New York City's Harlem and Bedford-Stuyvesant sections.

11. Mitchell Sviridoff, "The Urban Crisis in America," Remarks at William Hall High School, West Hartford, Connecticut, April 16, 1964, p. 7 (mimeographed).

12. Community Progress, Inc., *1965 Community Action Program Review* (New Haven: Community Progress, Inc., 1965), p. 7.

13. City of New Haven, Press Release, April 12, 1962, p. 9.

14. Robert Dahl, *Who Governs?*, pp. 130-137.

15. Ibid., pp. 64, 67-69.

16. Three additional parochial schools were included later in the project, all three of them associated with predominantly ethnic parishes: St. Rose (Italian); St. Stanislaus (Polish); St. Johns (Irish).

17. Mitchell Sviridoff, "First Annual Report of Program, Progress, Problems, and Possibilities," Address to the Annual Meeting of the Community Council of Greater New Haven, May 27, 1963, p. 19 (mimeographed).

18. The evaluation design called for two major surveys (N=circa 2,000) of teenagers in New Haven, with a control group of teenagers in Bridgeport, Connecticut. The first survey, to establish baseline data for measuring change, was conducted. The second survey, to determine what changes had occurred, never materialized. Results of the first survey, have not been widely publicized or circulated. An inquiry to CPI in 1970 revealed that a report had been prepared—though agency officials did not have a copy at hand.

19. Community Progress, Inc., *1965 Community Action Program Review* (New Haven: Community Progress, Inc., 1965), p. 7.

20. Ibid., p. 21.

21. Mitchell Sviridoff, "The Strategy of Change in New Haven," Remarks before the Annual Meeting of the American Orthopsychiatric Association, New York, New York, March 18, 1965, p. 5 (mimeographed).

22. Community Progress, Inc., "Final Report on a One Year CPI-OMAT Contract Dated January 29, 1963," New Haven, 1964, p. 10 (mimeographed).

23. Ibid., p. 11.

24. Ibid., p. 10.

25. Ibid., Appendix A.

26. In most cases, the demands from neighborhood workers were limited to verbal requests that the agency change its policy. The two most notable exceptions were: (1) the neighborhood lawyer involved in an interracial rape case (see above, p. 116) and (2) a Yale undergraduate, employed as a part-time neighborhood worker in the Hill section, who helped organize a militant neighborhood organization. In both cases personal persuasion failed and Sviridoff ultimately released the staff members concerned.

27. *The New Haven Register*, January 23, 1963.

28. The most interesting of these was an editorial, "Just Too 'Dern' Poor for Poverty Money?" in which *The Register* compared poverty in Martin County, Kentucky, with poverty in New Haven, and complained that New Haven, being comparatively well-off, did not warrant receiving more federal anti-poverty funds than Martin County. *The New Haven Register*, January 23, 1965. Federal "overindulgence" of New Haven is discussed on p. 144.

29. Most editorials were primarily cautionary in tone, counselling the community to keep a watchful eye on the activities of the New Haven project and CPI. *The New Haven Journal-Courier* and *The New Haven Register*, May, 1962, to December, 1964.

30. *The New Haven Register*, January 31, 1965.

31. James S. Coleman, *Community Conflict* (Glencoe, Illinois: The Free Press of Glencoe, 1959). As Coleman notes, local controversies often begin with rather specific issues and quickly broaden into more general matters. Normally these controversies center on new issues, new organizations, and new leaders. The Better Education Committee qualifies on all these counts. Both the issue and the organization were new, and the leaders, to use Coleman's terms, "were men who had not been community leaders in the past, men who felt none of the constraints of maintaining a previous position in the community."

32. *The New Haven Register*, January 20, 1965; January 25, 1965; May 12, 1965.

33. *The Hartford Courant*, June 29, 1968. The board acted under provisions of the Economic Opportunity Act, as amended in 1967. Under pressures from Southern Democrats and some big city Northern Democrats, the original Act was amended to curtail the independence of the hitherto independent local anti-poverty agencies. The 1967 amendment, dubbed the "boss and boll-weevil" amendment by Representative Charles Goodell of New York, authorized mayors and other elected local officials to take control of local community action programs. The history of the amendment is summarized in: Joseph Loftus, "How the Poverty Bill Was Saved in the House," *The New York Times*, December 25, 1967.

34. At issue, in addition, was a bitter personal dispute between the president of the New Haven Central Labor Council, AFL-CIO, who was the labor consultant to CPI, and New Haven's congressman.

35. The agency at this time was particularly vulnerable, I was told, because Sviridoff's replacement as executive director lacked two of his predecessor's important qualifications: a full-time commitment to the agency, and a thorough working knowledge of New Haven and Connecticut politics, Sviridoff's replacement, an individual of some stature in the labor movement, was brought in from out of state and reportedly divided his time between New Haven and his previous home base.

36. The National Advisory Commission on Civil Disorders, *Report of the National Advisory Commission on Civil Disorders* (Washington, D.C.: U.S. Government Printing Office, 1968), p. 71.

37. Ibid., p. 173.

38. Ibid., p. 325.

Chapter 9

1. Robert Dahl, *Who Governs?* (New Haven: Yale University Press, 1961); Nelson W. Polsby, *Community Power and Political Theory* (New Haven: Yale University Press, 1963); Raymond Wolfinger, *The Politics of Progress* (Englewood Cliffs, New Jersey: Prentice-Hall, Inc., forthcoming).

2. This literature is sufficiently familiar and need not be cited extensively here. Arguments supporting the view that social and economic elites control local—and other—levels of government can be found in: William Domhoff, *Who Rules America?* (Englewood Cliffs, New Jersey, Prentice-Hall, Inc., 1967); Thomas J. Anton, "Power, Pluralism and Local Politics," *The Administrative Science Quarterly* (March, 1963), pp. 426-457; and in Floyd Hunter's noted earlier study, *Community Power Structure* (Chapel Hill, North Carolina, University of North Carolina Press, 1953).

3. Robert Dahl, op. cit., p. 306.

4. Over the years, the decentralization of American politics and American government (and the depressing effect of decentralization on innovation and change) has been an enduring preoccupation of urban reformers and urban critics. Variations on W.B. Munro's 1916 lament that "even the best officials when hampered ad nauseam by checks and balances could accomplish few reforms worthwhile" can still be heard today. Some of these variations are cited above in note 52 to chapter 7.

5. The phrase is borrowed from Peter B. Clark and James Q. Wilson, "Incentive Systems: A Theory of Organizations," *The Administrative Science Quarterly* 6, No. 2 (September, 1961), p. 158.

6. Robert Dahl, op. cit., p. 309.

7. For a contrasting view of poverty, see Edward Banfield's recent provocative book, *The Unheavenly City* (Boston: Little, Brown and Company, 1970).

8. Peter Bachrach and Morton Baratz, "Two Faces of Power," *The American Political Science Review* 16, No. 4 (December, 1962), p. 949. See also Jack L. Walker, "A Critique of the Elitist Theory of Democracy," *The American Political Science Review* 60, No. 2 (June, 1966), pp. 285-295. For a critical analysis of the concept of indirect power see: James L. Payne, "The Oligarchy Muddle," *World Politics* 20, No. 3 (April, 1968), pp. 439-453; and Richard Merelman, "On the Neo-Elitist Critique of Community Power," *The American Political Science Review* 62, No. 2 (June, 1968), pp. 451-460.

9. *The New York Times*, April 8, 1970.

10. Morton Grodzins, *The American System: A New View of Government in the United States*, Daniel J. Elazar, editor (Chicago: Rand McNally and Co., 1966).

11. For a criticism of the federal government's overindulgence of New Haven, see William Buckley, Jr., *The Jeweler's Eye: A Book of Irresistible Political Reflections* (New York: G.P. Putnam's Sons, G.P. Putnam's Sons—Berkeley Medallion Edition, July, 1969), pp. 113-117. As I indicated in the text, federal policy, at least in anti-poverty, constituted a highly efficient use of public funds. Indeed, given the federal government's broader policy objective of extending and expanding governmental responsibility for the poor, concentrating funds in New Haven in this way was in a sense a very American, free-enterprise approach to "creeping socialism."

12. *The New Haven Register*, January 23, 1963.

13. Martin Rein and S.M. Miller, "Social Action on the Installment Plan," *Transaction* 3, No. 2 (January/February, 1966), p. 35.

14. The National Advisory Commission on Civil Disorders, *Report of the National Advisory Commission on Civil Disorders* (Washington, D.C.: U.S. Government Printing Office, 1968), p. 149. See also Allan Talbot, "The Lessons of New Haven, Erstwhile Model City," *Psychology Today* (August, 1968), pp. 23-27; and Fred Powledge, "New Haven: Triumph and Tragedy in Model City," *Washington Monthly* 2 (February, 1970), pp. 49-62.

15. The National Advisory Commission on Civil Disorders, op. cit., p. 149.

16. Ibid., p. 149.

17. Ibid., p. 147.

18. The section of the Hill neighborhood where the disorders were most intense had been the source of earlier outspoken criticism of both CPI and the mayor. See above, chapter 3. Unfortunately, neither the commission's report, nor the *Supplemental Studies* to the report thus far published, contain much information on the characteristics of riot participants, or on those who were sympathetic or unsympathetic to these participants. Most of those arrested in connection with the disorders were black (67.4%)—a percentage, however, that was low compared to other riot cities. But there was a substantial number of whites (23.8%) and "others" (8.9%). As a result it is difficult to tell, for example, whether the disorders were "non-racial" in the sense that whites and blacks joined together in rioting, or "inter-racial" in the sense that blacks and whites confronted each other. For data on arrests, see Robert M. Fogelson and Robert B. Hill, "Who Riots? A Study of Participation in the 1967 Riots," *Supplemental Studies for the National Advisory Commission on Civil Disorders* (Washington, D.C.: U.S. Government Printing Office, 1968), p. 246, Table 3.

19. Community Progress, Inc., *The Human Story, 1967* (New Haven: Community Progress, Inc., 1967), p. 36.

20. U.S. Bureau of the Census, *Current Population Reports*, Series P-60, No. 68, "Poverty in the United States: 1959-1968," (Washington, D.C.: U.S.

Government Printing Office, 1969). The bureau's measure of poverty is a "Poverty Index" based on such factors as family size, sex of family head, the age of family members, and the place of residence. The index is adjusted annually to reflect changes in the Consumer Price Index.

21. National family income data for 1965 are reported in: U.S. Bureau of the Census, *Current Population Reports*, Series P-60, No. 63, "Consumer Income" (Washington, D.C.: U.S. Government Printing Office, September 8, 1969).

22. Modeling of the New Haven sort is a widespread but little studied phenomenon in American politics. Model city charters, administrative codes, and ordinances abound, as do model state constitutions and state legislation. Little is known about the development or influence of these models, or about the groups such as the Advisory Commission on Intergovernmental Relations that promote them. Nor is there much systematic evidence on that often forgotten but nonetheless seemingly common attribute of American federalism, applying as much to the cities as to the states, alluded to in Justice Brandeis' dictum in *New State Ice Co. v Liebman*:

It is one of the happy incidents of the federal system that a single courageous state, if its citizens choose, may serve as a laboratory; and try novel social and economic experiments without risk to the rest of the country [*New State Ice Co. v. Liebman*, 285 U.S. Reports, 311 (1931)].

23. The political appeal of CPI-style reform is suggested by the programs for national action recommended by the Kerner commission. After citing the causes of urban disorders, among them the lack of resident participation in policy-making, the commission then recommended thirty-five programs in the area of education and employment, twenty-six of which were already in force in New Haven. The National Advisory Commission on Civil Disorders, op. cit., pp. 229-265.

Bibliography

1. Sources on Community Progress, Inc.

Most of the data for this study were gathered from agency sources, among them agency files, personal interviews with agency officials, and personal observation of agency activity. In this section of the Bibliography I have listed those sources I considered most important, including the references cited in the text. Internal staff documents, such as letters, memoranda, and reports are identified by Folder and Item number in the *File on the Formative Years of Community Progress, Inc.* This File is described in subsection (j) below.

(a) Community Progress, Inc.: Published Documents

Community Progress, Inc. *1965 Community Action Program Review.* New Haven: Community Progress, Inc., 1965, p. 45.

————. *The Human Story.* New Haven: Community Progress, Inc., 1966, p. 102.

————. *Opening Opportunities.* New Haven: Community Progress, Inc., 1963, p. 60.

————. *Program Report, Spring, 1964.* New Haven: Community Progress, Inc., 1964, p. 104.

————. *Directory of Community Resources for Youth in New Haven.* New Haven: Community Progress, Inc., 1965, p. 42.

————. *Community Progress.* 1963-1968. Monthly news bulletin published by Community Progress, Inc. Volume I, No. 1, December, 1963.

(b) Community Progress, Inc.: Public Addresses by Agency Staff Members

Hallman, Howard. "Social Reform in Urban Communities." Paper prepared for presentation to the Colloquium on Juvenile Delinquency, Youth Development Training Center, Western Reserve University, Cleveland, Ohio, May 14, 1964, p. 20.

Shiffman, Bernard. "The Human Aspects of Urban Renewal." Paper presented at the Sixth Annual Workshop, Associated Community Councils of Newark, Newark, New Jersey, April 27, 1963, p. 9.

Sviridoff, Mitchell. "CPI: Window Dressing or a Program with Meaning." Remarks before the Dixwell Renewal Forum, New Haven, Connecticut, November 12, 1962, p. 13.

————. "First Annual Report of Programs, Progress, Problems and Possibilities." Remarks before the Annual Meeting of the Community Council of Greater New Haven, New Haven, Connecticut, May 27, 1963, p. 23.

_____. "The Strategy of Change in New Haven." Remarks before the Annual Meeting of the American Orthopsychiatric Association, New York, New York, March 18, 1965, p. 8.

_____. "The Manpower Problem—A View from the Bridgehead." Remarks before the meeting of Ford Project Directors, San Juan, Puerto Rico, December 14, 1964, p. 14.

_____. "Yale and New Haven." Remarks before the Annual Banquet of the Yale Broadcasting Company, New Haven, Connecticut, May 27, 1964, p. 9.

_____. Remarks before the Dixwell Renewal Forum, New Haven, Connecticut, March 16, 1965, p. 6.

_____. "The Urban Crisis in America." Remarks, William Hall High School, West Hartford, Connecticut, April 16, 1964, p. 10.

_____. Address to the American Society of Planning Officials, 29th Annual Conference, Seattle, Washington, May 8, 1963, p. 14.

_____. Remarks before the Annual Conference of High School Guidance Counselors, New Haven, Connecticut, April 15, 1964, p. 10.

_____. Comments on a paper presented by Professor Joel Seidman, Annual Conference of Industrial Relations Research Association, Chicago, Illinois, December 28, 1964, p. 5.

_____. "Relationship of CPI to the Board of Education." Letter to the Editors of _The New Haven Register_ and _The New Haven Journal-Courier_, New Haven, Connecticut, February 18, 1965, p. 8.

(c) Community Progress, Inc.: Preliminary Project Proposals, June, 1959-December, 1961

"Prospectus for a Problem Family Study in New Haven, Conn.," June 5, 1959, p. 6. CPI File, Folder A, Item 1.

"A Program for Community Improvement in New Haven," January, 1960, p. 8. CPI File, Folder B, Item 1.

"Program for Human Development in New Haven," January 31, 1961, p. 23. CPI File, Folder B, Item 2.

"Application for a Ford Foundation Grant to Carry-Out New Haven's Comprehensive Program for Community Progress," March 19, 1961, p. 29. CPI File, Folder B, Item 3.

"Program for Human Development in New Haven," April 12, 1961, p. 9. CPI File, Folder B, Item 4.

"Program for Human Development in New Haven," April 25, 1961, p. 9. CPI File, Folder B, Item 5.

"A Program for Educational Improvement and Human Development in New Haven," May, 1961, p. 14. CPI File, Folder B, Item 6.

"A Program for Educational Improvement and Human Development in New Haven," June, 1961, p. 33. CPI File, Folder B, Item 7.

"Program for Community Development," August, 1961, p. 31. CPI File, Folder B, Item 8.

"Addendum to Program for Community Development," August, 1961, p. 5. CPI File, Folder B, Item 9.

"Program for Community Development," September, 1961, p. 19. CPI File, Folder B, Item 10.

"A Comprehensive Program for New Haven's Gray Areas," October 27, 1961, p. 31. CPI File, Folder B, Item 11.

"A Comprehensive Program for New Haven's Gray Areas," November 10, 1961, p. 36. CPI File, Folder B, Item 12.

"Account to the Ford Foundation of Fiscal and Personnel Support Needed," December 11, 1961, p. 5. CPI File, Folder B, Item 13.

"Summary of a Comprehensive Program for New Haven's Gray Areas," December, 1961, p. 18. CPI File, Folder B, Item 14.

(d) Community Progress, Inc.: Grant Applications

Application for a Ford Foundation Grant to Carry-Out New Haven's Comprehensive Program for Community Progress, April 4, 1962, p. 24. CPI File, Folder C, Item 7.

Community Progress, Inc. *New Haven Youth Development Program*. 4 vols. New Haven: Community Progress, Inc., 1963, p. 301. CPI File, Folder D, Items 1-4.

———. *Special Training Project for New Haven, Conn.: Proposal Submitted to the Office of Manpower Automation and Training*. New Haven: Community Progress, Inc., February 5, 1963, p. 8. CPI File, Folder G, Item 2.

———. *A Proposal for an Extension of the OMAT-CPI Demonstration Program in New Haven, Conn.* New Haven: Community Progress, Inc., May 17, 1964, p. 34. CPI File, Folder G, Item 5.

———. *Special Manpower Project*. New Haven: Community Progress, Inc., 1964, p. 25. CPI File, Folder G, Item 4.

———. *Application for Assistance Under the Economic Opportunity Act of 1964*. New Haven: Community Progress, Inc., October 2, 1964, p. 51. CPI File, Folder I, Item 6.

———. *Application for Community Action Grant Renewal*. New Haven: Community Progress, Inc., May 20, 1965, p. 63. CPI File, Folder I, Item 7.

_____. *Proposal for an Out-of-State Work Program.* New Haven: Community Progress, Inc., March 17, 1965, p. 17. CPI File, Folder N, Item 17.

_____. *Proposal to Establish a Regional Staff Development Institute for Community Action Programs.* New Haven: Community Progress, Inc., January 11, 1965, p. 15. CPI File, Folder M, Item 3.

_____. *Skill Center.* New Haven: Community Progress, Inc., January 29, 1965, p. 17. CPI File, Folder I, Item 2.

_____. *Proposal for an Out-of-School Work Training Program.* New Haven: Community Progress, Inc., September 29, 1964, p. 24. CPI File, Folder I, Item 3.

_____. *Proposal for an In-School Work Training Program.* New Haven: Community Progress, Inc., September 28, 1964, p. 28. CPI File, Folder I, Item 4.

_____. *Job Corps Screening Agency.* New Haven: Community Progress, Inc., December 3, 1964, p. 7. CPI File, Folder I, Item 5.

_____. *CPI II.* New Haven: Community Progress, Inc., 1964. CPI File, Folder G, Item 13.

_____. *CPI III.* New Haven: Community Progress, Inc., 1964. CPI File, Folder G, Item 17.

_____. *Summer Recreation Aide Proposal for In-School Youth.* New Haven: Community Progress, Inc., February 1, 1965, p. 15. CPI File, Folder I, Item 1.

_____. *Request for Renewal of Ford Foundation Grant for Period September 1, 1965 to August 31, 1968.* New Haven: Community Progress, Inc., July 6, 1965, p. 26. CPI File, Folder Q, Item 10.

(e) Community Progress, Inc.: Internal Agency Documents and Special Staff Reports

Brooks, Richard O. "History of the Development of the Legal Services Program by Community Progress, Inc. of New Haven, Connecticut." undated (circa January, 1965), p. 29. CPI File, Folder T, Item 2.

_____. "Analysis of the New Haven County Bar Association Vote on the Legal Services Program Sponsored by the Legal Assistance Association, Inc." March 20, 1965, p. 8. CPI File, Folder T, Item 6.

Brown, Milton. "Involvement of the Poor in Community Action Programs." 1964, p. 6. CPI File, Folder S, Item 7.

Community Progress, Inc. "First Annual Program Review for the Ford Foundation." New Haven, 1963, p. 190. CPI File, Folder Q, Item 1.

———. "Second Annual Program Review for the Ford Foundation." New Haven, 1964, p. 132. CPI File, Folder Q, Item 2.

———. "1965 Annual Report to the Ford Foundation: Financial Supplement." New Haven, 1965, p. 12. CPI File, Folder Q, Item 3.

———. "New Haven Youth Development Program: First Annual Progress Report." New Haven, 1964, p. 97. CPI File, Folder D, Item 5.

———. "Reflections on a Reform Movement." Addendum to the Second Annual Report to the Ford Foundation, New Haven, 1964, p. 12. CPI File, Folder Q, Item 5.

———. "Poverty and Urban Blight in New Haven." New Haven, 1964, p. 60. CPI File, Folder I, Item 8.

———. "Final Report on a One Year CPI-OMAT Contract Dated January 29, 1963." New Haven, 1964, p. 21. CPI File, Folder G, Item 1.

———. "Neighborhood Services for Wooster Square and Dixwell Neighborhoods." New Haven, August 15, 1963, p. 50. CPI File, Solder S, Item 1.

———. "Activities of the Neighborhood Services Staff, September 7, 1963 to October 31, 1964." New Haven, November 1, 1964, p. 51. CPI File, Folder S, Item 2.

———. "Administrative and Financial Aspects of the Large Family Housing Demonstration Program." New Haven, November 1965, p. 20. CPI File, Folder S, Item 3.

———. "The Legal Services Program." New Haven, January 24, 1964, p. 17. CPI File, Folder T, Item 4.

———. "Special Report: Involvement of the Poor in New Haven's Community Action Program." New Haven, 1965, p. 4. CPI File, Folder S, Item 5.

———. "Categorical State Aid to Education." New Haven, December 1, 1964, p. 9. CPI File, Folder L, Item 1.

———. "The Manpower Function at CPI." New Haven, October 10, 1962, p. 9. CPI File, Folder G, Item 20.

———. "Resident Participation Project: An Account of the Activities in New Haven to Expand and Formalize the Participation of CAP Area Representatives in the Community Action Program." New Haven, December 1, 1965, p. 14. CPI File, Folder S, Item 6.

———. "Summary of New Haven's Application for Financial Assistance Under the *Economic Opportunity Act* of 1964." New Haven, October 6, 1964, p. 3. CPI File, Folder I, Item 9.

———. "Community Action Summary." New Haven, December 1, 1965, p. 15. CPI File, Folder I, Item 10.

———. "Community Action Programs, *Economic Opportunity Act* of 1964:

Consolidated Budget for Fiscal Year January 1, 1965-August 31, 1965." New Haven, 1965, p. 14. CPI File, Folder I, Item 11.

_____. "Annual Report of the Controller." New Haven, October 1, 1964, p. 4. CPI File, Folder J, Item 1.

_____. "Report on the Relationship Between Community Progress, Inc. and the State Division of Vocational Education." New Haven, 1965, p. 17. CPI File, Folder G, Item 21.

_____. "The Role of the State Employment Service in the Development of the Community Action Program in New Haven." New Haven, May 3, 1965, p. 9. CPI File, Folder G, Item 22.

_____. "Community Action Manpower Plan." New Haven, February 1, 1965, p. 23. CPI File, Folder G, Item 23.

Hallman, Howard. "Planning with the Poor." New Haven, 1965, p. 41. CPI File, Folder S, Item 8.

_____. "New Haven's Attack on Poverty." New Haven, March 3, 1964, p. 8. CPI File, Folder I, Item 12.

_____. "Supplement Prepared for the Annual Program Review for the Ford Foundation." New Haven, May 1, 1965, p. 26. CPI File, Folder Q, Item 6.

(f) Community Progress, Inc.: Letters and Memoranda to and from Agency Officials.

Brooks, Richard O. Memorandum. "The Need for a Neighborhood Legal Service." October 7, 1964. CPI File, Folder T, Item 1.

_____. Letter to Professor James O. Freedman, University of Pennsylvania Law School (undated). CPI File, Folder T, Item 3.

Dewey, Mary, Director of the Connecticut State Employment Service. Letter to Seymour Wolfbein, U.S. Office of Manpower Automation and Training. April 23, 1964. CPI File, Folder G, Item 23.

_____. Memorandum to Joseph Purcell, Manager, Connecticut State Employment Service District Office, New Haven, Connecticut. April 9, 1964. CPI File, Folder G, Item 24.

Dineen, Francis X. Memorandum. "The Apprehension and Detention and Interrogation of Douglas Townsend, Age 14 Years." April 3, 1963. CPI File, Folder T, Item 8.

_____. Memorandum. "The Apprehension and Detention and Interrogation of Clinton Davis, Age 13 Years." January 15, 1964. CPI File, Folder T, Item 9.

Hallman, Howard. Letter to Isadore Wexler. December 6, 1960. CPI File, Folder A, Item 59.

———. Letter to Paul Ylvisaker. March 13, 1962. CPI File, Folder A, Item 43.

———. Memorandum to Thomas Appleby. February 1, 1962. CPI File, Folder A, Item 37.

———. Memorandum to Thomas Appleby, Harold Grabino, and Frank Harris. December 8, 1961. CPI File, Folder A, Item 25.

———. Memorandum to Edward Logue. September 20, 1959. CPI File, Folder A, Item 7.

———. Memorandum to Thomas Appleby. January 24, 1962. CPI File, Folder A, Item 82.

———. Memorandum to Thomas Appleby and Lawrence Paquin. January 24, 1962. CPI File, Folder A, Item 28.

———. Memorandum to the Files. November 20, 1961. CPI File, Folder A, Item 70.

———. with Frank Harris and Francis Looney. Memorandum to Edward Logue. December 28, 1959. CPI File, Folder A, Item 15.

Harris, Frank. Memorandum to Thomas Appleby and Howard Hallman. January 25, 1962. CPI File, Folder A, Item 83.

Logue, Edward. Memorandum to Francis Looney. December 6, 1959. CPI File, Folder A, Item 58.

Looney, Francis. Letter to Max Schwartz. June 19, 1959. CPI File, Folder A, Item 3.

McDaniel, Joseph M. Jr., Secretary of the Ford Foundation. Letter to Henry J. Pierce, Jr., President, Board of Directors, Community Progress, Inc. June 13, 1962. CPI File, Folder C, Item 12.

Rezendes, Dennis. Memorandum to Howard Hallman. August 30, 1961. CPI File, Folder A, Item 68.

Sirabella, Vincent. Memorandum. "Eli Whitney Technical School." January 1, 1963. CPI File, Folder G, Item 26.

Sviridoff, Mitchell. Memorandum to Staff. "The Legal Assistance Program." October 9, 1964. CPI File, Folder T, Item 10.

———. Memorandum. "Aid for Special School Programs for Cities Which Have Large Concentrations of Poverty Population." March 12, 1964. CPI File, Folder L, Item 2.

———. Letter to Richard Boone, Acting Director, Community Action Programs, U.S. Office of Economic Opportunity. January 21, 1965. CPI File, Folder G, Item 27.

Wirtz, Willard. Letter to Mitchell Sviridoff. February 27, 1964. CPI File, Folder G, Item 28.

(g) Community Progress, Inc.: Minutes of Meetings

Minutes of meeting of planning group assembled by Howard Hallman to discuss "A Program for Human Improvement in New Haven, Connecticut." January 5, 1961. CPI File, Folder A, Item 19.

Minutes of meeting of planning group assembled by Howard Hallman to discuss "A Program for Human Development in New Haven, Connecticut." February 23, 1961. CPI File, Folder A, Item 20.

Minutes of meeting held at the New Haven Redevelopment Agency to discuss "A Program for Community Development." August 24, 1961. CPI File, Folder A, Item 21.

Minutes of meeting with Ford Foundation staff to discuss New Haven's "Program for Community Development." November 20, 1961. CPI File, Folder A, Item 24.

Minutes of meeting between Ford Foundation staff and New Haven officials. January 10, 1962. CPI File, Folder A, Item 35.

Schedule of New Haven's Conference on a Comprehensive Program for the Gray Areas, January 9-10, 1962. CPI File, Folder B, Item 12.

Minutes of meeting held at the Ford Foundation to discuss New Haven's "Program for the Gray Areas." March 21, 1962. CPI File, Folder A, Item 34.

Summary Report of the meeting of the Special Committee on Categorical State Aid for Public Schools. January 6, 1965. CPI File, Folder L, Item 3.

Summary minutes of the Community Action Conference Panels of the First Annual Meeting of the National Association for Community Development. Washington, D.C., March 10-11, 1965. CPI File, Folder N, Item 2.

(h) Community Progress, Inc.: Miscellaneous Sources

Community Progress, Inc. Certificate of Incorporation. April 12, 1962. CPI File, Folder C, Item 9.

National Association for Community Development. Articles of Incorporation. March 11, 1965. CPI File, Folder N, Item 1.

(i) Community Progress, Inc.: Personal Interviews

Name	Position
Mrs. Ann Allen	Program Assistant, Manpower and Employment Program

Name	Position
David Altschuler	Special Assistant to the Director
Richard Belford	Chairman, Mayor's Committee on Equal Opportunities
George Bennett	Director, Manpower and Employment Program
Mrs. Louise Bernbaum	Program Assistant, Office of Public Information
Richard Brooks	Special Assistant to the Director
Milton Brown	Director, Neighborhood Services
Joel Cogen	General Counsel, New Haven Redevelopment Agency
Frank J. Corbett	Neighborhood Coordinator, Dwight Area
Edward DeLouise	Director, Division of Neighborhood Improvement, New Haven Redevelopment Agency
Mrs. Katherine Feidelson	Housing Coordinator, New Haven Redevelopment Agency
Thomas N. Flood	Neighborhood Coordinator, Hill Area
Donald Forest	Project Market Analyst, Manpower and Employment Program
Howard Hallman	Deputy Director
Frank Harris	Executive Secretary, Community Council of Greater New Haven
Robert Hearn	Research Assistant
Alexander Hart	Social Services Coordinator
William Iverson	Neighborhood Coordinator, Newhallville-Dixwell Area
Arthur Johnson	Manpower Associate for Youth Employment Programs

Name	Position
Joseph Marci	Trainer-Coordinator Supervisor
Mrs. Margaret McMillen	Public Information Coordinator
James Melillo	Comptroller
Alvin Mermin	Director, Office of Family Relocation, New Haven Redevelopment Agency
Edward Morrisey	Staff, Community Council of Greater New Haven
Miss Norma Panaro	Neighborhood Coordinator, Fair Haven-Wooster Square Area
Mrs. Jennifer Robbins	Program Assistant, Office of Public Information
Matthew Schecter	Training Assistant
Thomas Seessel	Special Assistant to the Director
William Shannon	Administrative Assistant, New Haven Redevelopment Agency
Bernard Shiffman	Director, Program Development and Training
Vincent Sirabella	Special Consultant on Labor and President of the New Haven Central Labor Council, AFL-CIO
Mitchell Sviridoff	Executive Director
Allan Talbot	Administrative Assistant, Office of the Mayor
Isadore Wexler	Special Consultant on Leisure Time Activities and Chairman of the Mayor's Committee on Physical Fitness and Leisure Time Activities
Miss May White	Consultant on Education Programs
William Will	Training Coordinator
Robert Wolfe	Director, New Haven Housing Authority

(j) Community Progress, Inc.: Files Pertaining to Community Progress, Inc. of New Haven, Connecticut, 1959-1966

Folder	Description of Folder	Number of Items
A	Documents on New Haven's early deliberations concerning the social and economic deterioration of the inner city.	250
B	Drafts of Applications for the original Ford Foundation Grant. Prior to April, 1962.	20
C	Grant Application, Grant Letter, Press Release regarding original Ford Foundation Grant. Includes Certificate of Incorporation.	15
D	Documents on Youth Development focusing on Juvenile Delinquency Grant from the U.S. Department of Health, Education and Welfare.	50
E	CPI-Miscellaneous Materials in Howard Hallman's Files. Before April, 1962. Clippings, drafts of letters.	100
F	CPI-Miscellaneous—continuation of Folder E.	50
G	CPI. Grant Applications, Reports and Letters to and from the Office of Manpower Automation and Training, U.S. Department of Labor (Office of Special Projects).	60
H	CPI. Manpower and Employment Program. Status Reports, Summaries of Meetings, and Policy Statements.	200
I	CPI. Grant Applications, Reports and Letters, Internal Staff Memoranda concerning the Economic Opportunity Act.	35
J	CPI. Internal staff documents on project Finances.	25
K	CPI. Internal staff documents on project Personnel.	15

Folder	Description of Folder	Number of Items
L	CPI. Documents relating to the passage of Conn. Pub. Act No. 523 (January Special Session, 1965). State Aid to Disadvantaged Children.	40
M	CPI. Documents relating to the establishment of a Regional Staff Development Institute for Community Action Programs.	3
N	CPI. Documents relating to the formation of the National Association for Community Development. Includes agricultural training proposal.	30
O	CPI. Public Addresses and Papers by staff members.	20
P	Reprints of articles on CPI. Includes term paper written at Columbia Law School.	19
Q	CPI. Annual Reports to the Ford Foundation. Includes documents relating to the Ford Foundation Grant Renewal in 1965.	15
R	CPI. New Haven Board of Education. Documents relating to the Board's programs supported by Ford, Juvenile Delinquency, and OEO funds.	15
S	CPI. New Haven's Inner-City Neighborhoods. Statistical data and documents relating to Resident participation in New Haven's anti-poverty project.	50
T	CPI. The Legal Program.	25

2. Books

Advisory Commission on Intergovernmental Relations. *Alternative Approaches to Governmental Reorganization in Metropolitan Areas*. Washington: Government Printing Office, 1962.

———. *Intergovernmental Relations in the Poverty Program*. Washington: Government Printing Office, 1966.

Allen, William Sheridan. *The Nazi Seizure of Power: The Experience of a Single German Town, 1930-1935*. Chicago: Quadrangle Books, 1965.

Anderson, Martin. *The Federal Bulldozer: A Critical Analysis of Urban Renewal.* Cambridge: MIT Press, 1965.

Application Galt. 87 S.Ct. 1428 (1967).

Banfield, Edward. *The Unheavenly City: The Nature and Future of Our Urban Crisis.* Boston: Little, Brown and Company, 1970.

Banfield, Edward and Wilson, James. *City Politics.* Vintage Book Edition. New York: Alfred A. Knopf, Inc. and Random House, Inc., 1966.

Beard, Charles. *American City Government: A Survey of Newer Tendencies.* New York: The Century Co., 1912.

Bibby, John and Davidson, Roger. *On Capitol Hill.* New York: Holt, Reinhart, Winston, Inc., 1966.

Bradford, Ernest S. *Commission Government in American Cities.* New York: The Macmillan Co., 1911.

Braybrooke, David and Lindblom Charles. *A Strategy of Decision: Policy Evaluation as a Social Process.* New York: The Free Press of Glencoe, A Division of the Macmillan Co., 1963.

Bremmer, Robert H. *From the Depths: The Discovery of Poverty in the United States.* New York: The New York University Press, 1956.

Bruere, Henry. *The New City Government: A Discussion of Municipal Administration Based on a Survey of Ten Commission Governed Cities.* New York: D. Appleton and Co., 1912.

Buchanan, James W., and Tulloch, Gordon. *The Calculus of Consent: Logical Foundations of Constitutional Democracy.* Ann Arbor: University of Michigan Press, Ann Arbor Paperback, 1965.

Buckley, William F. Jr. *The Jeweler's Eye: A Book of Irresistible Political Reflections.* New York: G.P. Putnam's Sons, G.P. Putnam's Sons-Berkeley Medallion Edition, 1969.

Coleman, James S. *Community Conflict.* Glencoe, Illinois: The Free Press, 1959.

Congressional Quarterly Service. *Federal Role in Education.* Washington: Congressional Quarterly Service, Inc., 1965.

_____. *Revolution in Civil Rights.* Washington: Congressional Quarterly Service, Inc., 1965.

_____. *Housing a Nation.* Washington: Congressional Quarterly Service, Inc., 1966.

_____. *Congress and the Nation: 1945-1964.* Washington: Congressional Quarterly Service, Inc., 1965.

Dahl, Robert. *Who Governs? Democracy and Power in an American City.* New Haven: Yale University Press, 1961.

Dahl, Robert and Lindblom, Charles. *Politics, Economics, and Welfare*. New York: Harper and Row, Publishers, Inc., 1953.

Dahlberg, Jane. *The New York Bureau of Municipal Research*. New York: The New York University Press, 1966.

Davies, Richard O. *Housing Reform During the Truman Administration*. Columbia, Missouri: University of Missouri Press, 1966.

Deming, Horace E. *The Government of American Cities: A Program of American Democracy*. New York and London: G.P. Putnam Son's, 1909.

Domhoff, William. *Who Rules America?* Englewood Cliffs, New Jersey: Prentice-Hall, Inc., 1967.

Donovan, John C. *The Politics of Poverty*. New York: Western Publishing Company, Inc., 1967.

Downs, Anthony. *Inside Bureaucracy*. Boston: Little, Brown and Co., 1967.

Fairlie, John A. *Local Government in Counties, Towns, and Villages*. New York: The Century Co., 1906.

Farrell, Gregory. *A Climate of Change*. Brunswick, New Jersey: Rutgers University Press, 1965.

Fenno, Richard F., Jr. *The Power of the Purse: Appropriations Politics in Congress*. Boston: Little, Brown and Company, 1966.

Fine, Sidney. *Laissez Faire and the General Welfare State: A Study of Conflict in American Thought 1865-1901*. Ann Arbor, Michigan: The University of Michigan Press, 1956.

Frazier, Franklin. *The Negro Family in the United States*. New York: The Dryden Press, 1948.

_____. *Black Bourgeoisie*. New York: The Free Press, A Division of the Macmillan Co., 1957.

Freedgood, Semour. "New Strength in City Hall," *The Exploding Metropolis*, ed. The Editors of Fortune. New York: Doubleday and Company, Inc., 1957, pp. 62-91.

Gans, Herbert. *The Urban Villagers: Group and Class in the Life of Italian Americans*. New York: The Free Press, A Division of the Macmillan Co., 1962.

Geismar, Ludwig and Krisberg, Jane. *The Forgotten Neighborhood: Site of an Early Skirmish in the War on Poverty*. Metuchen, New Jersey: The Scarecrow Press, 1967.

Glazer, Nathan and Moynihan, Daniel Patrick. *Beyond the Melting Pot: The Negroes, Puerto Ricans, Jews, Italians, and Irish of New York City*. Cambridge: MIT Press, 1963.

Goodnow, Frank J. *City Government in the United States*. New York: The Century Co., 1906.

———. *Municipal Government*. New York: The Century Co., 1909.

———. *Municipal Home Rule: A Study in Administration*. New York: Columbia University Press, 1903.

Gottman, Jean. *Megalopolis*. New York: Twentieth Century Fund, 1961.

Green, Christopher. *Negative Taxes and the Poverty Problem*. Washington: The Brookings Institution, 1967.

Grodzins, Morton. *The American System: A New View of Government in the United States*. Edited by Daniel J. Elazar. Chicago: Rand McNally and Co., 1966.

Handlin, Oscar. *The Newcomers: Negroes and Puerto Ricans in a Changing Metropolis*. Cambridge: Harvard University Press, 1959.

———. *The Uprooted: The Epic Story of the Great Migrations that Made the American People*. Boston: Little, Brown and Company, 1951.

Harrington, Michael. *The Other America: Poverty in the United States*. Baltimore: Penguin Books, 1962.

Hauser, Philip and Schnore, Leo F. eds. *The Study of Urbanization*. New York: John Wiley and Sons, Inc., 1965.

Howe, Frederic C. *Wisconsin An Experiment in Democracy*. New York: Charles Scribner's Sons, 1912.

———. *The Modern City and Its Problems*. New York: Charles Scribner's Sons, 1915

Hunter, Floyd. *Community Power Structure*. Chapel Hill: University of North Carolina Press, 1953.

Jacobs, Jane. *The Death and Life of Great American Cities*. Vintage Book Edition. New York: Alfred A. Knopf, Inc. and Random House, Inc., 1963.

Jennings, Kent M. *Public Administrators and Community Decision Making*. Washington: The Brookings Institution, 1963.

Kaufman, Herbert. *Politics and Policies in State and Local Government*. Englewood Cliffs, New Jersey: Prentice-Hall, Inc., 1963.

Key, V.O. "Government Corporations." *Elements of Public Administration*. ed. Fritz Morstein Marx. New York: Prentice-Hall, Inc., 1946, pp. 236-263.

Key, V.O. *Public Opinion and American Democracy*. New York: Alfred A. Knopf, Inc., 1963.

Lincoln, C. Eric. "The American Protest Movement for Negro Rights." *The American Negro Reference Book*. ed. John P. Davis. Englewood Cliffs, New Jersey: Prentice-Hall, Inc., 1966, pp. 458-483.

Lindblom, Charles. *The Intelligence of Democracy*. New York: The Free Press, A Division of The Macmillan Co., 1965.

Lipset, Seymour Martin. *Agrarian Socialism*. Berkeley: The University of California Press, 1949.

Lipset, Seymour Martin. "Bureaucracy and Social Change." *Reader in Bureaucracy*. ed. Robert Merton, Ailsa P. Gray, Barbara Hockey, and Hanan C. Selvin. Glencoe, Illinois: The Free Press, 1960, pp. 221-232.

Lomax, Louis. *The Negro Revolt*. New York: Harper and Row, Publishers, 1962.

Low, Seth. "An American View of Municipal Government in the United States." In *The American Commonwealth*, ed. James Bryce. 2 vols. 2nd ed. revised. New York: The Macmillan Co., 1891. Vol. 1, pp. 620-635.

Lowi, Theodore J. *At the Pleasure of the Mayor: Patronage and Power in New York City 1898-1958*. New York: The Free Press, A Division of the Macmillan Co., 1964.

Lubell, Samuel. *The Future of American Politics*. 2nd ed. revised. New York: Doubleday and Company, Inc., 1956.

Macchiavelli, Niccolo. *The Prince and the Discourses*. With an Introduction by Max Lerner. Modern Library Edition; New York: Random House, Inc., 1940.

Macdonald, Dwight. *The Ford Foundation: The Men and the Millions*. New York: Reynal and Company, 1956.

March, James and Simon, Herbert. *Organization*. New York: John Wiley and Sons, 1958.

Michels, Robert. *Political Parties*. Translated by Eden and Cedar Paul, with an Introduction by Seymour Martin Lipset. New York: The Crowell-Collier Publishing Co., 1962.

Miller, William Lee. *The Fifteenth Ward and the Great Society: An Encounter with a Modern City*. Boston: Houghton Mifflin Co., 1966.

Munro, William Bennett. *Principles and Methods of Municipal Administration*. New York: The Macmillan Co., 1916.

New State Ice Co. v. Liebman. 285 U.S. Reports 311 (1931).

Polsby, Nelson W. *Community Power and Political Theory*. New Haven: Yale University Press, 1963.

Popper, Karl. *The Open Society and Its Enemies*. 4th ed. revised. Vol. I: *The Spell of Plato*. Vol. II: *The High Tide of Prophecy: Hegel, Marx, and the Aftermath*. London: George Routledge and Sons, Ltd., 1962.

Rainwater, Lee and Yancy, William. *The Moynihan Report and the Politics of Controversy*. Cambridge: MIT Press, 1967.

Rourke, Francis E. *Bureaucratic Power in National Politics*. Boston: Little, Brown and Co., 1965.

Sayre, Wallace and Kaufman, Herbert. *Governing New York City: Politics in the Metropolis*. New York: Russell Sage Foundation, 1960.

Schattschneider, E.E. *Politics, Pressures and the Tariff: A Study of Free Enterprise in Pressure Politics, as Shown in the 1929-1930 Revision of the Tariff*. Brunswick, New Jersey: Prentice-Hall, Inc., 1935.

_____. *The Semi-Sovereign People*. New York: Holt, Reinhart and Winston, 1960.

Selznick, Philip. *Leadership in Administration: A Sociological Interpretation*. Evanston, Illinois: Row, Peterson, and Co., 1957.

Simon, Herbert, Smithburg, Donald and Thompson, Victor. *Public Administration*. New York: Alfred A. Knopf, Inc., 1952.

Talbot, Allan. *The Mayor's Game: Richard C. Lee of New Haven and the Politics of Change*. New York: Harper and Row Publishers, 1967.

Troeltsch, Ernst. *The Social Teachings of the Christian Churches*. 2 vols. Glencoe, Illinois: The Free Press of Glencoe, 1949.

Truman, David. *The Governmental Process: Political Interests and Public Opinion*. New York: Alfred A. Knopf, Inc., 1951.

Van Riper, Paul P. *The History of the United States Civil Service*. Evanston, Illinois: Row, Peterson, and Co.

Vose, Clement E. *Caucasians Only*. Berkeley: The University of California Press, 1959.

Weber, Max. *Essays on Sociology*. Edited by H.H. Gerth and C. Wright Mills, New York and London: The Oxford University Press, 1958.

White, Morton and White, Lucia. *The Intellectual Versus the City*. Cambridge: MIT Press, 1962.

Wildavsky, Aaron. *The Politics of the Budgetary Process*. Boston: Little, Brown and Company, 1964.

Wilson, James Q. "The Negro in American Politics." *The American Negro Reference Book*. ed. John P. Davis. Englewood Cliffs, New Jersey: Prentice-Hall, Inc., 1966, pp. 431-457.

3. Articles

Anton, Thomas J. "Power, Pluralism, and Local Politics." *Administrative Science Quarterly* (March, 1963), pp. 426-457.

Asbell, Bernard. "Dick Lee Discovers How Much Is Not Enough." *The New York Times Magazine* (September 3, 1967).

Bachrach, Peter and Baratz, Morton. "Two Faces of Power." *The American Political Science Review* 61, No. 4 (December, 1962), pp. 947-952.

_____. "Decisions and Non-Decisions: An Analytical Framework." *The American Political Science Review* 17, No. 3 (September, 1963), pp. 632-642.

Cahn, Edgar and Cahn, Jean. "The War on Poverty: A Civilian Perspective." *Yale Law Journal* 73 (1964), pp. 1317-1352.

Cater, Douglas. "The Politics of Poverty." *The Reporter* (February 13, 1964), pp. 16-20.

Chase, Edward T. "The Job-Finding Machine: How to Crank It Up." *Harpers Magazine* (July, 1964), pp. 31-36.

"Citizens Participation in Urban Renewal." Law Note. *Columbia Law Review* 66 (March, 1966), pp. 485-607.

Congressional Quarterly Service. "Urban Problems and Civil Disorder." *Congressional Quarterly Weekly Report* 25, No. 36, Part I (September 8, 1967), pp. 1707-1767.

Dahl, Robert. "A Critique of the Ruling Elite Model." *The American Political Science Review* 52, No. 2 (June, 1958), pp. 463-469.

_____. "Further Reflections on the Elitist Theory of Democracy." *The American Political Science Review* 60, No. 2 (June, 1966), pp. 296-305.

_____. "The City in the Future of Democracy." *The American Political Science Review* 61, No. 4 (December, 1967), pp. 953-970.

Eisenberg, Warren. "Bungle in the Jungle." *Greater Philadelphia Magazine* 39 (December, 1964), pp. 96-109.

Glazer, Nathan. "To Produce Creative Disorder. The Grand Design of the Poverty Program." *The New York Times Magazine* (February 27, 1966).

Goldberg, Arthur. "Equal Justice for the Poor, Too." *The New York Times Magazine* (March 15, 1964).

Goodwin, Richard. "Reflections on Vietnam." *The New Yorker Magazine* (April 16, 1966).

Grant, Daniel R. "Urban and Suburban Nashville." *Journal of Politics* 17 (February, 1955), pp. 82-99.

Gulick, Luther. "Metropolitan Organization." The American Academy of Political and Social Science, *Metropolis in Ferment* (November, 1957), pp. 57-66.

Herson, Lawrence. "The Lost World of Municipal Research." *The American Political Science Review* 51, No. 2 (June 1957), pp. 330-345.

_____. "In the Footsteps of Community Power." *The American Political Science Review* 55, No. 4 (December, 1961), pp. 817-830.

Jasek, Edward. "The New Left in New Haven." *The New Haven Register* (January 1, 1966).

Jones, Victor and Kaufman, Herbert. "The Mystery of Power." *The Public Administration Review* 14 (Summer, 1954), pp. 205-212.

Kibbee, Joel M. "The Scope of Large-Scale Computer Based Systems for Governmental Functions." The American Academy of Political and Social Science, *Governing Urban Society: New Scientific Approaches* (June, 1967), pp. 181-196.

Knoll, Erwin and Whitecover, Jules. "Politics and the Poor: Shriver's Second Thoughts." *The Reporter* (December 30, 1965), p. 23 ff.

Kopkind, Andrew. "Poor Politics." *The New Republic* (June 25, 1966), p. 15 ff.

Kristol, Irving. "It's Not a Bad Crisis to Live In." *The New York Times Magazine* (January 27, 1967).

Levitan, Sar A. "Poverty: Survey and Outlook." *Science* (May 13, 1966), p. 901 ff.

Lewis, John D. "Democratic Planning in Agriculture." *The American Political Science Review* 35, No. 2 (June, 1941), pp. 232-249.

Loftus, Joseph. "How the Poverty Program Was Saved in the House." *The New York Times* (December 25, 1967).

Merelman, Richard. "On the Neo-Elitist Critique of Community Power." *The American Political Science Review* 62, No. 2 (June, 1968), pp. 451-460.

Moynihan, Daniel Patrick. "Urban Conditions: General." he American Academy of Political and Social Science, *Social Goals and Indicators for American Society* (May, 1967), pp. 159-177.

Ostrom, Vincent, Tiebout, Charles and Warren, Robert. "The Organization of Government in Metropolitan Areas." *The American Political Science Review* 55, No. 4 (December, 1961), pp. 831-842.

Payne, James. "The Oligarchy Muddle." *World Politics* 20, No. 3 (April, 1968), pp. 439-453.

Powledge, Fred. "New Haven: Triumph and Tragedy in Model City." *Washington Monthly* 2 (February, 1970), pp. 49-62.

Price, Hugh Douglas. Review of "Who Governs?" by Robert Dahl. *Yale Law Journal* 71 (1962), pp. 1589-1596.

Rein, Martin and Miller, S.M. "Social Action on the Installment Plan." *Transactions* 3, No. 2 (January/February, 1966), pp. 31-38.

Shaetsley, Paul. "White Attitudes Toward Negroes." *Daedlus* (Winter, 1966), pp. 217-238.

Spivak, Jonathan. "Manpower Morass." *The Wall Street Journal* (July 13, 1967).

Talbot, Allan. "The Lessons of New Haven Erstwhile Model City." *Psychology Today* (August, 1968), pp. 23-27.

Velie, Lester. "Stepping Stones from the Slums." *Readers Digest* (October, 1963), pp. 175-180.

Walker, Jack L. "A Critique of the Elitist Theory of Democracy." *The American Political Science Review* 60, No. 2 (June, 1966), pp. 285-295.

Wolfinger, Raymond. "Reputation and Reality in the Study of Community Power." *The American Sociological Review* 25 (October, 1960), pp. 636-644.

4. Newspapers, Periodicals, Radio and Television

Congressional Quarterly Service. *Congressional Quarterly Weekly Reports*. Vols. XX-XXVI. Washington: Congressional Quarterly Service, Inc., 1962-1968.

Dull, Jim. "Point of View." Radio Station WELI, New Haven, Connecticut. Transcript of Broadcast of June 15, 1965, p. 5 (mimeographed).

The Gallup Report. 1964-1966.

The Hartford Courant. 1966-1968.

Morgan, Edward T. "Edward T. Morgan and the News." The American Broadcasting Company. Transcripts of Broadcast of March 17, 1964 (mimeographed).

The New Haven Journal-Courier. 1962-1966.

The New Haven Register. 1962-1966.

The New Republic. 1962-1966.

The New York Times. 1962-1968.

The Reporter. 1962-1966.

The Wall Street Journal. 1962-1968.

WELI. Radio, New Haven, Connecticut. 1962-1966.

WNHC-TV. New Haven, Connecticut. ABC Affiliate. 1962-1966.

WTIC. Radio, Hartford, Connecticut. 1966-1968.

WTIC-TV. Hartford, Connecticut. CBS Affiliate. 1966-1968.

5. Public Documents

City of New Haven. *Journal of the New Haven Board of Aldermen*. 1952-1965.

City of New Haven. New Haven Board of Education. *Proposals for Promoting Equality of Educational Opportunity and Dealing with the Problems of Racial Imbalance*. 1964.

_____. *Blueprint for Better Education*. 1961.

City of New Haven. New Haven Board of Finance. *Budget of the City of New Haven: General Fund, Bond Fund, Capital Budget.* 1951-1966.

City of New Haven. Office of the Development Administrator. *Dixwell Development and Renewal Plan.* August, 1960.

_____. *Redevelopment and Renewal Plan for Wooster Square Project, as Amended, October, 1961.* October, 1961.

_____. *Renewal and Redevelopment Plan for Dwight Area.* January, 1963.

_____. *Redevelopment and Renewal Plan for the Church Street Renewal Area, as Amended July, 1960.* July, 1960.

City of New Haven. Office of the Mayor. *Annual Report of the City of New Haven, 1966.* October 30, 1966.

Joint Federal-State Action Committee. *Final Report of the Federal-State Joint Action Committee to the President of the United States and the Chairman of the Governor's Conference.* Washington: Government Printing Office, 1960.

Municipal Code Corporation. *Charter of the City of New Haven, Connecticut.* Talahassee, Florida: Municipal Code Corporation, 1962.

The National Advisory Commission on Civil Disorders. *Report of the National Advisory Commission on Civil Disorders.* Washington, D.C.: U.S. Government Printing Office, 1968.

The National Advisory Commission on Civil Disorders. *Supplemental Studies for the National Advisory Commission on Civil Disorders.* Washington, D.C.: U.S. Government Printing Office, 1968.

State of Connecticut. Business and Industrial Development Division of the Connecticut Development Commission. *Connecticut Market Data. Regional, State, and Town Statistics: Consumer and Industrial Markets.* 1963.

State of Connecticut. Connecticut Development Commission. *Urban Renewal in Connecticut: Statistical Report.* Hartford, June, 1964.

State of Connecticut. Economic Planning and Development Committee. *Report of the Connecticut Economic Planning and Development Committee.* 1960.

State of Connecticut. Juvenile Court for the State of Connecticut. *Annual Report.* 1962-1966.

State of Connecticut. Public Act 523. January Special Session, 1965.

U.S. Bureau of the Census. *Country and City Data Book, 1952.* Washington: Government Printing Office, 1952.

_____. *County and City Data Book, 1962.* Washington: Government Printing Office, 1962.

_____. *Current Population Reports.* Series P-60, No. 63. "Consumer Income." Washington, D.C.: U.S. Government Printing Office, 1969.

———. *Current Population Reports*. Series P-60, No. 68. "Poverty in the United States: 1959-1968." Washington, D.C.: U.S. Government Printing Office, 1969.

U.S. House of Representatives. Committee on Education and Labor. *Economic Opportunity Act of 1964. Hearings Before the Subcommittee on the War on Poverty Program of the Committee on Education and Labor on H.R. 10440.* 88th Cong., 2d Sess., 1964.

U.S. House of Representatives. *Economic Opportunity Amendments of 1965.* Report No. 428. 89th Cong., 1st Sess., 1965.

U.S. House of Representatives. Committee on Education and Labor. *1966 Amendments to the Economic Opportunity Act of 1964. Hearings Before the Subcommittee on the War on Poverty of the Committee on Education and Labor on Examination of Facts Which Have Developed Under the Administration of the Act.* 89th Cong., 2d Sess., 1966.

U.S. House of Representatives. Committee on Education and Labor. *Manpower Development and Training Act Amendments of 1966. Hearings Before the Select Subcommittee on Labor of the House Committee on Education and Labor on H.R. 14690.* 89th Cong., 2d Sess., 1966.

U.S. Office of Economic Opportunity. *Community Action Program Guide.* February, 1965.

U.S. President. The President's Commission on Law Enforcement and the Administration of Justice. *The Challenge of Crime in a Free Society.* Washington: Government Printing Office, 1967.

U.S. Public Law 87-274.

U.S. Public Law 87-145.

U.S. Public Law 88-452.

U.S. Senate. Committee on Labor and Public Welfare. *Youth Employment Act. Hearings Before the Subcommittee on Employment and Manpower of the Committee on Labor and Public Welfare on S. 1.* 88th Cong., 1st Sess., 1963.

6. Other Sources

(a) Reports

City of New Haven. Redevelopment Agency. Office of Family Relocation. "Where Families Have Moved from Redevelopment Projects and Highway Construction Areas," April 30, 1964. CPI File, Folder A, Item. 18.

Ford Foundation. "Ford Foundation Urban and Regional Program Grants, 1955 through February 28, 1961." CPI File, Folder A, Item 38.

Hill Neighborhood Union (New Haven, Connecticut). "Complaint to the Office of Economic Opportunity Regarding the Failure of Community Progress, Inc. to Comply with the Requirements of the *Economic Opportunity Act* and the *Community Action Program Guide*." July 23, 1965. CPI File, Folder S, Item 1.

Institute of Public Administration. *Developing New York City's Human Resources: Report of a Study Group of the Institute of Public Administration to Mayor John Lindsay*. New York: Institute of Public Administration, June, 1966.

Little, Arthur D. "Administrative Organization of the School System in New Haven, Connecticut." August, 1961.

United Funds and Councils of America, Inc. *Interagency Communications in New Haven, Connecticut*. New York: United Funds and Councils of America, Inc., January, 1958.

U.S. Conference of Mayors. Community Relations Service. Community Action in New Haven. Washington: U.S. Conference of Mayors, March 5, 1965.

(b) Unpublished Material

Barber, James D. "Predictions from Pluralism." New Haven: Yale University, Department of Political Science, 1965.

Harris, Frank. "Let's Fish or Cut Bait." Paper read before meeting of Pinewood Institute, Plymouth, Massachusetts, July 26, 1963.

Hilles, Frederick. "The Creation of a Program in Social Renewal." Research Paper submitted to a Seminar in Urban Renewal, Columbia Law School, February, 1963.

Miller, Meredith Sawyer. "Residential Planning Areas for New Haven." Unpublished Master's Thesis, Department of City Planning, Yale University, 1961.

Nagel, Paul. "What is the Place of Social Welfare in the Kind of Community We Want." Paper read before the meeting of Pinewood Institute, Plymouth, Massachusetts, July 26, 1963.

Wilson, James Q. "Innovation in Organization: Notes Toward a Theory." Paper prepared for delivery at the annual meeting of The American Political Science Association, New York City, September 3-6, 1963.

———. "Problems in the Study of Urban Politics." Paper prepared for delivery at Conference in Commemoration of the 50th Anniversary of the Department of Government, Indiana University. Bloomington, Indiana, November 5-7, 1963.

198

Wolfinger, Raymond. "The Politics of Progress." Unpublished Ph.D dissertation, Department of Political Science, Yale University, 1961.

Ylvisaker, Paul. "The Approach of the Ford Foundation to the Problems of American Cities." Address to the 29th Annual Conference of the National Association of Housing and Redevelopment Officials. Seattle, Washington, October 1, 1963.

(c) Pamphlets

Community Council of Greater New Haven, Inc. *Directory of Community Resources for Health, Welfare and Recreation*. New Haven: Community Council of Greater New Haven, Inc., 1962.

League of Women Voters of New Haven. *New Haven: A Handbook of Local Government*. New Haven: League of Women Voters of New Haven, 1963.

New Haven Democratic Town Committee. *Promises Made . . . Promises Kept*. New Haven: New Haven Democratic Town Committee, 1965.

United States Chamber of Commerce. *Modernizing Local Governments*. Washington: United States Chamber of Commerce, 1967.

About the Author

Russell D. Murphy is an Associate Professor of Government at Wesleyan University. A graduate of St. John's Seminary in Brighton, Massachusetts, Mr. Murphy attended the North American College in Rome and received his M.A. from Boston College and PhD from Yale University. As a graduate student at Yale, he served for two years as a Research Associate with New Haven's Community Progress, Inc. His study, originally completed as a dissertation in the Department of Political Science at Yale, won the American Political Science Association's 1968 Leonard D. White Award for the "best dissertation submitted in the field of public administration."

Mr. Murphy resides in Middletown, Connecticut with his wife and four children. He is currently Research Director for The Twentieth Century Fund-supported Study of Mayoral Leadership.

Index